3302191242

Sigmund

C000048433

Sigmund Freud and the History of Anna O.

Reopening a Closed Case

Richard A. Skues

First published in hardback 2006

First published in paperback 2009 by

PALGRAVE MACMILLAN

Palgrave Macmillan in the UK is an imprint of Macmillan Publishers Limited, registered in England, company number 785998, of Houndmills, Basingstoke, Hampshire RG21 6XS.

Palgrave Macmillan in the US is a division of St Martin's Press LLC, 175 Fifth Avenue, New York, NY 10010.

Palgrave Macmillan is the global academic imprint of the above companies and has companies and representatives throughout the world.

Palgrave® and Macmillan® are registered trademarks in the United States, the United Kingdom, Europe and other countries.

ISBN-13: 978–0–230–00530–3   hardback
ISBN-10: 0–230–00530–6   hardback
ISBN-13: 978–0–230–22421–6   paperback
ISBN-10: 0–230–22421–0   paperback

This book is printed on paper suitable for recycling and made from fully managed and sustained forest sources. Logging, pulping and manufacturing processes are expected to conform to the environmental regulations of the country of origin.

A catalogue record for this book is available from the British Library.

Library of Congress Cataloging-in-Publication Data

Skues, Richard A., 1953–
   Sigmund Freud and the history of Anna O : reopening a closed case / Richard A. Skues.
       p. cm.
   Includes bibliographical references and index.
   ISBN 0-230-00530-6 (cloth) 0-230-22421-0 (pbk)
       1. Hysteria—Case studies. 2. Psychoanalysis—Case studies.
3. Freud, Sigmund, 1856–1939. 4. Pappenheim, Bertha, 1859–1936.
5. Breuer, Josef, 1842–1925. Studien über Hysterie. I. Title.

RC532.S48 2006
616.85′24—dc22   2006045226

10   9   8   7   6   5   4   3   2   1
18   17   16   15   14   13   12   11   10   09

Printed and bound in Great Britain by
CPI Antony Rowe, Chippenham and Eastbourne

For Susie, without whom…

The relevant methodology can be summed up in four principles: (1) Never take anything for granted. (2) Check everything. (3) Replace everything in its context. (4) Draw a sharp line of distinction between the facts and interpretation of the facts.

Henri F. Ellenberger, introduction to *The Discovery of the Unconscious* (1970)

Alle Männer vom Fach sind darin sehr übel dran, daß ihnen nicht erlaubt ist, das Unnütze zu ignorieren.
(All specialist scholars are at a great disadvantage in that they are not allowed to ignore what is useless.)

J. W. von Goethe, *Maximen und Reflexionen* (Posth.)

Contents

Preface

Die größten Schwierigkeiten liegen da, wo wir sie nicht suchen.[1]

    J. W. von Goethe, *Maximen und Reflexionen* (1829)

This book is intended as an attempt at historical demystification: the deconstruction of a legend of psychoanalysis. The legend concerns Anna O., the patient whose real name was Bertha Pappenheim and whose case study stands at the head of Freud and Breuer's *Studies on Hysteria*, first published in 1895. Josef Breuer treated Bertha Pappenheim from the end of 1880 until June in 1882, but it was not until ten years later and after considerable pressure from Freud that he agreed to publish an account of it in their joint work, first in a *Preliminary Communication* at the beginning of 1893, and then more fully two years later. In 1895 Breuer and Freud used this case as an illustration of their success in the alleviation of hysterical symptoms by means of a new method of treatment. This method, it was claimed, had been elaborated by Breuer in the course of the treatment of his patient when he discovered that her hysterical symptoms disappeared once she had related all the circumstances of their occurrence right back to the event that precipitated them. Once the emotions attached to this original experience had been allowed free expression through being articulated in speech, then the affect would no longer constitute the energy base that sustained the hysterical symptom in question. Although this 'talking cure' had been initiated by his patient, Breuer began to apply it systematically to relieve her symptoms one by one, and then Freud himself, having heard about the case directly from Breuer shortly after its conclusion, tried the method on patients of his own several years later. The case histories of Anna O. and four patients of Freud's own formed the backbone of the *Studies on Hysteria*, which also included a theoretical chapter by Breuer, and one on psychotherapy by Freud.

For Freud this work was to become one of the foundation stones of psychoanalysis. It represented the first faltering steps towards the full elaboration of the discipline that was to become almost synonymous with his own name, and the basis of everything that came after. Freud's relationship with Breuer did not survive the completion of their book, and even at its publication he had a very clear view about its inadequacies. Yet at the same time the systematic attempt to make the hysterical symptom intelligible, and thus to attain control over it, was what marked the new method as the embryonic form of psychoanalysis. Seen in this light, Anna O. becomes the first psychoanalytic patient, even though her treatment was to predate the nominal birth of Freud's new science by some 15 years or so. When Freud in later years was to credit Breuer with having inaugurated psychoanalysis in all but name, it was his treatment of Anna O. that justified this. Both within Freud's lifetime and ever since, there are few histories of psychoanalysis that do not begin by mentioning Breuer's treatment of Anna O. as the event that stands at its origins.

Yet if for psychoanalysis the Anna O. case was one of its earliest triumphs, there are today few historically informed commentators on the discipline who do not regard it with considerable scepticism, and this sometimes amounts to a claim of outright fraud on the part of Breuer and Freud. Since Ernest Jones recorded in the first volume of his biography of Freud in 1953 that Freud had told him that there were aspects of the conclusion of the case that had not been published, that Breuer brought the treatment to an end prematurely as a result of an emotional entanglement between himself and his patient, and that she herself suffered relapses that necessitated her institutionalisation, other accounts have compiled on these foundations a case which makes it appear that Breuer's treatment was little short of catastrophic. In the early 1970s the pioneering historian of dynamic psychology, Henri Ellenberger, discovered that shortly after the ending of her treatment with Breuer, Bertha Pappenheim had gone to stay in a sanatorium in Switzerland. He discovered an original report by Breuer and supplementary case notes by a doctor at the sanatorium which indicated that Bertha was still suffering considerably. Building on this, Breuer's biographer, Albrecht Hirschmüller, also found out that Bertha was repeatedly hospitalised in Vienna during the succeeding five years. All these circumstances, along with a number of comments that came to light in Freud's correspondence with various of his followers over the years, conspired to paint a picture of the Anna O. case that was radically at odds with the received version that had engrained itself in conventional psychoanalytic history.

There are few writers nowadays who make more than a passing reference to the case of Anna O. without also mentioning this body of evidence and commentary that has come to the fore in the last 50 years and which seems to cast such doubt not only on the original treatment of the patient but also on the integrity of both Breuer and Freud in their sustained assertion that this treatment was a success. Freud's own position is perhaps even more precarious than Breuer's in that even though he seemingly knew the case was highly problematic, and revealed as much in private to several of his followers over the years, he also apparently continued to maintain in public the façade that represented Anna O. as the founding patient of psychoanalysis. To the extent that this case is now thought to be a dramatic failure, Freud's testimony rebounds back ironically as an astringent commentary on the value of the science and therapy that was his life's work.

The substantive thesis to be argued in this book is that this picture of the Anna O. case, constructed by the last 50 years of Freud scholarship, is in all fundamentals wrong and itself represents a modern-day fiction about the origins of psychoanalysis. To that extent the burden of this thesis signifies not so much a rewriting of history, as almost an attempt to reverse it. To many, this may seem at the outset to be not just a monumental but a hopeless task, for the modern story of Anna O. is deeply rooted in the critical literature on psychoanalysis and appears to be so well founded in contemporary historical scholarship as to be almost beyond correction, let alone radical rejection. Yet such an undertaking is necessary. Conventional histories of psychoanalysis have been subject to harsh criticism, and often not without justification, by those who have seen them as little more than apologies for a discipline that needs to bury the realities of its past and to replace them with reassuring myths about its origins. Yet there is no point in substituting one set of comfortable fictions for another, for this is what recent histories of the Anna O. case have become. There is no single author of these fictions, but in the accretions of the myth over the last few decades the new tale of Anna O. has evolved to become the story that many – particularly critics of psychoanalysis – wish to retell and to hear retold. It will be argued here that this is a story that does not withstand close scrutiny.

It is now necessary to reassess the evidence and to try to recapture what we can of the Anna O. case as it took shape and played its leading role in the development of psychoanalysis in the 1880s and 1890s. This must be done by examining this evidence as far as possible in its original setting and with an awareness that the case can properly be evaluated only when one is sensitive to the historical circumstances that gave rise to it and to the nature and purpose of the documents that constitute its legacy. This book will therefore present an historical reconsideration of the case and its data, concentrating particularly on the circumstances surrounding the ending of the treatment and its aftermath, for this is the key battleground marked out by the case's critics. It is therefore hoped that it will be by the persuasiveness of the historical reconstruction and its consequences for our reading of the case that the book's success or failure will be judged.

This project has been several years in the making and could not have been completed in its present form without the support and assistance of a number of friends, colleagues and acquaintances. The late and much-missed Terry Tanner was the first to hear an outline of the thesis, and his encouragement was an important stimulus to its elaboration in print. To Dr Sonu Shamdasani grateful thanks are due both for being the first reader of an early draft of this book and for his incisive comments and criticisms which helped immeasurably to clarify and strengthen its argument. Anthony Stadlen and Peter Swales have not only assisted on specific points but also provided a constant background of discussion, stimulation and support both for this project and in the field of Freud studies in general, which has been of incalculable benefit. Dr Wilhelm Hemecker gave invaluable assistance with some difficult issues of translation, and comparable help was also provided on particular points by Dr Ernst Falzeder, Professor Johannes Reichmayr and Julia Swales. Professor George Makari and Professor Peter Rudnytsky both provided valuable comments on the penultimate draft of the book as a whole. Dr Gerald Kreft was exceptionally accommodating in assisting with the illumination of the 'Edinger connection', while Dr Michael Schröter provided indispensable help with elucidating aspects of Max Eitingon's paper on Anna O. Thanks are also due to Professor Stephen Frosh for his supportive comments on an earlier draft of the text and likewise to Professor Edward Timms for helping to highlight the particular pitfalls that await the non-specialist historian in this domain. Julia Brown's consummate skill and professionalism helped in no small way with the completion of this whole project. While this book would not have been published in its final form without the assistance of all those named above, responsibility for its shortcomings remains solely with the author.

Introduction: The Changing History of a Case History

Das eigentlich Unverständige sonst verständiger
Menschen ist, daß sie nicht zurechtzulegen wissen,
was ein anderer sagt, aber nicht gerade trifft, wie er's
hätte sagen sollen.[1]
     J. W. von Goethe, *Maximen und Reflexionen* (1824)

It was Freud himself who first made the claim that Breuer's case of
Anna O., published in 1895 in the *Studies on Hysteria*, represented the
inaugural moment of psychoanalysis. As early as 1904 there appeared a
minor publication in which Breuer's patient features in this role (Freud,
1904), but then five years later he placed her at the head of a much
more public retrospective account of the development of psychoanalysis, the first lecture that he gave at Clark University on his trip to the
United States in 1909:

> If it is a merit to have brought psycho-analysis into being, that merit
> is not mine. I had no share in its earliest beginnings. I was a student
> and working for my final examinations at the time when another
> Viennese physician, Dr. Josef Breuer, first (in 1880–2) made use of
> this procedure on a girl who was suffering from hysteria. (Freud,
> 1910, p. 9)

This lecture is just one of the first of several occasions where Anna O.
features in Freud's expositions of psychoanalysis as the case that exemplified the initial success from which first Breuer and he together, then
later he alone, developed what was to become the new science of
the mind, and following Freud's lead it became almost obligatory for
Anna O. to figure somewhere in the opening paragraphs or pages of the

1

many secondary accounts of the development of psychoanalysis that were to be written by both followers and critics. All in all, it is with some justification that Mark Micale has described her as 'probably the single most famous patient in the annals of hysteria' (Micale, 1995, p. 27).

Yet in the first volume of his biography of Freud in 1953, Ernest Jones drew into the light of day a radically different account of the termination of the Anna O. case from that which had previously been current. Jones made two major alterations to the way in which the story had traditionally been told. The first concerned the relationship between Breuer and his patient. According to Jones, Freud had told him that Breuer had become completely preoccupied with Anna O. to the point where his wife became jealous, unhappy and morose. When Breuer became aware of his wife's feelings he decided to break off the treatment and announced this to his patient, who by this time was much better. The same evening, however, he was called back because Anna was in a greatly excited state and apparently just as ill as ever. In fact she was in the throes of an hysterical childbirth, the culmination of a phantom pregnancy that had been developing during Breuer's lengthy treatment of her. Profoundly shaken by this, Breuer managed to calm his patient down, but then fled the house, embarking the next day on a trip to Venice with his wife which was to result in the conception of a daughter (Jones, 1953, pp. 246–7).

This story is corroborated, according to Jones, by the correspondence between Freud and his fiancée, Martha Bernays, dating from second half of 1883, a year after the treatment ended, which also reveals something of the complications the affair had caused for Breuer in his domestic life:

> Confirmation of this account may be found in a contemporary letter Freud wrote to Martha which contains substantially the same story. She at once identified herself with Breuer's wife, and hoped the same thing would not ever happen to her, whereupon Freud reproved her vanity in supposing that other women would fall in love with *her* husband: 'For that to happen one has to be a Breuer.' (p. 247)

In addition to this significant variation from the way in which the treatment terminated according to Breuer's published account, Jones had even more to reveal. In fact not only had the treatment been broken off in this dramatic and unsatisfactory manner, but its conclusion did not by any means mark the end of the patient's suffering. Basing himself on the privileged access that he had been afforded to Freud family correspondence, Jones wrote:

> The poor patient did not fare so well as one might gather from Breuer's published account. Relapses took place, and she was removed to an institution in Gross Enzersdorf. A year after discontinuing the treatment Breuer confided to Freud that she was quite unhinged and that he wished she would die and so be released from her suffering. She improved, however, and gave up morphia. A few years later Martha relates how 'Anna O.', who happened to be an old friend of hers and later a connection by marriage, visited her more than once. She was then pretty well in the daytime, but still suffered from her hallucinatory states as evening drew on. (Jones, 1953, p. 247)

Although there had been previous hints in the published literature[2] that Breuer's account of the Anna O. case may have been in some respects less than complete, Jones's version, apparently resting on the impeccable sources of an oral account from Freud and unpublished family letters from the 1880s, was the first to make explicit significant additional information about the case, and this in a way which challenged to a marked extent Breuer's own version of events as published in 1895.

It did not require a great deal of research to demonstrate that Jones's version was not wholly reliable. Henri Ellenberger's discussion of the Anna O. case has little time for it, and he suggests that it is 'fraught with impossibilities' (Ellenberger, 1970, p. 483). In the first place Breuer's daughter was born on 11 March 1882 and could thus not have been conceived after the termination of the treatment in June of that year. Secondly, there was never a sanatorium in Gross Enzersdorf, and it was likely that there was a confusion here with the sanatorium at Inzersdorf. However, Ellenberger could find no trace of any case history of Bertha Pappenheim in its archives. He therefore concluded that: 'Jones' version, published more than seventy years after the event, is based on hearsay, and should be considered with caution' (pp. 483–4).

Two years later, however, Ellenberger was to transform the study of the case quite dramatically when he published a new review of it which benefited from significant additional data. Ellenberger was able to ascertain from the embossment on a photograph of Bertha in the possession of one of her biographers that the picture had been taken in the German town of Konstanz in 1882, and from that he tracked down in the Sanatorium Bellevue in the neighbouring Swiss town of Kreuzlingen a transcript of an original case report on her, written by Breuer and originating from Bertha's stay in the sanatorium between 12 July and 29 October 1882, shortly after his treatment of her had ended. Ellenberger summarises both the Breuer report and also a supplementary report written by one of the doctors at the sanatorium covering the period of Bertha's stay there.

Ellenberger's general conclusion on the basis of this new evidence is as follows:

> Thus, the newly discovered documents confirm what Freud, according to Jung, had told him: the patient had not been cured. Indeed, the famed 'prototype of a cathartic cure' was neither a cure nor a catharsis. Anna O had become a severe morphinist and had kept a part of her most conspicuous symptoms (in Bellevue she could no longer speak German as soon as she put her head on the pillow). Jones's version of the false pregnancy and hysterical birth throes cannot be confirmed and does not fit into the chronology of the case. (Ellenberger, 1972, p. 279)

With this decisive summary by Ellenberger, most of the pieces of what has by now become almost the standard picture of the case among historically knowledgeable commentators on the origins of psychoanalysis were put into place. All further evidence that has come to light since then has generally been regarded as merely reinforcing the impression of the picture that Ellenberger constructed. Indeed Micale hardly exaggerates when he judges that: 'Ellenberger's discovery that Pappenheim did not recover after her long, intense private psychotherapy, as Breuer and Freud contended, but rather suffered serious and prolonged relapses has by now been integrated into the historical literature of psychoanalysis' (Micale in Ellenberger, 1993, p. 398). Albrecht Hirschmüller, following in Ellenberger's footsteps, found and published other relevant documents, including a supplementary report on the patient by Breuer dating from mid-June 1882, and he also discovered from the records of the Inzersdorf sanatorium in Vienna that Bertha had been a patient there on three occasions between July 1883 and July 1887. Prepared to give more credence to Jones than had Ellenberger, Hirschmüller saw this as evidence in support of Jones's account of the later course of Bertha Pappenheim's illness, and as leading to a potential indictment of Breuer's integrity:

> All this goes to show that years after Breuer's treatment Bertha was still in fact struggling to regain her health. [...] Thus despite the clearly unsatisfactory developments in the patient's condition

following termination of his own treatment, he gave an account in the *Studies* which tended to suggest that his patient had completely recovered. In view of this we should not be surprised that Breuer delayed so long before publishing his account of the case, quite contrary to his normal practice. (Hirschmüller, 1989, p. 116)

John Forrester was able to draw on some of the hitherto unpublished correspondence between Freud and his fiancée that had informed Jones's version of events and reached an even more starkly expressed conclusion about Breuer's publication of the case history:

Certainly that case could never be regarded as a complete success, as we have seen: Bertha was confined to a sanatorium after the abrupt ending of her treatment, and her condition continued to deteriorate. Freud wrote to Martha some months later:

'Bertha is once again in the sanatorium in Gross-Enzersdorf, I believe. Breuer is constantly talking about her, says he wishes she were dead so that the poor woman could be free of her suffering. He says she will never be well again, that she is completely shattered.'

All of this material reinforces the impression gained from Ellenberger's important paper that Breuer's treatment of Anna O. was in large part a medical disaster, however many symptoms were disposed of through the talking cure. (Forrester, 1990, pp. 25–6)

In his own extensive discussion of the case Malcolm Macmillan summarised his view of the outcome of the treatment in this way:

Breuer himself was wrong in implying Anna O. was cured. Although neither described in his published account nor referred to publicly by him or Freud, within five weeks of the close of treatment Anna O. had the first of four relapses. On July 12, 1882, she was admitted to the Sanatorium Bellevue, Kreuzlingen, Switzerland, where she remained until October 29, 1882 (Ellenberger 1972; Hirschmüller 1978, pp. 152–6, 362–4). Many symptoms remained; the hysterical features, speech disorders, alterations of consciousness, and the facial neuralgia. It was not surprising that she was described as criticizing 'in an unfavourable manner the inadequacy of science in the face of her suffering' (Hirschmüller 1978, p. 364). Her symptoms seem not to have changed by the time she was discharged from Bellevue. (Macmillan, 1997, p. 9)

Han Israëls, reaching much the same general conclusion, also implicates Freud directly in the misreporting of the case: 'Freud therefore knew that Anna O. had in no way been completely cured after the treatment by Breuer, but he revealed this to only a few confidants' (Israëls, 1999, p. 146). Moreover: 'Freud pretended at the time never to have understood Breuer's delay [in publishing]; but one good reason at least was very well known to him, namely that the treatment of Anna O. had in no way led to a cure. However, Freud always kept this secret in public' (p. 154).

Mikkel Borch-Jacobsen has taken the matter further by producing additional evidence not previously debated in the public domain, but which predates Jones's 1953 account. He includes a citation of C. G. Jung first brought to light by Ellenberger, but has more:

> As early as 1916, in his book *The History and Practice of Psychoanalysis*, Poul Bjerre noted almost in passing, 'I can add that the patient was to undergo a severe crisis in addition to what was given out in the description of the case. Since then, however, she has lived, and still lives in the best of health and in widespread activity.' And Carl Jung, in a private seminar of 1925, went even farther. Referring to confidential remarks made by Freud about the 'untrustworthiness' of some of his early case histories, Jung stated: 'Thus again, the famous first case that he [Freud] had with Breuer, which has been so much spoken about as an example of a brilliant therapeutic success, was in reality nothing of the kind.' In fact so little does the whole business appear to have been kept a secret within Freud's inner circle that Marie Bonaparte, upon returning from Vienna, where Freud had told her 'the Breuer story,' noted in her diary on December 16, 1927, 'The rest is well known: Anna's relapse, her fantasy of pregnancy, Breuer's flight.' (Borch-Jacobsen, 1996, pp. 29–30)

Borch-Jacobsen's book-length treatment of this case has continued the snowballing trend of the criticism of Breuer and Freud in recent years. He devotes an early chapter to summarising the evidence found by Ellenberger and Hirschmüller, adding his own commentary and highlighting the way it all demonstrates how Breuer's marvellous tale, which was almost too good to be true, was in fact not true at all (Borch-Jacobsen, 1996, p. 21). Despite the fact that Freud would have been completely aware of the whole situation, this did not deter him from pressing Breuer to publish the case, nor from making false claims himself about Breuer's method (p. 26). As far as Borch-Jacobsen is concerned, it is simply not true that Breuer's treatment ever got rid of Anna O.'s symptoms:

> This fact became well known in 1953, when Ernest Jones revealed it publicly in the first volume of his biography of Freud, and it has since been amply corroborated by the painstaking research of Henri Ellenberger, Ellen Jensen, and Peter Swales, among many others. No one today can remain unaware that the treatment of Anna O. [...] was very different from what Breuer and Freud have told us about it – so different, in fact, that we can legitimately wonder what remains of modern psychotherapy's origins myth, now that the historians of psychoanalysis have so thoroughly debunked it. (pp. 9–10)

This is certainly a reasonably accurate representation of the summary judgement that seems to follow from the last 50 years of historical discussion of the Anna O. case, and while there may be some remaining discussion about particular details or about the wider implications of the case for the discipline of psychoanalysis that was to emerge from it, the general story that Borch-Jacobsen summarises has not as a whole been disputed – indeed it has so much come to be seen as the inescapable outcome of the amassing evidence over the years as to appear almost beyond argument. Edward Shorter, for example, basing his conclusion solely on a comparison of Breuer's published case study with the original notes found by Ellenberger and needing no more than a footnote to do it, is able to demonstrate Breuer's published version variously as 'partly fanciful' (1997a, p. 367) and 'largely confabulated' (1997b, p. 23).

Yet this book will contest precisely this story of the end of the treatment and what came after. The original documents from the 1880s unearthed by Ellenberger and Hirschmüller will be re-examined and compared with what both Freud and Breuer were subsequently to publish. It will be argued that judged on the basis of currently available external evidence the case study Breuer published in 1895 cannot be deemed to be seriously misleading, that the evidence that Jones first alluded to in 1953 does not sustain the position that is generally predicated on it, that the arguments of more recent scholars have been based on supposition and insufficiently critical attention to detail and context, and that the accumulating story that Borch-Jacobsen eloquently characterises as representing the debunking of a myth, is itself much less securely founded than the supposed fable it is intended to replace. In the course of this re-examination of the evidence and of the way it has been cumulatively misconstrued over the past several decades, we shall try to reach a more balanced appraisal of the Anna O. case in an attempt to prevent the last half century of mystification continuing for another 50 years.

Before embarking on this excursion, however, a few notes of caution should perhaps be entered in order to prepare the reader for what to expect in the following pages. In the first place the general argument of this book necessarily tends towards a negative thesis. That is to say, there will be no great revelation of new evidence in support of an entirely novel view of the Anna O. case; rather the main object is to demonstrate that the theses on the case proposed in the recent second-ary literature cannot in general be sustained. Perhaps even more cir-cumspectly it should be said that the evidence and argument to be found in these studies, even where consistent with particular known facts, do not for the most part point inexorably in the direction that their authors would like them to go. In summary, while the general proposition that Breuer's case was a failure and that he and Freud knew this cannot entirely be discounted as a matter of principle – often a problem when trying to prove a negative – the totality of the evidence that is so far available is not sufficient to establish that it is in all prob-ability correct, or even that it is likely to be right. While there are a few pieces of new empirical evidence brought to light in the course of the book, the general method of demonstration of the argument relies for the most part on a systematic exposition and critical re-evaluation of existing data. An unfortunate feature of this totality of evidence that is inclined to frustrate those seeking certainty and conviction is that its component parts are often ambiguous and capable of several variant interpretations when abstracted from the full picture. But all too often a drive to certainty and conviction has marked the strivings of some commentators who press their own interpretation of individual data to a conclusion that at first sight might seem inevitable, whereas in fact – so it will be argued – this is often at the expense of alternative and equally plausible interpretations that have the additional merit of being consistent with the evidence as a whole.

If the overall effect of the argument, in so far as it is successful, is to re-establish the reliability of the published case study of Anna O. and to rescue it from its detractors (Freud in some respects included), the sta-tus of what is here being reinstated itself requires a degree of careful delineation. While the present study revisits the Anna O. case history, it does not do so in the cause of a general vindication of Breuer's (and sub-sequently Freud's) analyses of it, nor, in a similar vein, does it stand as an investigation of what 'really' happened in Breuer's treatment of his patient, understood with the benefit of hindsight. The early psychoanalytic literature on the case, including the published case study itself, is littered with diagnostic and therapeutic categories and practices that are very much of their time, and if a comparable case were to be found today the conceptual vocabulary used to account for it would be very different from that used by Breuer and Freud in the 1880s and 1890s. That much we can say with a fair degree of confidence. But the adequacy or otherwise of this lexicon for sustaining a present-day account of Bertha Pappenheim's afflictions and their treatment is not a systematic subject of investigation here for a number of reasons. First of all, while a modern retrospective analysis would no doubt supplant a number of elements of Breuer's case study, it would not be able to do so in such a systematic manner as to render an account and explanation that would be on the whole any more credible than those offered at various points by Breuer and Freud themselves. This is not to mount an objection in principle to medical retro-diagnoses, for on occasions these can be successfully undertaken. But in this particular case there is not the unequivocal evidence to make an alternative diagnosis to the kind made by Breuer that can be sustained with any great plausibility.

A quite extensive subset of the secondary literature on the case has precisely this concern to propose alternative retro-diagnoses of Anna O.'s afflictions to that of 'hysteria', the condition attributed to her by Breuer. This includes schizophrenia (Goshen, 1952, p. 831), tuberculous meningitis (Thornton, 1986, p. 131), temporal lobe epilepsy (Orr-Andrawes, 1987), depression (Merskey, 1992), drug intoxication and withdrawal with related mood disorders (Pollock, 1984, p. 32; Orr-Andrawes, 1987, p. 397; de Paula Ramos, 2003, p. 246) and various other imaginatively constructed alternatives in Rosenbaum and Muroff, (1984).[3] It has also been suggested that Anna O. was simulating her illness by Swales (1986), Schweighofer (1987), Borch-Jacobsen (1996) and Shorter (1997b), which too is a retrospective rediagnosis of course, since it challenges Breuer's own opinion that there was anything wrong with his patient at all.

One difficulty with these reinterpretations is that it is doubtful whether in a case that is as manifestly complicated as Anna O.'s it is possible to reach a corrective diagnosis within the framework of modern medical science after more than one hundred years on the basis merely of the documentary evidence that survives. The immense strides that medical science has taken during the last century have been in part dependent on increasingly sophisticated diagnostic techniques, but these are not often required to operate in the absence of the patient and with all the signs of their illness available only in the form of a few literary traces. It would be a bold modern clinician indeed who would reach a new diagnosis with confidence, and the very variety of the alternatives that have been so far offered suggests that if the science of documentary rediagnosis does eventually produce a new conclusion about Anna O. sufficiently persuasive to command widespread agreement, it has not done so as yet. Moreover, this continuing uncertainty should not just be seen as a result of a dearth of reliable data. It is also a feature of the current state of psychiatry – or more broadly conceived, sciences of the 'person' – that means that retro-diagnoses of such cases are bound to remain problematic. For it is by no means clear that modern diagnostic categories in this general terrain are any more secure from the hazards of social and historical contingency than their nineteenth-century counterparts. One does not have to subscribe to a crude social relativism to recognise that particularly in a domain where diagnoses are allocated on the basis of observation of the patient's behaviour and mental capacities and where these are necessarily linked to normative judgements about what constitutes the relative 'acceptability' of particular forms of conduct and mental function, the modern psychiatric map may well have moved as far again in a few decades time as it has in the last one hundred years. When one adds to this the continuing instability and lack of uniformity of current psychiatric theory and practice, any attempt to state definitively what, if anything, was 'really' wrong with Anna O. is bound to remain, at least for the time being, little more than an entertaining parlour game.

There is a further reason for not overestimating what is to be gained from attempted retrospective diagnosis. With regard to expanding our understanding of Breuer's treatment of his patient it is in large part beside the point. For even if it could be proved with the benefit of modern medicine and a good deal of hindsight that Anna O. was afflicted by a specific condition that was unknown to Breuer and those around her, the very fact that this was an unknown (or at least undiagnosed) state means that our knowledge of this can add very little to the description and analysis of their actions at the time. What is important is the diagnostic and treatment categories and options that were available to Breuer and his contemporaries, and especially in this particular case how these came to be woven into the development of what was eventually to become psychoanalysis.

On the other hand, it does not do to be too purist about knowledge with hindsight as such, since this is what forms a large part of the historical enterprise itself. If 'rediagnosis' of Anna O.'s condition is understood more broadly than the mere production of an alternative clinical conclusion, then this can indeed have a significant effect on the way we now approach the case, and certainly this has been a principal thrust of recent critical writing on the case. For if it can be shown that what was really in play in it was different from the way it was represented by the key figures, notably Breuer and Freud, and that they actually knew this to be so, then this compels us to adopt a fundamentally different stance both in relation to the case itself and their part in its history. Much of the literature prefaced in this introduction is a critical rediagnostic literature in this wider sense, in that it not only adopts as its objective the task of challenging and correcting the testimonies of contemporary actors from the viewpoint of what purports to be the better knowledge of the present, but often does so with the clear implication (even where not explicitly stated) that this better knowledge was actually available to or even intentionally suppressed by the actors involved. To the extent that their testimonies might now be demonstrated to have been knowingly at variance even with the way things appeared at the time, then not only their accuracy, but also the good faith of their authors is impugned, and this radically shifts the focus of inquiry away from the true nature of Anna O.'s illness and onto those authors themselves. While this perspective is by no means universal in the recent secondary literature, it is certainly widespread and is one of the main reasons why what is at stake in the Anna O. case is not just the accuracy of a written case history but the whole integrity of the enterprise that was to become psychoanalysis, given that such significant issues of legitimacy surround one of its key foundational moments. It is in this specific, broader sense that the challenge of retrospective diagnosis is taken up by the project of this book and forms the focus of its historical investigations.

Narrowly conceived, this book might be viewed primarily as an attempt to revisit and reconstitute the events leading up to the publication of the Anna O. case in 1895. It might be seen as a reinvestigation of the narrative surrounding the three key figures of Josef Breuer, Sigmund Freud and Bertha Pappenheim: two nineteenth-century Viennese doctors and a patient. And in certain sense of course this would be an accurate perception. But there is another sense in which this is not simply the retelling of a medical course of treatment, and in many respects neither Bertha Pappenheim nor Josef Breuer are the key players in the bigger historical picture that has emerged since their own parts in it were long past. Pappenheim of course established her own reputation independently of her engagement with Breuer in the 1880s, though this is not in any way a concern of this book, and Josef Breuer had a public reputation that was greater than Freud's own at the time they worked in collaboration. But had it not been for the fact that Sigmund Freud, the Viennese neurologist who published a book with Josef Breuer in 1895, went on to become the same Sigmund Freud who established psychoanalysis and who marked Breuer's treatment of his patient as the founding moment of his discipline, things would have been very different. Few today would have heard of Breuer, no one would have known of Bertha Pappenheim's treatment by him, and the whole occurrence would have been nothing more than a small footnote in the history of dynamic psychology. The accumulated history of the case is therefore not just the history of a treatment of a young Bertha Pappenheim by her general practitioner, Josef Breuer, in the Vienna of the early 1880s. Rather it consists in large part of a retro-spective revaluation of this episode through the agency of what was then still yet to come, and is thus a prime example of what is expressed much better in German in the concept of *Nachträglichkeit*, a notion that Freud of course understood very well. So the history that is written here is not primarily the story of Bertha Pappenheim and her family doctor, but of Anna O.; it concerns not just Sigmund Freud the ambitious neurologist, but Sigmund Freud the founder of psychoanalysis. It is the history of psychoanalysis that forms the backdrop for the interplay between these two, almost mythical figures of Freud and Anna O., and it is against that history that their own must nowadays be seen. But the last 50 years of the history of the Anna O. case have seen it steadily closed down, as a new orthodoxy of historical sediment has gradually hardened around it in the multiple accounts of the failure of the case that permeate the secondary literature. For the most part this now pre-vailing narrative appears so solid that its closure seems almost beyond challenge. The principal task of this book is to see if perhaps the case can still nevertheless be reopened and the history reformed.

Part I The Evolution of the Case

Ausgezeichnete Personen sind daher übler dran als andere; da man sich mit ihnen nicht vergleicht, paßt man ihnen auf.
(Outstanding people are therefore in a worse case than others; as we don't compare ourselves with them, we try to catch them out.)

J. W. von Goethe, *Maximen und Reflexionen* (1821)

1
The 1882 Documents

Der Augenblick ist eine Art von Publikum: man muß
ihn betrügen, daß er glaube, man tue was, dann läßt er
uns gewähren und im Geheimen fortführen, worüber
seine Enkel erstaunen müssen.[1]
J. W. von Goethe, *Maximen und Reflexionen* (Posth.)

It is undeniable that the historical study of the Anna O. case was
transformed when Henri Ellenberger (1972) managed to trace in the
archives of the Sanatorium Bellevue in the Swiss town of Kreuzlingen a
transcript of an original case report on Bertha Pappenheim written by
Breuer, and again when Albrecht Hirschmüller (1989), building on
Ellenberger's achievements, found and published other relevant
documents, including a further, supplementary report by Breuer. The
original case report, apparently written in mid-1882 after Breuer had
completed his treatment of Anna O., but before her stay in Kreuzlingen,
is important because it serves as a point of comparison with what Breuer
eventually came to publish in 1895, and has the potential either to lend
additional credence to the published version of the case or to undermine it. And this is the way that the first report is most often read by
scholars: using it only in relation to the published version and not
considering it as a text in itself. The difference is subtle, but important.
If one reads a document solely in conjunction with another, then there
is a danger of seeing only the points in that first text which have a
marked relation to or disjunction from the second, and of missing its
own internal relations and tensions which have a standing that is independent of any other particular external reference point. To understand
as much as possible about the Anna O. case and the way it was perceived
at the time, one must consider the contemporary documents on their

own terms, and not just by comparison with what was to be written more than a decade later.

If one reads the transcript of Breuer's original case notes, intent on setting aside as far as possible the published report, there is in fact a striking complexity and unevenness in the description of Bertha Pappenheim's illness and in the categories and concepts with which Breuer depicts and accounts for it, which is somewhat lost in the later version. In order to understand more clearly how it appeared to Breuer during the time he was working with his patient it is necessary to enter into his own narrative of the illness and examine its structures, rhythms, stresses and lacunae uncontaminated by a knowledge of what the case was subsequently to represent. In this way it is possible to perceive subtleties and inflections that might otherwise be missed, which then in turn may shed light on the origins and novel characteristics of later accounts. In order that we may better understand the end of the treatment, let us therefore begin our re-examination of the case by considering its emergence in Breuer's earliest surviving written account of the development of the illness and the course it followed.

In the 1882 report we find the division of Bertha Pappenheim's illness into the four phases that Breuer later gives in the published version. In the earlier account he mostly gives only the chronology rather than a brief description of the principal characteristic of each period, which comes only in 1895 (Hirschmüller, 1989, p. 278; Breuer and Freud, 1895, p. 22). The first 'latent' stage began in the middle of July 1880 and lasted until about 10 December. The second phase lasted until the death of Bertha's father in April 1881. The third extended from April to December 1881 and the final period terminated with the end of the treatment in June 1882.

In his original case history, Breuer begins his description of the first period of Bertha's illness with an account of its onset on the night of 17 July 1880, when she was nursing her sick father. He recounts the incident that was not only to mark the beginning of the illness but was also (as we learn from the published case history) to re-emerge at its climax some two years later. This was the occasion when Bertha's right arm became anaesthetised as she sat with it hanging over the back of her chair by her father's bed. She gradually fell into a state of absence and eventually hallucinated black snakes crawling out of the walls, with her own fingers transformed into small snakes. Although she tried to pray, she was unable to utter any word, except in English (Hirschmüller, 1989, p. 278). But as Breuer continues to recount a number of Bertha's more extravagant symptoms from the early stages of her illness, we must take care not to miss that these are in fact not the main focus of his initial narrative. The principal feature of her illness to which Breuer is drawing attention is the recurrent absences that Bertha was to suffer. After the events by the bedside, Breuer continues: 'On another day she was brought to such a state of absence...'; and then: 'The absences (time missing) giving rise to some sort of hallucination gradually multiplied...'; followed by: 'In one deep absence she did not recognise her father or understand when he asked her a question...' (pp. 278–9). These absences were the framework within which the individual symptoms (the hallucinations, aphasia, deafness, rigidity of the arm and so on) developed.

Why is this important? Mainly because of what comes next, when we are told: 'In such a way there appeared an extraordinary multitude of *hystericis*, always first in an affect or absence, which then recurred ever more frequently...'[2] This makes clear the idea that the states of absence were the conditions under which individual hysterical symptoms always appeared first of all, rather than being hysterical symptoms themselves.[3] And Breuer goes on to list a number of further symptoms, mainly relating to visual deficiencies, but also including deafness, lack of understanding, aural hallucination, limb contractions, coughing and an inability to speak.

At this very first point of elucidation of a detail of Breuer's case notes it is perhaps worth pausing to face at the outset the very real difficulties involved in being clear about exactly what was signified by the diagnosis of hysteria. In the first place we are confronted with the diagnosis of a condition which no longer has currency in modern medical discourse in the way it did in Breuer's time, so there is an immediate problem of unfamiliarity. Secondly, this does not, however, mean that we suffer accordingly from an absence of detail about the condition; on the contrary we have a surfeit of information which nevertheless does not necessarily make precise understanding correspondingly easier. In the last 30 years or so there has grown a torrent of research and publication of historical work on hysteria in all its aspects, and an indication of the range and extent of this may be gleaned from Mark Micale's invaluable series of essays (Micale, 1995). But as Micale notes (p. 11) much of this work has been disparate, fragmented and uncoordinated, and a clear synthesis of the history of hysteria is not currently to be had. To a large extent this reflects not a deficit in the literature but the elusive nature of its object. For one of the characteristics of hysteria which makes it today such an apparently endless source of new historical work is that even in its time it was shifting and uncertain in its application. As a diagnostic category, not only could it be used to explain physical maladies that could not otherwise be accounted for, but it also frequently encompassed deviant or eccentric character traits. In several respects it straddled the persistent duality of mental and physical pathology; its aetiology was uncertain and contested, and its treatment equally so. When to this is added disagreements within branches of the medical profession, between individual doctors and researchers and even national and regional variations, the exact significance of any particular diagnosis of hysteria can be difficult to determine.

Breuer's diagnosis of Bertha Pappenheim as suffering from hysteria therefore has to be set in the most general terms in the context of what this diagnosis would mean to a typical Viennese general practitioner in the early 1880s and also how he would expect it to be understood by his professional contemporaries. This is the approach taken by Albrecht Hirschmüller (1989, pp. 86–95) in his preamble to the study of Breuer's treatment of Bertha. After noting that in the broadest terms hysteria was considered to be a general affection of the nervous system and possessing no definite localisation within it, he notes that the foremost researchers on the subject in Vienna at the time were Moriz Benedikt and Moritz Rosenthal and that their work may have represented the principal stimulus to Breuer's own development in neurology (pp. 87–8). This is eminently reasonable, but when we then go on to learn of theoretical differences between Benedikt and Rosenthal, and also of the importance of work by Maximilian Leidesdorf, Theodor Meynert and Richard von Krafft-Ebing, each having its own distinct character, the question of whom Breuer, as a non-specialist, will have regarded as an authority on particular points becomes very murky.

The approach taken here will therefore be as far as possible to grasp Breuer's understanding of Bertha's malady by paying particular attention to the detail of his own exposition in all its apparent peculiarities, rather than forcing an assimilation between what he says and what we think we know about either hysteria in general terms, or about Bertha's illness. The importance of this for a correct understanding of Breuer's approach to the Anna O. case may be seen in this very first point we have noted, in the distinction between his patient's absences and the hysterical symptoms themselves. Unless we are clear at the outset that the absences were part of the predisposing conditions of the hysterical symptoms, but did not themselves belong to these symptoms, then we shall be led quite astray when it comes to grasping exactly what it was that Breuer and Freud were later to claim about the success of the new method of treatment in this case.

The phenomena that Breuer describes as Bertha's 'absences' are in no sense a novel feature of the case, for analogous states were legion in the literature in Breuer's time in cases of doubling of personality, spontaneous somnambulism, trance states and so on. Such absences or incipient disintegrations of personality were widely seen as the seedbed in which more florid behaviours could take root, hysterical symptoms among them. But the absences and similar phenomena were by no means regarded as the prerogative of hysterics or even intrinsically as signs of pathology. It is likely that Breuer adopted the specific term 'absence' (originally given in French) by analogy with epileptic absence, or *petit mal*,[4] but attached no great theoretical weight to it except as a means of describing succinctly what appeared to be happening to Bertha. Some years later of course the absences were to transmute into the 'hypnoid states' that we find in the *Studies on Hysteria* (and which will be discussed below), where their role as a precondition for the development of hysterical symptoms is more clearly defined, but even there, they are not to be confused with the hysterical symptoms themselves.

This distinction between Bertha's mental state as exemplified by her absences and her other symptoms finds an echo shortly afterwards in the report when Breuer recounts how he first visited his patient at the end of November because of her cough. 'It was a clear case of tussis hysterica; however I classified the patient immediately as mentally ill on account of her strange behaviour' (p. 280). Here too he distinguishes between (indeed contrasts) two facets of Bertha's condition: she did not merely suffer from an hysterical cough but also from mental illness, diagnosed as such because of 'strange behaviour'. Although the distinction is clearly made, its nature is ambiguous. Breuer could simply be contrasting a localised hysterical symptom in the form of the cough, and a different set of hysterical symptoms affecting Bertha's mental condition: what he was later to describe as 'slight hysterical insanity' (p. 293) or a 'psychosis of a hysterical nature' (p. 295). In this context it is more likely that a more fundamental distinction is being drawn. On the one hand, there is hysteria conceived as an underlying general affection of the nervous system, manifesting itself in this case in the form of an hysterical cough, and, on the other, mental illness conceived as a quite different kind of diagnostic category. It is important to bear in mind at this point that during the nineteenth century hysteria was generally considered a somatic complaint and not a mental illness as such. Micale, for example, is insistent about this:

Moreover – and the point cannot be emphasised strongly enough – hysteria, throughout the greater part of its history, has been interpreted by medical observers as a wholly *somatic* derangement. Currently, we view the disorder as an intensely psychological condition; but until the turn of the last century it was understood as a physical infirmity with a specific projected pathophysiological mechanism: a wandering womb, ascending uterine vapors, irritable ovaries, digestive or menstrual turmoil, a spinal or cerebral lesion, and so forth. (Micale, 1995, p. 111)

As the nineteenth century progressed and hysteria became more commonly assimilated specifically with neuroses, its somatic nature became entrenched as it was deemed an affection of the nervous system, albeit that this might be a 'functional' aberration with no visible lesions. To be sure, it was possible for the hysterical condition to give rise to psychical effects, and a 'psychosis' (defined, unlike today, merely as a disturbance of psychical function) could certainly be a symptom of a severe hysteria, yet the condition itself was not conceived essentially to be one of 'mental' rather than 'nervous' illness. Although by the 1880s it was also common for psychiatric conditions to be regarded as the result of brain pathologies, the connotations of 'mental illness' were then still quite different from those of neurosis. Not only was mental illness tainted by being historically the province of the traditional alienist based in an asylum, but there also existed the popular conception that insanity was an hereditary condition, whereas this was not necessarily so with nervous illness. The implications of a diagnosis of mental illness were therefore potentially quite different from one of neurosis.[5] When Breuer draws a clear contrast between Bertha's hysterical cough and her mental illness, this distinction alluded to merely through the use of the simple 'however' could be quite crucial for the way in which we understand him feeling his way towards a diagnosis.[6] By the time he wrote his 1882 report Breuer seems to have concluded that Bertha's disturbances of psychical functioning were not the result of 'mental illness' as such, but could be accounted for by the diagnosis of hysteria, but it cannot be assumed that this was clear to him at the outset. The fact that in April 1881 he called in Richard von Krafft-Ebing (at that time Professor of Psychiatry in Graz) rather than a nerve specialist suggests that he might still have thought of her as potentially a psychiatric case. In the light of contemporary ideas that mental illness was more likely than neurosis to be an hereditary condition it is also interesting that he pays particular attention at the start of his 1882 report to Bertha's 'moderately severe hereditary handicap' (Hirschmüller, 1989, p. 276). This survives into the published case history of 1895 (Breuer and Freud, 1895, p. 21) and in fact it is the only one of the cases in the *Studies* to begin in such a manner.[7]

This parallel and contrast between the two groups of symptoms continues when Breuer describes the second period of the illness, starting when Bertha took to her bed on 11 December. A series of severe disturbances developed in succession, including headaches, visual difficulties, muscle weakness, contractures and anaesthesias. But then Breuer changes register and concentrates on his patient's mental state and the symptoms that led him to think of this as 'severely disordered' (p. 281): her changes of mood, anxiety, her pining for her father, stubbornness, hallucinations and so on. In between these states there were periods of lucidity in which Bertha talked of herself having two selves, and Breuer then states for the first time his conclusion: 'It became more and more evident, as we have just said, that she had two quite separate states of consciousness which tended to differ more sharply the longer the illness lasted' (ibid.)

In Breuer's description of Bertha's condition, the supposedly hysterical phenomena constitute at this stage merely one group of symptoms among several others in what evidently appeared to him to be a quite complex disease picture. At this juncture in the report, and presumably at the equivalent stage of the illness, he gives no clear diagnosis. As Hirschmüller points out (p. 109), although Breuer had diagnosed Bertha's cough as hysterical, he was clearly in some doubt as to whether hysteria could account for the whole of her condition, and for a time he entertained the possibility of tubercular meningitis. The second period, after she had confined herself to bed, was in some respects the most difficult of the whole illness and it was only the fact that he noticed an increase in her psychic activity during her most severe absences, along with an alleviation of her aphasia, that then led Breuer eventually to record a diagnosis of hysteria (p. 283).

But no one reading this report carefully and on its own terms could conclude for one moment that Breuer thought of Bertha's condition as either a wholly somatic or a purely mental illness. Nor does he invoke the diagnosis of hysteria to account for the whole of her condition – it is merely a label that groups together and helps him make sense of some of her symptoms. Here we have to take into account the quite fluid state of the diagnostic categories available to Breuer at this time, and the equally eclectic manner in which he adopted them. Although hysteria could be considered as a general neurosis, as a condition of the whole nervous system, its symptoms could also be manifested in disturbances limited to particular nerve fields, such as cramps, paralyses and so on.

This would include localised 'functional' disturbances that could be traced to no corresponding localised nerve damage. Therefore so far as hysteria could have psychical symptoms as well, it potentially straddled the terrain of both the psychiatrist and the neurologist (see Hirschmüller, 1989, pp. 88, 362, n. 12). In Breuer's report on Bertha Pappenheim we can see these various conceptualisations at work in his hesitation over the diagnosis and his initial separation of Bertha's mental condition (especially her absences) from her more localised hysterical symptoms. Breuer could by no means take it for granted that just because a particular symptom was clearly hysterical (the cough, for example) then hysteria would necessarily suffice as a general diagnosis of her whole condition. Neither a general psychosis (conceived as a general disturbance of psychical function) nor a severe somatic condition with psychical effects could be ruled out as present and, in effect, forming the bedrock for the more delimited hysterical symptoms.

Eventually Breuer did seem to settle on a general diagnosis of hysteria, but doing so was little more than stating a conclusion that there was no clearly diagnosable alternative somatic pathology that could give rise to the behavioural and localised symptoms. Moreover, there is no sign in the report that such a diagnosis led to a clear programme of treatment. Indeed, in Breuer's narrative of the illness from December 1880 until the death of Bertha's father in April 1881 there are only two indications of a therapeutic intervention on Breuer's part. The first came after his patient had been offended by her father, refused to ask after him and then suffered a complete aphasia for two weeks. Breuer compelled Bertha to speak of her father and this resulted in a partial lifting of the aphasia (p. 282). The second intervention came when Breuer realised that Bertha gained relief in the evenings when she was able to tell stories that were triggered by the repetition to her of keywords she had uttered during the daytime. 'The fact that her increased psychic activity during these absences was accompanied by temporary disappearance of the aphasia, together with the whole situation, led me to record a diagnosis of hysteria' (p. 283). As Hirschmüller comments (p. 109), these two factors suggest that Breuer was led to aetiological conclusions about the illness on the basis of the effects of specific therapeutic interventions.

We should note, however, that there is very little evidence of a determined therapeutic régime for Bertha during this period of her illness. In the spring of 1881 her most severe symptoms had declined to the point where she was able to leave her bed again for the first time on 1 April. But there is no indication from the case report that this was anything other than a spontaneous recovery. Even if we make allowances for the psychical relief obtained from the evening story-telling, this would not account for the partial but sustained lifting of the aphasia, nor the disappearance of the contractures and strabismus (p. 283).

The gradual recovery was abruptly interrupted by the death of Bertha's father on 5 April and the illness entered a new phase, where for the best part of the day she was in a state of absence, relieved only in the evenings when she had given an account of what had been troubling her during the daytime. In spite of the evening euphoria her condition deteriorated, and after increasing agitation and attempts at suicide she was forcibly taken to the Inzersdorf sanatorium, just outside Vienna, on 7 June 1881 (p. 286).

At the point in Breuer's report where he tells of Bertha's removal to Inzersdorf, at what one would normally assume to be the lowest ebb in her condition, there is a sudden change of mood, for he continues:

> Frl. Pappenheim's illness from July 1880 to June 1881 had at all events passed its peak in the winter, insofar as the contracture of all extremities, the almost complete aphasia and the numerous visual disorders constituted such a peak. The regression and restriction of anaesthesia and contracture to the right side, the return of speech (albeit involving the loss of her German mother tongue), the vanishing of strabismus and conjugate deviation of the eyes and the restoration of vision (still clouded by a number of varying disorders, though in most respects normal), all meant that her illness had passed its peak, so far as somatic – though purely functional – disorders were concerned; thus the unknown disease must have withdrawn to the left half of her brain. The psychic illness had reached its peak in June, passing it a few days after her removal to Inzersdorf. (p. 286)

There are a number of points in this passage that are worthy of particular note. First, although Bertha had just been forcibly removed to a sanatorium, the somatic aspects of her condition had shown a gradual but marked improvement since the winter months. Secondly, there is no evidence that the improvement in these specific symptoms was the result of any deliberate programme of therapy. The 'unknown disease' had simply passed its peak. Thirdly, Breuer here distinguishes again between the somatic condition and Bertha's psychic illness, although even in the latter respect the worst was over a few days after she arrived at Inzersdorf. Her removal to Inzersdorf was therefore not prompted by a general deterioration in her condition – quite the contrary – but, as far as we can tell from Breuer's report, by an acute crisis in her 'psychical' symptoms in the wake of her father's death.[8]

The rest of the original report is largely taken up with events between Bertha's admission to Inzersdorf and the end of the year. Breuer recounts his attempts to provoke Bertha's evening story-telling and a number of incidents where there seemed to be a marked alleviation of her symptoms. After a visit to Vienna at the end of August, Bertha finally returned to her mother at the beginning of November, but there followed a worsening of her condition, and particularly of her mental state (p. 289). Here, at the end of the third period of Bertha's illness, Breuer's account breaks off and we may legitimately feel disappointed at not having the original account of the fourth phase.

What, therefore, can we learn from the original case report about Breuer's contemporaneous explanations of the symptoms and their removal? First, we may note that there is nothing in the way of an elaborated theoretical apparatus of explication. There is no mention of 'catharsis' nor any hint of a novel explanatory framework to which Breuer might have been driven by the peculiarities of the case. This in any case, as Kurt R. Eissler has pointed out (2001, p. 72), would not be expected in what was essentially a set of descriptive, clinical referral notes for a professional colleague, rather than a research paper. On the other hand, this is not to say that there are no observations of regularities, and there are indeed indications that Breuer could discern some pattern to the origin of the symptoms and the way they disappeared. He reveals that from August 1881 the evening stories increasingly became reports of Bertha's hallucinations and of things that had annoyed her (Hirschmüller, 1989, p. 277). This idea is repeated and elaborated when we learn that:

> Similarly, if she held back from giving expression to annoyance she would suddenly develop a cramp in the [musculi] orbicul[ares] palpebrar[um], but this would disappear when – with difficulty at first, and with some help from myself – she gave an account of the incident. Real amaurosis, which appeared genuine to very different kinds of test, developed similarly due to affection[9] and disappeared following narration of the incident. The first old symptom to be eliminated in this way was the contracture of the right leg, which had already diminished spontaneously. (pp. 288–9)

The same idea recurs when we are told: 'Inhibitions or acts of will (drinking or closing her eyes to suppress tears) which occur due to affects get stuck, as it were, until narrated away' (p. 289).

It is therefore very clear that in 1882 Breuer assigned a role to suppressed affect in the production of at least some of Bertha's symptoms, and in removing them to the narration of the originating event that had caused the emotional response, although there is no explanation of the supposed mechanism of this.[10] The nearest we come to any sign of a systematic pro-gramme of treatment is when Breuer writes that when Bertha returned to live with her mother at the beginning of November 1882 he thought he might make a gradual improvement in her condition by means of the daily stimulus of the 'talking cures' (p. 289). There is no mention in the document of any hypnotic induction on Breuer's part; the only mention of hypnosis refers to Bertha's own evening hypnotic state (ibid.) Nevertheless, there is an indication, from a letter that Breuer wrote around that time to Robert Binswanger about the prospect of placing Bertha in Binswanger's sanatorium in Kreuzlingen for a period of convalescence away from her family, that her general condition had started to improve, implying that at least in some respect Breuer considered that the worst was over, even if this turned out not to be sustained (pp. 292–3).

There are two further points to note from the original documents. Although Breuer and Dr Breslauer (at Inzersdorf) had been prescribing chloral for some time to induce sleep, the follow-up case notes written by Dr Laupus, after Bertha had gone to the Bellevue sanatorium in the summer of 1882, reveal that at this time she was also taking morphine. At the point of admission, Bertha had stopped taking chloral, but increasing doses of morphine had been necessary to relieve the pain of a trigeminal neuralgia which had been quite severe during the previous six months (p. 290). There is no mention of this in Breuer's report because it does not cover the period after December 1881. But if Laupus attributed the morphine doses to neuralgia, there must remain some uncertainty about this because in a brief preliminary report on Bertha, written by Breuer in June 1882 before he wrote the longer version for Binswanger, he records that in recent months his patient had been receiving injections of morphine not for neuralgia, but to counter severe convulsions (p. 295). It may be the case that as far as Breuer was concerned, the original reason for the morphine had been the facial neuralgia, but that the convulsions had overtaken this as a reason. By October 1882, the neuralgia had in any event become again the pre-dominant reason for Bertha taking morphine, as evidenced by a letter from Bertha's mother to Binswanger (p. 303). Despite the uncertainty about this in the documents, there is no evidence that morphine had been prescribed as a means of treatment of Bertha's hysteria. The significance of this will be discussed below.

The second point concerns the extent to which the diagnosis of hysteria covered all of Bertha's symptoms. This is not a question of whether she 'really' suffered from hysteria – since such questions of retrospective diagnosis are here mostly futile – but whether at the time all the symptoms were accounted for by the category of hysteria by those treating her. The indications on this remain unclear. Breuer very neatly summarises her illness as a 'very severe neurosis and psychosis of a hysterical nature' (p. 295) when he writes his brief referral report to Binswanger in June 1882, and we have noted that a diagnosis of hysteria is included in his longer report. But whether this was consistently thought to cover all of her ailments seems more doubtful. In the first place there is the trigeminal neuralgia just alluded to, which began (along with facial spasms) in the spring preceding the onset of her hysterical affliction (p. 278). While there was evidently some debate between the doctors as to whether it was of infra-orbital or zygomatic origin (p. 290),[11] there appears never to have been any question of it being hysterical, although Bertha's mother did consider it to be related to her 'psychic processes' (p. 301). This was in response to Binswanger's own proposal to treat the neuralgia by surgery, so he certainly did not entertain a diagnosis of hysteria on this point. Then there is the question of some of Bertha's other physical symptoms: her muscle weakness and her contractures. The evidence is ambiguous about aspects of these. Breuer was in no doubt that some of these somatic disorders were purely functional (p. 286) and some appeared to be susceptible to being talked away when Bertha gave an account of the incident that led to their onset. Breuer refers to the elimination of the contracture of the right leg in this context (p. 289). More problematic are the contractures of the left extremities and weakness of the anterior neck muscles. These symptoms first appeared after the patient had taken to her bed in December 1880 (p. 280) and disappeared, apparently spontaneously, shortly before the death of her father the following April (p. 283). However, when Breuer discusses these symptoms in the published case history he expresses his doubts as to whether they had the same origin as the others:

> I distinguish them from the other phenomena because when once they had disappeared they never returned, even in the briefest or mildest form or during the concluding and recuperative phases, when all the other symptoms became active again after having been in abeyance for some time. In the same way, they never came up in

the hypnotic analyses and were not traced back to emotional or imaginative sources. I am therefore inclined to think that their appearance was not due to the same psychical process as was that of other symptoms, but is to be attributed to a secondary extension of that unknown condition which constitutes the somatic foundation of hysterical phenomena. (Breuer and Freud, 1895, pp. 44–5)

This tentative attribution of these symptoms to the somatic foundation of the hysterical phenomena leaves a question unclear. Is this foundation the putative hysterical predisposition or hysterical illness as such, or is Breuer postulating some other underlying condition from which the psychical mechanism of hysterical symptoms can manifest itself? The passage echoes similar phrases in Breuer's 1882 report that suggest that while a significant proportion of Bertha's symptoms could be explored interactively through Bertha's self-hypnoses and regarded as a product of her emotional or imaginative life, this did not exhaust the phenomena of her illness, and neither could 'hysterical symptom' be used by itself as the sole descriptive category to encompass the entirety of her condition. In 1882 Breuer had recorded a diagnosis of hysteria to account for some of the symptoms, yet when the somatic symptoms receded somewhat he speculated that 'the unknown disease must have withdrawn to the left half of her brain' (Hirschmüller, 1989, p. 286).

If we try to summarise what may be gleaned from the 1882 documentation about Bertha Pappenheim's illness we might say that it followed a course from July 1880 until June 1882, with its most severe somatic symptoms occurring around the end of 1880 and its most severe psychic symptoms occurring around June 1881. Although most of the symptoms appeared to Breuer to be hysterical, this diagnosis could not with certainty account for all of them, and in particular the trigeminal neuralgia and some of the limb contractions and muscular weakness seemed to Breuer not to have an hysterical origin. Some of these latter appeared to be a secondary effect of the underlying somatic condition which were also the bedrock for the hysterical symptoms, and which disappeared as the essentially unknown illness pursued its natural course.

As far as therapeutic measures were concerned, these seem to have been relatively narrow in range. The drug treatment that Bertha received was merely palliative: the chloral was to induce sleep, while the morphine was to reduce pain from the neuralgia or later to suppress convulsions. Neither drug was a principal means of treating the hysteria itself. Breuer's most significant therapeutic intervention was of course to aid his patient by facilitating the narration of her 'stories'. At first these were elaborations of her phantasies, but they developed into accounts of incidents that provoked strong emotion and which seemed to lie at the root of her symptoms. But it is only in the published case history that we learn more of both the extent of this practice and the technique; in the original case notes there is little indication of this.[12] In order to save time, Breuer hypnotised his patient during his daytime visit and elicited from her the series of events surrounding the multiple appearances of a particular recurrent symptom; Bertha would elaborate on these in the evening session. The numerous instances that Breuer refers to in the case of just one symptom are revealing of the extent he was prepared to go with Bertha in pursuing her narratives (Breuer and Freud, 1895, p. 36) but further discussion of this at this point would take us a little too far from what we learn from the contemporary documentation.

The ending of Breuer's treatment of Bertha Pappenheim remains as the last issue that must be addressed in the light of what these original documents can tell us. Unfortunately they reveal very little about this, mainly because the final part of Breuer's own report on the case is missing and it is necessary to glean what we can from the rest of the brief reports and letters. Inevitably we are drawn here to the later, retrospective accounts of the conclusion of the treatment to supplement what meagre clues are left to us in the earlier documents.

The nearest we have to a contemporaneous reference comes from the opening sentence of the short report that Breuer wrote in June 1882 to refer Bertha to the Sanatorium Bellevue in Kreuzlingen. He writes: 'Fräulein Bertha Pappenheim, 23 years old, is convalescing from very severe neurosis and psychosis of a hysterical nature (with no element of sexuality throughout the whole illness)' (Hirschmüller, 1989, p. 295). The key word here of course is 'convalescing'. As Eissler has pointed out (2001, p. 72), Breuer clearly has in mind that his patient is over the worst of her illness and has entered into a period of recovery. There is every indication too that he regarded his own role as complete. This is supported by the fact that as the two preceding letters indicate, there was an uncertainty about when Bertha was to go to Kreuzlingen because she was minded (and was clearly in his view well enough) to visit relatives in Karlsruhe first. Breuer even entertained the prospect that she might dispel her remaining psychoses[13] and manage to withdraw her morphine dose while she was there (Hirschmüller, 1989, p. 294). As she departed from Vienna for Karlsruhe on 19 June (ibid.) and began her stay in Kreuzlingen on 12 July (Ellenberger, 1972, p. 274) it appears that Bertha stayed in Karlsruhe for about three weeks.

It may also be significant that immediately after the treatment was ended on 7 June, Breuer appears to have recommended, or at least acquiesced in, withdrawal from some of the narcotics, possibly with a view to bringing the treatment to a more complete closure. In the letter to Binswanger written in the middle of June 1882 and in the report of a few days later Breuer mentions that Bertha did not receive her chloral dose for four successive nights, but this threatened quite a severe reaction and was not sustained. Breuer also expresses an expectation, however, that weaning from the drugs will not be too difficult once Bertha is able to apply her own strong will to this (Hirschmüller, 1989, pp. 294, 296). On the balance of probability this is surely most likely to have been one of the principal benefits expected from her admission to the Sanatorium Bellevue. Schweighofer is in no doubt about this: 'From Breuer's letters it emerges unambiguously that withdrawal from chloral and morphine was to be the primary goal of the cure in Kreuzlingen' (Schweighofer, 1987, p. 64). Gerhard Fichtner appears to have drawn a similar conclusion (in Freud and Binswanger, 2003, p. xiii), as has Eissler (2001, p. 72). If this is so then it puts a very different complexion on the stay at the Sanatorium Bellevue from that which is commonly presented in the secondary literature. However, when considered as a whole, all the documents prior to the stay at Kreuzlingen speak against withdrawal from chloral and morphine being the sole objective of the visit; general recovery and convalescence was clearly equally important.

This issue of narcotic withdrawal is directly reflected in the most significant medical report that we have relating to Bertha's stay in the Sanatorium Bellevue: that written by Dr Laupus, which he appended directly to the end of the transcription of Breuer's own referral report. It consists of approximately 2½ pages (compared with the 21½ of Breuer's) and was intended, as is stated in its first sentence, as a summary of the 'Course of her illness during her stay in "Bellevue" from 12 July to 29 October 1882' (Hirschmüller, 1989, p. 290). Nearly two pages of this report are dedicated to a description of Bertha's somatic symptoms, dealing overwhelmingly with her facial neuralgia and the attempts to control this by the use of morphine. We learn here that the facial neuralgia appeared at the same time each evening and that after a period of a few weeks in which this was within tolerable limits, the pain grew worse and the resulting spasms led to closure of the eyes and consequent loss of sight until this was relieved by morphine. There is no mention at all of hysteria or hysterical symptoms throughout this initial discussion, and it is only in the last two paragraphs of the report, consisting of just over half a page, that the topic emerges. Here, in the context of a discussion of her psychical state, Laupus perceived undoubted signs of mental imbalance, yet even here, where he notes that the patient 'displayed unmistakable signs of hysteria' (p. 291) this is because of the 'unmotivated fluctuation of her moods', including hostile irritation to others and states of depression. Laupus also reports a lack of insight into the severity of her nervous condition, as evidenced by her formulation of unrealistic plans as well as by her excessive mourning for her dead father. What is noticeably absent, however, is any continuation of the ornate array of symptoms that had been described by Breuer. Only right at the end of Laupus's report does he mention aspects of Bertha's behaviour that are familiar from Breuer's case report: the free-ranging phantasies of her private theatre and finally the evening occurrence of the loss of her mother tongue:

> This phenomenon occurred regularly each evening in such a way that as soon as the patient's head was laid on a pillow she could no longer either understand or speak the German language. If she was speaking German at the time, the sentence would be finished in English. She would also speak and understand French on these occasions, though this did cause her trouble on some evenings. (ibid.)[14]

Just these few lines are all that are dedicated to any remaining hysterical symptoms that have become so well known to us through Breuer's report and later case study. And this was all that Laupus had to say about such symptoms as had persisted during the course of the illness throughout the patient's three-month stay in Bellevue. This medical report, dispassionately appraised, is in no way consistent with the conventional picture of Bertha suffering from the after-effects of Breuer's failure to deal with persistent hysterical symptoms for months afterwards. It is much more in harmony with Schweighofer's observation that the sanatorium treatment concentrated on fighting the facial neuralgia, and consequently on the narcotic dependence (Schweighofer, 1987, p. 65). Ellenberger's summary is quite to the point here: 'Someone who would know of Anna O only what Breuer related in the *Studies in Hysteria* would hardly guess that it is a follow-up of the same patient after she had undergone Breuer's "cathartic cure"' (Ellenberger, 1972, p. 277).

The information that we have from other sources about Bertha's progress after Breuer's treatment was finished is fragmentary and uneven, with a great deal of latitude available for a variety of interpretations. The bare facts seem to be as follows. In her own report on her condition, probably dating from no earlier than the beginning of October 1882[15] Bertha describes her regular inability to speak German, which arises every evening as soon as she lies back in bed. This normally lasts for a number of hours. She also reports that she had still suffered from her absences in the first two months of her stay, but there had been none for some weeks. Although she does not discuss it at length, she also notes that she is still afflicted by 'strong neuralgic pain' (Hirschmüller, 1989, p. 297). By the time she left Bellevue at the end of October 1882, largely at her own insistence, it was clear that the attempt to wean her from morphine had been a failure and that the pain she suffered as a result of her neuralgia was still acute. In the extant correspondence published by Hirschmüller, Bertha's neuralgia and the morphine treatment appear recurrently. After she left Bellevue she went to stay again with her relatives in Karlsruhe (pp. 304–5) travelling to Frankfurt for three days round about Christmas time and then to Mainz towards the end of December (p. 307). In her letter from Karlsruhe to Robert Binswanger in November 1882, Bertha herself complains of her continued dependence on morphine: 'As for my health here, I can tell you nothing which is new or favourable. You will realize that to live with a syringe always at the ready is not a situation to be envied' (p. 306). In January 1883 we learn from a letter from her cousin, Fritz Homburger, to Binswanger that she was still experiencing no improvement: 'The neuralgic pains persisted; so far as I was able to detect them I thought I noticed an improvement of late, though Bertha herself denied this was so' (p. 307). As far as Bertha's remaining hysterical symptoms are concerned, there is very little information. As has been noted, in his report at the end of her stay at Bellevue, Laupus mainly concentrates on the attempt to wean her from the drugs and on her neuralgia, but he does comment towards the end that she displayed genuine signs of hysteria, although this is stated in relation to her fluctuating moods, rather than any more extravagant symptoms. His report concludes, however, by noting the fact that she still regularly lost the use of her mother tongue each evening, resorting to English or French (pp. 291–2). This same symptom is mentioned in January 1883 by Fritz Homburger, in the letter just referred to, although it seems to have ameliorated since Bertha's own notes on it the previous autumn, lasting for about an hour each evening (p. 307).

If we depend solely on the evidence presented in the documentation from 1882 and 1883, there are at this stage a number of conclusions about the final stages of Bertha's illness that it seems reasonable to draw. We know that Breuer's treatment came to an end in June 1882 and that after a three-week stay with relatives in Karlsruhe she went to Kreuzlingen to convalesce. There is no direct indication at all that Breuer decided to break off the treatment prematurely for any reason. Indeed there is nothing to contradict the assertion that Breuer made in 1895 that it was Bertha herself, rather than Breuer, who decided to end the treatment by 7 June, the anniversary of her committal to Inzersdorf (Breuer and Freud, 1895, p. 40). Her residual hysterical symptoms on leaving Breuer consisted of a 'slight hysterical insanity' (p. 293) exhibited in various pieces of odd behaviour, although Breuer also expected that in her new surroundings among her relatives in Karlsruhe this would all disappear and that the prognosis was favourable (p. 295). When she arrived in Kreuzlingen, after visiting her relatives, there is evidence that she still suffered severely from trigeminal neuralgia, and for this reason she was dependent on morphine, although between leaving Breuer and arriving at the Sanatorium Bellevue she appears to have dispensed with the chloral that she had previously been taking as a sedative (Hirschmüller, 1989, p. 296).

According to Dr Laupus's report at the end of October Bertha suffered from unmotivated mood swings, which Laupus read as a sign of hysteria, and she also underwent bouts of depression. The only other sign of hysteria was that she lost the ability to speak German each night – on Bertha's own report, for some hours – although three months later even this had declined to a brief period each evening. With the exception of the neuralgia and the consequent narcotic dependence, neither of which were considered to be hysterical, a disinterested observer would conclude from the testimony of her doctors and relatives, as well as her own account, that compared with the severities of the afflictions that had burdened her just a few months previously Bertha had managed almost a full recovery. Even though by the end of her stay at Bellevue she was not free of pain and the consequent drug dependence and neither had she regained a state of psychical equilibrium, there is nothing in this documentation so far to indicate that Breuer's care of his patient before her convalescence period could be considered a radical failure, nor that her general condition would be expected to do anything other than continue to improve. The picture we can piece together from this is entirely consistent with Breuer's summary in 1895: 'After this she left Vienna and travelled for a while; but it was a considerable time before she regained her mental balance entirely' (Breuer and Freud, 1895, pp. 40–1).

2
Subsequent Evidence

Diejenigen, welche widersprechen und streiten, sollten
mitunter bedenken, daß nicht jede Sprache jedem ver-
ständlich sei. Es hört doch jeder nur, was er versteht.[1]
J. W. von Goethe, *Maximen und Reflexionen* (Posth.)

Up to this point we have been concentrating on documents
contemporaneous with Bertha Pappenheim's illness and its immediate
aftermath. But what of evidence from the period after 1882? Further
details about her fate were uncovered by Albrecht Hirschmüller when
he found records from the Inzersdorf sanatorium from the mid-1880s.
They revealed that apart from her spell there in 1881, Bertha spent three
further periods in the sanatorium: from 30 July 1883 to 17 January
1884, from 4 March 1885 to 2 July 1885 and from 30 June 1887 to 18
July 1887. Each time the diagnosis is given as 'hysteria', and the result
of the examination of her mental state is recorded as 'somatic illness'.
On the first and third occasions she is described as 'recovered', but on
the second only as 'improved'. On the first two occasions it appears that
the admission was sought by herself and her mother, rather than
resulting from a doctor's referral, but on the third she was referred by
Dr Carl Bettelheim (Hirschmüller, 1989, pp. 115–6).[2]

Bertha appears to have returned from Mainz to Vienna sometime
around the beginning of 1883 because she is mentioned in a letter that
Martha Freud wrote to her sister, Minna Bernays, on 22 January 1883. She
says: 'Also Bertha is back again and is reported to be completely cured;
I have not yet been there to see her' (Freud and Bernays, 2005, p. 47).
In just over six months, however, Bertha was back at the Inzersdorf
sanatorium. Shortly afterwards, in a letter of 5 August, Freud reported to
his fiancée that he had spent the day with Breuer and had learnt that:

Bertha is once again in the sanatorium in Gross-Enzersdorf,[3] I believe. Breuer is constantly talking about her, says he wishes she were dead so that the poor woman could be free of her suffering. He says she will never be well again, that she is completely shattered. (Cited in Forrester, 1990, p. 26)

This of course is the same letter that Jones cited in his own revision of the Anna O. story (Jones, 1953, p. 247) and it does indeed sound as though Bertha's situation was fairly desperate. But the information we have here is not at all specific about the exact nature of her complaint. It is true that the sanatorium diagnosis was 'hysteria', but in itself this means very little. It may well be that this is nothing more than a carrying forward of the dominant diagnostic category from her previous stay, rather than a fresh diagnosis of a presenting problem. The note of 'somatic illness' against her mental state is equally unilluminating, but it does raise the distinct possibility that the cause of her admission was not a resurgence of her major hysterical symptoms but a return or aggravation of her facial neuralgia, with all the implications for her morphine addiction that this would imply. If this was compounded with a renewed state of depression it could certainly be consistent with Breuer's report to Freud. Compare Freud's second-hand account of Bertha's misery with what Laupus had written the year before in his report on her stay in Bellevue: 'Under the burden of neuralgia, even when this was relieved by morphine, she could express despair of a happier future...' (Hirschmüller, 1989, p. 292). The likelihood is that it was the sheer physical pain of her neuralgic symptoms which was the cause of her misery, rather than any continuation of her hysterical loss of language, which by all accounts caused her little discomfort or distress even when she was aware of it. We should note that in Bertha's own report on her language problem that she had written a year previously she records: 'The whole going on is not accompanied from the slightest physick sensation; no pain, no oppression or giddyness are to be felt. From the point of any such symptomes the whole thing could pass very well without its being from me remarked at all...' (Hirschmüller, 1989, p. 297; the misspellings are Bertha's own). There is no sign in this that this aspect of her hysteria caused her any immediate suffering at all. At any rate, there are no grounds for assuming that in August 1883 Bertha's wretched state was a direct consequence of a therapeutic failure on Breuer's part a year earlier in relation to her hysterical symptoms.

By 31 October 1883, nearly three months later, Freud is able to report further to his fiancée in a vein that is entirely consistent with the picture of Bertha we have just constructed: 'It will surely interest you that your friend Bertha P. is doing well in the Enzersdorfer institution, is getting rid of her pains and her morphine poisoning, and is rapidly gaining weight' (Freud, cited in Borch-Jacobsen, 1996, p. 40). There is no indication here either that Bertha's presenting problems had been a continuation or renewal of her hysterical symptoms. By 13 January 1884, after she had left Inzersdorf, Breuer is able to write to Binswanger: 'I saw the young Pappenheim girl today. She is in good health, no pains or other troubles' (Hirschmüller, 1989, p. 310).

After this stay in Inzersdorf, Bertha was to spend a further four months there from March up until the beginning of July 1885, but towards the end of the following year, Martha Freud wrote to her mother and sister in a letter of 28 November 1886: 'I have also been to Bertha's this week, but only saw her mother, who was very friendly. B. is apparently extraordinarily well; she is now learning dressmaking to pass the time'.[4]

On Sunday 30 January 1887 Sigmund and Martha were invited to dinner by Emma Pappenheim, Bertha's cousin. The dinner was to celebrate the engagement of Emma's husband's cousin, Betti Berger, to the musicologist Guido Adler. In a letter of 1 February 1887 Martha wrote to her mother and described the event. In the course of the letter she notes that Bertha and her brother Wilhelm had been there and it appears that this was the first occasion on which she had seen her since her illness. She continues: 'Bertha announced herself directly for the other afternoon here for tea, and in fact she came yesterday with her cousin Anna. Both were very sociable, and plump Willi collected them. Bertha is quite like before in her essential character; in her appearance she has aged very much; her hair is almost completely grey and the sparkle has completely gone from her eyes.'[5] The essence of Martha's observation here is that Bertha's illness has taken its toll. Then four months later, on 31 May 1887, Martha again wrote to her mother: 'At midday yesterday Bertha visited me for a moment, but she is quite miserable again: after 5 in the evening she gets into one of her states and is then quite useless. During the whole day she is smart and well, but apparently does not eat anything at all again – that is so terribly sad isn't it?'[6]

If we are to rely on Martha's report it would appear that Bertha's poor condition has been fluctuating rather than constant: she twice uses the word 'again', suggesting that there has been some remission for a period of time. What is most interesting of course is the reference to Bertha's 'states'. This is the letter that Jones relied on in his account of Bertha's progress, but it is different from what he reports in one crucial respect: Jones writes that Bertha still suffered from her 'hallucinatory states'

(Jones, 1953, p. 247), but this is not borne out by the letter itself, which makes no reference to hallucinations. In fact it is not totally clear whether Martha's allusion to Bertha's 'states' carries with it any precise indication at all of what we might understand the term to denote from a detailed knowledge of the case history. Martha's allusion could be no more than a passing reference to an emotional state, such as depression or anxiety. But even if we do stretch a point and assume that Martha and her mother shared a common understanding of the details of Bertha's past problems, the most that we can reasonably infer from Martha's elliptical description is that the 'states' refer to Bertha's absences – we have no indication at all as to what they may have entailed beyond this. It cannot safely be assumed that they marked a continuation or a return of her inability to speak German, for example, or any of her other peculiar symptoms described by Breuer. In any case, it must also be remembered that as far as Breuer's original report is concerned, the absences were the seedbed for her hysterical symptoms: what he later came to see as the hypnoid states within which the hysterias were able to take root. But they were not, as far as Breuer was concerned, hysterical symptoms themselves. We shall return to the significance of this later, but for now it must merely be noted that although Bertha was clearly not fully and permanently recovered from her illness in May 1887, the character, duration and extent of this relapse presently remain largely unknown. Whatever the nature of her ailment it is presumably likely that this was the reason for her third known return to Inzersdorf at the end of June 1887, on Bettelheim's referral, but its severity was nevertheless not sufficient to keep her there for more than two and a half weeks.

On the basis of all the available contemporaneous documentation it is clear that as late as 1887 Bertha Pappenheim was still not fully cured of all aspects of whatever had afflicted her in the period from the summer of 1880 until June 1882, the time during which she was under Breuer's care. But after January 1883, when Fritz Homburger refers to Bertha's inability to speak German for about an hour each evening, there is no specific reference in the extant available literature to any of the very particular hysterical symptoms that Breuer referred to as having been present during the major period of her illness. There is evidence that after Breuer finished treating her she still suffered from facial neuralgia, from the consequences of morphine addiction and even perhaps from her 'states' or absences, but there is no evidence that the hysterical symptoms which Breuer considered to be the target of his successful intervention during his period of treatment continued to exist.

The conclusion that Bertha Pappenheim had effectively recovered from the hysterical symptoms for which she received treatment from Breuer must of course remain in principle a provisional one, in the sense that evidence may well come to light which shows that her hysterias continued beyond the beginning of 1883. Should such evidence at some future point be uncovered, then this conclusion will have to be revised. But at present it does not exist, and so any contention that Bertha Pappenheim was not for all practical purposes relieved of her hysterical symptoms within a short time of her leaving Kreuzlingen goes further than the presently available contemporaneous evidence will sustain.

3

The Publication of the Case Study

Wenn ein paar Menschen recht miteinander zufrieden
sind, kann man meistens versichert sein, daß sie sich
irren.[1]

    J. W. von Goethe, *Maximen und Reflexionen* (Posth.)

Sceptical readers will no doubt at this point wish to raise objections on
a number of grounds. In the first place, even if the above argument is
conceded as far as the empirical facts are concerned, is it not still the
case that Bertha Pappenheim continued to suffer from hysterical symptoms after the conclusion of the treatment by Breuer? After all, she
undoubtedly suffered from the loss of her native tongue as much as six
months after Breuer finished treating her, and after he said that the case
had been brought to a successful conclusion. Was not Breuer totally
disingenuous in omitting from the case history any mention of her subsequent institutionalisation, or her neuralgia, or her dependence on
chloral and morphine? How is all this consistent with the idea that
Breuer's treatment was effective, an outcome that is quite clearly the
implication of the published case history, as well as other published
statements made by Freud in subsequent years? In focusing on these
questions we are now beginning to move from what it is possible to
infer from the evidence relating to the case of Bertha Pappenheim that
was unpublished in her lifetime to an evaluation of the published
claims about her mythical alter ego, Anna O. The evidence so far has
been largely gleaned from documents that were never intended for
publication and which date from 1882–87. At the point where the documentary record becomes very thin, the case begins to appear in the
published record and it is possible to trace some of the history of this
from the point where the original source material breaks off in 1887

through the period leading up to the publication of the full case study in the *Studies on Hysteria* in 1895.

The place to start in our assessment of this material is Freud's article on hysteria that he published in 1888 in Albert Villaret's *Handwörterbuch der Gesamten Medizin*, for it is here that Freud makes his first published reference to Breuer's new method of treating hysteria. After discussing the treatment of hysterical symptoms by a method of hypnotic suggestion, Freud writes:

> It is even more effective if we adopt a method first practised by Joseph Breuer in Vienna and lead the patient under hypnosis back to the psychical prehistory of the ailment and compel him to acknowledge the psychical occasion on which the disorder in question originated. This method of treatment is new, but it produces successful cures [*Heilerfolge*] which cannot otherwise be achieved. (Freud, 1888, p. 56)

In fact apart from this direct reference to Breuer there are a number of other points in this article where we may see clear parallels with what he had already written in his discussion of the case in 1882. Freud's brief allusion to Breuer's method of treatment occurs in the final part of the article, very near the end of the section entitled 'Treatment of the Neurosis', but the whole of this section merits attention.

At its outset Freud makes a threefold distinction: 'from the standpoint of treatment three tasks must be separated: the treatment of the hysterical disposition, of hysterical outbreaks (*acute hysteria*), and of individual hysterical symptoms (*local hysteria*)' (p. 53). He then deals with each of these in turn. In the case of the first he concedes frankly that the hysterical disposition cannot be done away with, but that one can take prophylactic measures to guard against hysterical outbreaks. The situation appears to be little better in the case of acute hysterias: 'the physician's task is a hard one: it is easy to make mistakes and successes are rare' (p. 54). In fact what Freud has to offer here is little more than the well-known conventional treatments: removal of the patient from their regular conditions (in particular away from the immediate family circle) and then the usual panoply of massage, electrotherapy, hydrotherapy, gymnastics and the Weir Mitchell rest cure. It is when we come to the third aspect that Freud suddenly says something that is quite striking in the context of our reading of the 1882 reports of Bertha Pappenheim's treatment:

> The treatment of individual hysterical symptoms offers no prospect of success so long as an acute hysteria subsists: symptoms that have been got rid of return or are replaced by new ones. Finally both

physician and patient grow weary. The position is different if the hysterical symptoms represent a residue of an acute hysteria which has run its course, or if they appear in a chronic hysteria, owing to some special exciting cause, as localizations of the neurosis. (p. 55)

This distinction between the individual hysterical symptoms and the acute hysteria itself, which has its own course to follow, reflects exactly the distinction made by Breuer between Bertha's hysterical symptoms, which were amenable to treatment by the talking cure, and the 'unknown' illness, which formed the basic condition of these symptoms and which climaxed and declined according to its own rhythm and apparently independently of any therapeutic intervention. Freud's claims for the efficacy of treatment are therefore quite limited: treatment can only realistically be aimed at the residual symptoms of acute attacks, but not at the hysterical condition itself. In reading this whole section, including its reference to the use of hypnosis and suggestion, as well as the passing reference to Breuer's new method, we must therefore be careful to see it only as an outline of the possible treatments for individual hysterical symptoms in patients where the principal, underlying hysterical illness has run its course. It does not purport to represent a radical cure for hysteria as such.

This finds an echo just over four years later in the concluding passage of the *Preliminary Communication*:

It is of course true that we do not cure hysteria in so far as it is a matter of disposition. We can do nothing against the recurrence of hypnoid states.[2] Moreover, during the productive stage of an acute hysteria our procedure cannot prevent the phenomena which have been so laboriously removed from being at once replaced by fresh ones. But once this acute stage is past, any residues which may be left in the form of chronic symptoms or attacks are often removed, and permanently so by our method, because it is a radical one; in this respect it seems to us far superior in its efficacy to removal through direct suggestion, as it is practised today by psychotherapists. (Breuer and Freud, 1895, p. 17)[3]

Just as clear is the concluding passage of the lecture that Freud gave in January 1893 and which was exactly contemporaneous with the *Preliminary Communication*:

You must not suppose, then, that very much has been gained by this for the therapeutics of hysteria. Hysteria, like the neuroses, has its deeper causes; and it is those deeper causes that set limits, which are often very appreciable, to the success of our treatment. (Freud, 1893, p. 39)

So right from the outset, Breuer's new method of treatment is heralded as being little more than a particularly effective clearing-up operation, thus enabling in Anna O.'s case the whole hysteria to be brought to a close. This idea is again repeated in Freud's own much longer discussion in his final chapter in the *Studies on Hysteria* where he sets out at great length the intrinsic limitations as well as some of the strengths of the method of treatment. It is at its strongest in the final period of an illness as it is running its course:

> Where a period of hysterical production, an acute hysterical parox-ysm, has been overcome and all that is left over are hysterical symptoms in the shape of residual phenomena, the cathartic method suffices for every indication and brings about complete and permanent success. (Breuer and Freud, 1895, p. 262)

But in particular Freud also emphasises the method's lack of effect in cases of acute hysteria:

> Where we meet with an acute hysteria, a case which is passing through the period of the most active production of hysterical symp-toms and in which the ego is being constantly overwhelmed by the products of the illness (i.e. during a hysterical psychosis), even the cathartic method will make little change in the appearance and course of the disorder. (p. 263)

This surfeit of quotations from Freud and Breuer's writings of the period has been necessary to counter a commonly held fiction about the treat-ment of Anna O. This is the idea that Freud and Breuer claimed that the latter's treatment of his patient resulted in a 'cure' of her condition. Of course one can use the word 'cure' to apply simply to a régime of treatment, and in this sense the word is unobjectionable here. But if what is implied is the sense in which 'cure' constitutes an outcome of a process of treatment that restores the patient to full health through the effective elimination of the underlying disease state, then it is a complete misnomer in this context. Such a conception is most clearly seen in Henri Ellenberger's pat conclusion to his own analysis of the evidence that 'the famed "prototype of a cathartic cure" was neither a cure nor a catharsis' (Ellenberger, 1972, p. 279). This notion that the cathartic method aimed to 'cure' its recipients of their affliction is one much depended on by Ellenberger himself and almost endlessly repeated, it seems, by others ever since.[4] Once it is possible to show that the patient was subsequently hospitalised, then the case against Breuer and Freud almost seems to be made. But the textual evidence simply does not support such a fanciful exaggeration of the claim. Breuer's new method no more aimed to cure hysteria than insulin is aimed at curing diabetes, or aspirin a head cold. All of these published general estimates, from 1888 to 1895, of the strengths and weaknesses of Breuer's method are completely consistent with what we know to have been the case with Anna O., and it is therefore difficult to see how either Freud or Breuer could be accused of claiming more for this case than can be sustained by the evidence.[5]

The continuing sceptic will no doubt nevertheless insist that however much the general claims for the new method might be hedged round with cautionary warnings, Breuer's own account of Anna O.'s treatment and her return to health is fundamentally misleading in that it gives no hint of anything that we can now ascertain from the contemporary documentation about how long and arduous his patient's road to full recovery actually was.

The extent to which one subscribes to such a view will depend not only on how carefully and closely one reads the published text, but also on how one situates it in the context of the rest of the project that the *Studies on Hysteria* constituted. Further than this it will depend on certain other assumptions shared by Freud, Breuer and their medical contemporaries, but perhaps not by present-day, non-medical critics. The key passages in the actual case study are those where Breuer describes the final stage of the treatment on 7 June 1882, the anniversary of the day the previous year when Bertha had been forcibly moved to Inzersdorf. Having described how each individual symptom disappeared after the patient recounted its first occurrence, Breuer moves to the termination of the treatment:

In this way too the whole hysteria concluded.[6] The patient herself had formed a strong determination that the whole treatment should be finished by the anniversary of the day on which she was moved to the country. [...] On the last day [...] she reproduced the terrifying hallucination which I have described above and which constituted the root of her whole illness. During the original scene she had only been able to think and pray in English; but immediately after its reproduction she was able to speak in German. She was moreover free from the innumerable disturbances which she had previously exhibited. After this she left Vienna and travelled for a while; but it was a considerable time before she regained her mental balance entirely. Since then she has enjoyed complete health. (Breuer and Freud, 1895, pp. 40–1)

There can be no doubt that the way the ending of the treatment is described by Breuer is rather curious, even leaving aside any external evidence independent of the published case study. At this culmination we are told that she reproduced the scene by her father's sick bed, which was at the root of her whole illness, and re-experienced both the hallucination of the snakes with death's heads and the aphasia that had gripped her at the time. Immediately after this, however, not only was she able to speak German, but, even more dramatically she was free from all the other disturbances that she had exhibited.[7] Breuer returns to this in the very last paragraph of his report, noting that the final scene was accompanied by a considerable disturbance of the patient and a worsening of her psychical state (p. 47). If here we are being told that after nearly two years of illness, which reached the levels of severity that Breuer describes in the case study, the patient underwent such a momentous climax and then immediately emerged from it as though she had never been ill and with no subsequent recurrence of any of the symptoms at any time or in any form, then this is indeed asking a great deal of the modern reader to believe. Even leaving aside the peculiarities to the present-day, conventional, medical sensibility of Anna O.'s manifest symptoms, this conclusion contradicts our whole idea of how a severe mental disturbance, indeed almost *any* kind of illness, comes to a close. We shall return to this problem below.

In addition to this there are a number of what appear to be glaring contradictions in the report. For example, there is the claim that after the occurrences of each individual symptom had been recounted in reverse order, going back to the time of its first appearance, the symptom was permanently removed (*für immer behoben*) (p. 35) and the comparable claim that this permanent removal resulted when the stimuli arising from the secondary state of consciousness were given verbal utterance in hypnosis (p. 46). How are these claims to be reconciled with the statement that during the concluding and recuperative phase all the symptoms became active again after being in abeyance for some time (*nach längerem Schlummer*) (p. 44)? Either their initial removal was permanent, or it was not. Or what about the statement that Anna O. was completely unsuggestible (p. 21)? How does this fit with the fact that Breuer always gave his patient a suggestion in the evening that on going to sleep she would not be able to open her eyes until he himself opened them the following morning (p. 38)? Or with his statement that the disappearance of the symptoms could very well be explained by suggestion (p. 43)? And how, in its turn, is this to be squared with Breuer's confident assurance that the removal of the stimuli of the illness after verbal utterance in hypnosis was not an invention that he had imposed on the patient by suggestion (p. 46)?

At a distance of more than one hundred years there is no incontestably clear way for the historian to resolve these contradictions. On the question of suggestion, for example, it is quite possible that Breuer had in mind slightly variant applications of the term, depending on whether it was direct suggestion in the course of ordinary conversation, auto-suggestion, suggestion under hypnosis, or inadvertent suggestion that he was referring to. But even if this may in principle be the case, there is no obvious way to be sure which particular application was intended in each context, or even to be reasonably certain that Breuer was as careful, unambiguous and free of inconsistency as we might wish.

Perhaps the most palpable contradiction lies within the very passage we have quoted at length, where Breuer describes the end of the treatment. Immediately after he has declared that Anna was free from the innumerable disturbances she had previously exhibited, indeed in the very next sentence, he says that it was a considerable time before she regained her mental balance entirely (pp. 40–1). If she was free from all the disturbances, then how could she not, by definition, already have regained her mental balance? Alternatively, if she was still afflicted, she could hardly be free from disturbance. The fact that the two poles of this contradiction are located so close to one another suggests that Breuer would have to have been exceptionally careless in his writing to produce such an inconsistency, if in fact this is what is represented here. Then again, it is also possible that to Breuer there was no inconsistency, and that what he thought indicated a lack of mental balance was not included in the category of 'innumerable disturbances' caused by the hysteria. We have already noted that in his original report Breuer draws a distinction between Bertha's mental problems and her hysterical symptoms, and does not assimilate one to the other (Hirschmüller, 1989, p. 281). Dr Laupus's Kreuzlingen report, on the other hand, appears to take a different position, where his patient's mood swings are what substantiate his diagnosis of hysteria (p. 291). Amid these uncertain and shifting categories there is much room for indeterminacy in any particular reference. For example, it could also be that Breuer was distinguishing individual hysterical symptoms from the 'absences' that had been the seedbed where these symptoms grew. Another possibility is that the regular, daytime, structured occurrence of the symptoms was finally broken by the last treatment session and that this pattern never re-established itself. This would at least be consistent with Bertha's own testimony in the autumn of 1882 that her inability to speak German, which had been continual, had been broken four months previously, and now only recurred in the evening. While a number of alternatives may be hypothesised, it must be conceded that there is at present no means to settle this matter with any great confidence.

For the same reason that it seems impossible to determine a constructive resolution to the problem of interpretation, we should also be diffident about fixing on an entirely negative reading. So even if we were to go so far as to decide that these apparent anomalies are to be considered as contradictions, we are in no position to conclude whether they are the result of carelessness, disingenuous presentation of the argument, misrepresentation of the evidence, exaggerated claims, or whatever other charge of disapproval we may be tempted to level at Breuer. While such apparent contradictions within the very same text appear to us to be so obvious, this should not lull us into assuming that they would have been just as clearly problematic to Breuer or his immediate audience. As retrospective interpreters of Breuer's writing, we are desperate for a textual gloss that would help us to solve these riddles, but they may not have appeared as puzzling to Breuer or his contemporary readers because of their implicit knowledge of what would be intended, based on a set of assumptions that we no longer possess. It may even be that the degree of what we would call consistency, or diligence at the level of detail, was simply not a matter of concern for Breuer and his contemporaries in the way that we, as historians today, are driven to demand. There is no point in expecting an almost forensic degree of accuracy in such writings when they were produced for strictly medical reasons and not for the purpose of retrospective quasi-legal testimony.

Underlying these considerations is the question of what in this particular case could reasonably be claimed as a successful outcome, and here we need to allow a wide degree of latitude of interpretation where the possibilities are so various. We have already established that there could be no intentional claim that the treatment should end in a 'cure', in the sense of an eradication of the general pathological state, but beyond this, what would be a reasonable set of assumptions about whether the programme of treatment was sufficiently successful that it could be terminated without undue hazard? The implausibility to present-day assumptions of the idea that the symptoms of such an illness should suddenly cease has already been registered, yet surely we are not being too rash to presuppose, somewhat sceptically, that a similar set of assumptions would also be shared by Breuer's contemporaries, and that if this idea were directly suggested to them they would also have baulked at it.

Contemporary evidence suggests, however, that this is not at the case. Similarly sudden cures are well attested to in the literature of the time, particularly in cases diagnosed as hysteria. In his series of lectures given in the 1880s, for example, Jean-Martin Charcot refers to a case involving a sudden remission of paralysis after convulsions (Charcot, 1991, p. 258) and acknowledges similarly rapid recoveries after the experience of a strong emotion in a religious ceremony or some other event that appeals strongly to the imagination (p. 336). Hippolyte Bernheim, again in the 1880s, reports a number of such cases in his *Suggestive Therapeutics*. In his general discussion of the application of suggestion to therapeutics he refers to a wide variety of literature relating sudden recoveries, as well as citing three cases of his own (Bernheim, 1890, p. 199). Otto Wetterstrand gives similar accounts of treatments of his own patients, which not only resulted in a remarkably sudden recovery, but also carry features where, as in the case of Breuer, an over-literal reading might produce a sense of contradiction. For example Wetterstrand reports the case of a nine-year-old child suffering from excruciating neuralgia as a result of poor tooth condition:

> I hypnotised her; somnambulism resulted. The toothache as well as the neuralgic pains had disappeared as by magic when she awoke. The pains did not return for a single instant. She was hypnotized twice after that. (Wetterstrand, 1902, p. 18)

Similarly in the case of a woman of 56 with a severe facial neuralgia:

> The patient was hypnotized for the first time on May 5, 1889, with immediate success. I judged it necessary to continue my suggestions, in all, ten times more. (p. 23)

In both of these cases, not only was the relief from pain quite sudden, but Wetterstrand in spite of his own testimony of the immediate success of his method, also notes the continuation of the treatment, for reasons that he does not give.

Even the ostensibly unlikely resolution of Anna O.'s condition on a predetermined date has its counterpart in Wetterstrand. In a case of chronic hysterical attacks in a married woman in her twenties he reports:

> When I asked her, during the hypnotic sleep, what day these attacks would cease, she answered: 'The 27 of February.' Such was really the case. She has not had another attack thus far (February, 1890). Of course one should not consider her answer as to the exact time, as clairvoyance, but as unconscious auto-suggestion. (p. 53)

The point of these examples is to illustrate that not only were recoveries of the rapidity that Breuer describes not uncommon, but that in other similar cases it would be not unusual to continue treatment despite the dramatic nature of the success. On the other hand of course it would not necessarily be expected that after the point where direct medical intervention in a severe illness ceases then there should subsequently be no recurrence at all of any of the symptoms nor any sign of any residue. In the medical circles of the time, just as today, such a prospect would be unreasonable. But if this is so, then we should not automatically judge Breuer's claim about the restoration of his patient's wellbeing as if it implied such an expectation. After all there is no record in the contemporary reviews of any incredulity about the apparent suddenness of the cure, or any questioning of how this might be compatible with continuing 'mental imbalance'. It is only the separation of the case study from its original murky medical context and its subjection to ahistorical textual criticism with accompanying tests of courtroom exactitude that makes such anomalies appear so stark and unyielding. Breuer's text should be judged in accordance with the purposes for which it was written, and not by standards that are alien to it.

As we know from Breuer's supplementary report on Bertha Pappenheim from June 1882, he thought of his patient as a convalescent (Hirschmüller, 1989, p. 295) and this is at least in part consistent with his statement in the published case history that she had not yet recovered her mental balance. The notion of convalescence at the time implied, as it does today, that the immediate course of the illness is past, and yet that a full recovery has still to take place.[8] While this paradoxically implies both the absence of illness and also the lack of full health, the normal expectation would be a gradual recovery over time, though not necessarily ruling out occasional setbacks. Improvements will not always be uniform and symptoms on the wane may nevertheless flare up again under certain conditions. The literature of rapid recovery cited above is replete with such examples, even following quite dramatic recuperations. Understood in this context there is no clear contradiction between a sudden recovery, continuing mental imbalance, convalescence and a generally successful programme of treatment.

Yet in the particular case of Bertha there are further considerations, for we also know from the contemporary documents that she had other problems: not only was she tormented by an acute facial neuralgia, but she was dependent on both chloral hydrate and morphine. There is always a potential issue of course, when a patient is suffering from more than one affliction, as to which symptom is attributable to which pathology. In this specific case there is the additional difficulty that whereas Breuer had judged that the hysterical symptoms had been sufficiently dealt with to allow his own treatment to finish, there is also the possibility that her remaining problems interfered with and exacerbated the residual effects of the hysteria or the underlying condition that had produced it. In practical terms this could have meant that although the hysteria had effectively run its course and the patient would otherwise have made a fairly rapid full recovery, in the situation of a continuing pathology of another form it could be impossible to tell which residual symptoms were attributable to which condition. We have no direct evidence of this from the case notes and correspondence of course, because we have very little evidence of continuing symptoms that appear to have been hysterical.

However, the drugs on which Bertha Pappenheim was dependent could well have produced precisely this problem, and here we have some indirect evidence to draw on. If we return to Freud's article on hysteria for Villaret, where he mentions Breuer's new method, we find that he discusses the wisdom of treating hysteria by means of internal medication. He is quite emphatic that this is not a desirable practice and he adds a particular note in relation to narcotics: 'To begin with, internal medication is to be disrecommended here, and narcotic drugs are to be warned against. To prescribe a narcotic drug in an acute hysteria is nothing less than a serious technical mistake' (Freud, 1888, p. 55). But of course this is exactly what had happened in the case of Bertha Pappenheim. During the course of her acute hysteria and during the period she was convalescing she was taking heavy doses of both chloral hydrate and morphine. It is true that these were not directly prescribed for the hysteria itself, but there is no doubt that Freud and (presumably) Breuer will by now have seen this narcotic intake as having had a detrimental effect on Bertha's recovery. Earlier in the article Freud is just as explicit about the inadvisability of treating hysteria by means of internal medicaments. Commenting on the shifting of symptoms in response to miscellaneous external influences, he writes that this is remarkable 'in view of the fact that a hysterical nervous system offers great resistance as a rule to chemical influence by internal medication and reacts in a positively perverse manner to narcotics such as morphine and chloral hydrate' (p. 48).

Whether Breuer believed at the time she was being treated that narcotics were contraindicated in cases of hysteria is not clear, but it is difficult to see how Freud could have held the view that he did in 1888 without also regarding Bertha Pappenheim's intake of narcotics as having potentially had a damaging effect on her hysterical symptoms. This means that he and Breuer would have had reasonable grounds for attributing any continuing symptoms during the convalescent period, or even any temporary resurgence of individual symptoms during the concluding phases of the treatment, to the effects of the narcotics, or at least for suspecting that they had played a part. Drawing a general conclusion in 1895 about the usefulness of the cathartic method, they would therefore have parallel grounds for thinking that Breuer's treatment programme could have been even more successful than it had been if his patient had not been taking these drugs.

But if the retrospective view of the hysteria is complicated by the accompanying drug dependence and facial neuralgia, there is a residual matter to do with the latter which requires attention in the light of certain passages in the *Studies on Hysteria*. It has been noted in the discussion of the original case notes that there never appeared to be any reference to Bertha's facial neuralgia as an hysterical symptom and there is no record of it being treated in any other way than as a purely somatic manifestation. This is certainly consistent with its receiving no mention in the published case study, but is it also consistent with what Breuer and Freud write about neuralgia elsewhere in their joint work? For in the *Preliminary Communication*, for example, neuralgia features at the heart of one of the authors' central claims about the scope of their discovery:

> Our experiences have shown us, however, that the most various symptoms, which are ostensibly spontaneous and, as one might say, idiopathic products of hysteria, are just as strictly related to the precipitating trauma as the phenomena to which we have just alluded and which exhibit the connection quite clearly. The symptoms which we have been able to trace back to precipitating factors of this

sort include neuralgias and anaesthesias of very various kinds...
(Breuer and Freud, 1895, p. 4, emphasis in original)

Later on in the book (pp. 176–9) Freud describes how one of his
patients, Cäcilie von M., suffered for many years from a recurrent and
violent facial neuralgia, which appears to have been very similar to
Bertha Pappenheim's affliction. In this case her teeth had originally
been held responsible and several of them had been extracted, although
this resulted in no alleviation of the affliction. But after the pain had
seemed to respond to Freud's hypnotic treatment he began to have
doubts about the genuineness of the neuralgia, and when it recurred
again a year later he recovered from his patient during a period of nine
days a series of traumatic scenes containing supposed insults which she
had experienced over many years. Freud believed that the insults had
been experienced by Frau Cäcilie as a 'slap in the face' and that the neuralgia had resulted as a symbolic conversion of these slights. Although
he does not give an indication of the therapeutic outcome of his
approach, he was clearly prepared to integrate the neuralgia into his
overall treatment of his patient's hysteria in a way that Breuer does not
discuss in the case of his own patient.

Yet there is a passing mention of neuralgia in the Anna O. case, which
suggests that perhaps Breuer did use his new method of treatment in a
comparable fashion, and this on the face of it makes his omission of the
chronically severe continuation of Bertha's facial neuralgia after his
treatment had finished, rather more striking. For he writes: 'In this way
her paralytic contractures and anaesthesias, disorders of vision and
hearing of every sort, neuralgias, coughing, tremors, etc., and finally her
disturbances of speech were "talked away"' (p. 35).

To begin to understand the apparent inconsistencies here, it needs to
be appreciated that 'neuralgia' did not have quite the same application
at the end of the nineteenth century as it does today. Nowadays the
term is usually used to refer to pain that follows the path of specific
nerves, and trigeminal neuralgia is perhaps the most common example
of this. But from early in the nineteenth century 'neuralgia' was used
not only to refer to precise, localised afflictions of this kind, but also in
a more generic sense which has today lost its currency in conventional
medicine. A large number of conditions were thought of as 'neuralgias',
to the point where practically any pain in the body that could not be
linked to a definite cause was labelled as a neuralgia (Alam and Merskey,
1994, p. 433). The term was also one of a range of concepts, along with
hysteria, hypochondria and spinal irritation, that were invoked to

account for chronic pains that showed no sign of lesion in their immediate vicinity (Hodgkiss, 1991). A range of possible models could be drawn on to explain the influences of the mind on the body in the experiences of such pains (ibid.) and as the century passed this became the case too with neuralgia specifically, which it was thought possible for emotional and mental factors to bring about (Alam and Merskey, 1994, pp. 454–8). Although some of these notions survived well into the twentieth century, this broad application of 'neuralgia' tended to decline as knowledge of the nervous system increased, and this went along with a reluctance to use the term for conditions that could not be supported by known anatomical patterns. The accompanying twentieth-century readiness to describe mysterious pains as 'psychogenic' also contributed to the narrowing of the term's application, for it had been more comfortable in the nineteenth century to lend them more of an organic air by means of the somatically-based disease category of neuralgia (p. 471).

The common practice of describing as neuralgia a wide variety of pains occurring practically anywhere in the body which could not be attributed to a definite cause can be seen in Freud's and Breuer's uses of the term in a number of passages. In the *Preliminary Communication*, for example, it is clearly this generic sense of pain that is referred to when they say that their method has enabled the tracing back to a precipitating trauma of such symptoms as 'neuralgias and anaesthesias of very various kinds'. This does not mean that all neuralgias are hysterical, nor that their method is applicable to all neuralgias, but merely that their method has been productively employed on some neuralgias (understood simply as painful sensations) and some anaesthesias (understood as absences of sensation).

In the case of Cäcilie von M., Freud describes how what appeared at first sight to be a conventional trigeminal neuralgia turned out to have a strong hysterical component to it and thus to be as susceptible to treatment as any other hysterical symptom would be. When he therefore refers to having doubts about the 'genuineness' of the neuralgia this does not mean that the pain was not real, or even that it was not a neuralgia, but that it was a case of hysterical neuralgia, rather than one originating from a specific lesion. As for Breuer's reference to Anna O's 'neuralgias', he gives no clear indication in the case study what these could be, since beyond a passing reference to a 'left occipital headache' (Breuer and Freud, 1895, p. 23) there is very little to suggest that pain was a key feature of her array of hysterical symptoms. Nor are there any additional clues in the case notes, beyond the very brief mention of the facial neuralgia as having occurred in the spring preceding her illness, and even then it is described as 'transitory' (Hirschmüller, 1989, p. 278). But the vague reference to a plurality of pains clearly does not encompass the facial neuralgia which plagued Bertha Pappenheim for many years and which Breuer and all the other doctors with whom she came into contact never seemed tempted to consider as hysterical. For him it appears to have been a separate issue from the rest of her illness: there is no evidence in any documentation of his attempting treatment of this affliction by his new method or by anything other than conventional means. In the context of the varied and shifting notions of 'neuralgia' that were prevalent at the time we cannot see these multiple references to it in Freud's and Breuer's writings as evidence of anything other than precisely this breadth of application. But the evidence about it suggests that Bertha Pappenheim's very clearly delineated facial neuralgia fell into a different category altogether and would not readily be subsumed under the heading of a vague and unspecified series of pains and discomforts that might be susceptible to psychical treatment.

In summary therefore, the published case history of 1895 gives a clear impression that Breuer's treatment of Anna O. was a success. Of this there can be no doubt. The key question is: What could reasonably constitute such a success, and thereby justify their implied claim? There is no question of Freud and Breuer's having asserted that Breuer's method cured his patient in the sense of eradicating the underlying disease condition; in fact they are quite explicit that the method was powerless to do this. Success was judged in terms of its ability to remove symptoms that were persisting as the hysterical illness itself pursued its course and gradually waned. Breuer's success in removing each symptom and establishing the conditions for it not to recur each day according to the normal pattern of his patient's illness was sufficiently striking and sustained for him to claim the value of the method and for Freud in particular to think that this could be repeated with other patients. Two factors that were particular to Bertha Pappenheim's case could have conspired to complicate the treatment in practical terms, but were not sufficient to undermine theoretical confidence in the effectiveness of the method. First, she suffered from other, non-hysterical symptoms: in particular, facial neuralgia. Secondly she was dependent on a high intake of narcotics which, at least by 1888, were thought to have a detrimental effect on hysterics. Both of these considerations, if Breuer and Freud judged them to have been significant in Bertha's case, could have been sufficient to render her recovery more gradual and uneven than would otherwise have been the case, but because they were extraneous to the hysteria, neither would have compromised their view of the essential success of the new method of treatment of hysterical symptoms that Breuer discovered with his patient.

In fact there was a third factor in play that later on would have appeared to Freud to have had a disruptive effect on the ending of the treatment and yet not affect the basic validity of its approach. This factor was to become central to his gradually evolving dispute with Breuer and the eventual breakdown of their relationship. This was the question of Bertha Pappenheim's emotional entanglement with her doctor. In the final section of his contribution to the *Studies on Hysteria* Freud raises as an obstacle to the cathartic treatment the situation where a patient has a dread of losing her independence in relation to the doctor, indeed of becoming sexually dependent on him, or the situation where a patient begins to transfer onto the physician ideas that arise from the content of the analysis (Breuer and Freud, 1895, pp. 301–2). This issue of what was later to become known as the problem of the transference is one which we must now explore in greater detail, for it is central to Freud's own retrospective view of Breuer's treatment of his patient.

4
Freud's Account: Reconstructions

Was man mündlich ausspricht, muß der Gegenwart,
dem Augenblick gewidmet sein; was man schreibt
widme man der Ferne, der Folge.[1]
    J. W. von Goethe, *Maximen und Reflexionen* (Posth.)

The reader who is familiar with the secondary literature on the Anna O. case and who is perhaps still sceptical of the general argument mounted so far will probably consider as valid grounds for objection the fact that Freud himself was one of the principal people to question the success of Breuer's treatment of Anna O. Was it not Freud who circulated the stories about Bertha Pappenheim's hysterical childbirth and who maintained that the patient was not in fact cured in the way the published case suggests? There is without doubt an issue of substance here, but it is necessary to look closely at the evidence to establish exactly what was said, under what circumstances and to whom. It is here that we begin to move beyond the published case history itself and begin to look at Anna O.'s fate in Freud's subsequent publications, as well as the accounts that began to circulate informally among his close colleagues.

If Freud was the first to cast Anna O. as the founding patient of psychoanalysis he was also first in line to question in print exactly what Breuer had accomplished in his treatment of her. In 1914 he wrote:

In his treatment of her case, Breuer was able to make use of a very intense suggestive *rapport* with the patient, which may serve us as a complete prototype of what we call 'transference' to-day. Now I have strong reasons for suspecting that after all her symptoms had been relieved Breuer must have discovered from further indications the sexual motivation of this transference, but that the universal nature of this unexpected phenomenon escaped him, with the result that, as though confronted by an 'untoward event',[2] he broke off all further investigation. He never said this to me in so many words, but he told me enough at different times to justify this construction [*Kombination*] of what had happened. (Freud, 1914, p. 12)

In 1925, he again wrote rather cryptically:

But over the final stage [*Ausgang*] of this hypnotic treatment there rested a veil of obscurity, which Breuer never raised for me; and I could not understand why he had so long kept secret what seemed to me an invaluable discovery instead of making science the richer by it. (Freud, 1925, pp. 20–1)

Later in the same work Freud reveals a little more by linking this mystery to Breuer's resistance to the theory of the sexual aetiology of neuroses and again to the question of the transference:

He might have crushed me or at least disconcerted me by pointing to his own first patient, in whose case sexual factors had ostensibly played no part whatever. But he never did so, and I could not understand why this was, until I came to interpret the case correctly and to reconstruct [*rekonstruieren*], from some remarks which he had made, the conclusion [*Ausgang*] of his treatment of it. After the work of catharsis had seemed to be completed, the girl had suddenly developed a condition of 'transference love'; he had not connected this with her illness, and had therefore retired in dismay. (p. 26)

These elliptical hints foreshadow an account of the end of the treatment that Freud was to give to Stefan Zweig in 1932, where he mentions the hysterical childbirth that Jones later reported in his biography. In the letter to Zweig he writes:

What really happened with Breuer's patient I was able to guess later on, long after the break in our relations, when I suddenly remembered something Breuer had once told me in another context before we had begun to collaborate and which he never repeated. On the evening of the day when all her symptoms had been disposed of, he was summoned to the patient again, found her confused and writhing in abdominal cramps. Asked what was wrong with her, she replied: 'Now Dr B.'s child is coming!'

At this moment he held in his hand the key that would have opened the 'doors to the Mothers', but he let it drop. With all his great intellectual gifts there was nothing Faustian in his nature. Seized by conventional horror he took flight and abandoned the patient to a colleague. For months afterwards she struggled to regain her health in a sanatorium.

I was so convinced of this reconstruction [*Rekonstruktion*] of mine that I published it somewhere. Breuer's youngest daughter (born shortly after the above-mentioned treatment, not without significance for the deeper connections!) read my account and asked her father about it (shortly before his death). He confirmed my version, and she informed me about it later. (Freud, 1961, pp. 408–9)

It was James Strachey, the editor of the Standard Edition of Freud's works, who first linked together the published passages from 1914 and 1925 and the story told by Jones. In a footnote to Breuer's chapter at the point where Anna O.'s treatment ends he recounts how Freud himself had once told him about the 'hiatus in the text' and about the 'strong unanalysed positive transference of an unmistakably sexual nature' (Strachey in Breuer and Freud, 1895, pp. 40–1). But he also noted in a letter to Ernest Jones that he had always been in doubt as to whether this was a story that Breuer had told Freud, or whether it was what he inferred: a 'construction' (Strachey, cited in Borch-Jacobsen, 1996, p. 39). As is quite evident from the above quotations, a 'construction' or, to use Freud's own word, a 'reconstruction' is precisely what it was, and in all the evidence we have that stems directly from Freud's pen, he never disguises this.[3] It is therefore unfortunate that Ernest Jones omitted to highlight the speculative nature of Freud's reconstruction in his biography, but rather relayed the story with no hint that its accuracy might be doubted. The reasons for this are not clear – it may be that Freud withheld this aspect of his story from Jones, or it could perhaps have been simple carelessness on Jones's part. In any event, as first suggested by Ellenberger (1970, p. 483) Jones's version is sufficiently inaccurate in at least some of its supplementary details for it not to be considered unquestioningly reliable even in those respects where we have no direct evidence to refute it. The most that can be said for it is that in its main features it is not contradicted by Freud's own account as set out in his letter to Zweig.

Although we have only these three texts written by Freud telling us directly what he may have inferred about the ending of the treatment, there are several references to the undisclosed conclusion in the testimony and publications of others, which clearly have their origin in what their authors had learnt from Freud either at first or second hand. The first of these, while quite an equivocal document in this respect, nonetheless has one or two notable points.

In 1998 Albrecht Hirschmüller published a newly discovered paper on the Anna O. case written by one of Freud's most loyal disciples, Max Eitingon, (Hirschmüller, 1998; Eitingon 1998). The paper, a typescript found in an archive in Jerusalem, is marked 'Vienna, October 1909' and is written in lecture format rather than as a draft for publication. Having ruled out its presentation at one of the weekly Wednesday meetings of the Vienna Psychoanalytic Society, Hirschmüller surmises that it was most probably given at one of Freud's Saturday evening teaching sessions held in the winter semester of 1909–10 in the psychiatric clinic of the General Hospital, since Freud mentions in a November letter to Karl Abraham that he was currently holding his lectures in the form of seminars (Hirschmüller, 1998, pp. 10–11). Hirschmüller is surely correct here because in a letter to C. G. Jung on 21 November, written two days before the Abraham letter, Freud refers to the content of his university sessions: 'So far I have had two of the case histories from the *Studies* brought up to the level of our present knowledge...' (Freud and Jung, 1974, pp. 266–7).

This reference to the *Studies* corresponds completely with the content of Eitingon's paper, for it is a reading of the Anna O. case history retrospectively interpreted in the light of the state of psychoanalytic theory and practice in 1909. Looked at in this way Eitingon is able to perceive all kinds of things invisible to Breuer but now clearly apparent in the light of the latest psychoanalytic knowledge. Quite predictably at the forefront of this is the sexual element of the case, whose existence had been explicitly denied by Breuer. Eitingon not only perceives the sexual factors at play, but sees the manifestations of a specifically infantile sexuality and the emergence in Anna of a set of incestuous notions in relation to her father. Most of the details of this rereading do not concern us for the present purposes, but there are one or two aspects that are worthy of note.

Eitingon proffers an explanation of the decisive moment of the very beginning of the illness at her father's bedside, when Anna was possessed of an hallucination of snakes. According to Eitingon, the unconscious incestuous content of her daydreams became ever more intensive as she nursed her father and these were reinforced by a convergence with an infantile memory of a similar situation which provoked an intense repression of the whole set of desires, which then itself returned in a disguised form in the shape of the hallucination. This critical moment therefore amounted to nothing less than an incestuous coition phantasy (Eitingon, 1998, pp. 19–20). The corollary of this seems to follow naturally for Eitingon, for if the beginning of the illness represented a phantasy of coition, then the period of weakness, abstinence from food and confinement to bed that followed, he suggests, bears more than a passing resemblance to a phantasy of pregnancy (p. 20). Now this is not at all the same thing as the acting out of a phantasy of childbirth, such as Freud describes in his letter to Zweig and which Eitingon never mentions, but it does provide a context for the place of such a phantasy once it is set in the framework of this particular retrospective reinterpretation of the case. Not only that, but Eitingon takes the analysis one stage further in making explicit Breuer's role as surrogate father for Anna after her own father died. Breuer was not solely the only person at times from whom she would take food, but he also engaged himself with her in her 'private theatre'. In fact Eitingon goes so far as to suggest that her father's death made such a relatively slight impression on her because in her unconscious mind he was not dead, and moreover while he was still alive he had been replaced by another, better father in the form of Breuer (p. 23). So in constructing an incestuous phantasy of coition with her father, followed by a pregnancy phantasy with Breuer in addition taking the father's place, Eitingon sets the scene for the birth of Anna's and Breuer's phantasy baby, which Freud was later to deliver in his own retrospective constructions.

But how far can it be assumed that Freud actually subscribed to the details of Eitingon's construction? In his 1914 account of the case, Freud leaves us in little doubt about his own view of the merits of this kind of retrospective reinterpretation, even though he is rather unusually coy in alluding to the incestuous content of the bedside phantasy:

> Anyone who reads the history of Breuer's case now in the light of knowledge gained in the last twenty years will at once perceive the symbolism in it – the snakes, the stiffening, the paralysis of the arm – and, on taking into account the situation at the bedside of the young woman's sick father, will easily guess the real interpretation of her symptoms; his opinion of the part played by sexuality in her mental life will therefore be very different from that of her doctor. (Freud, 1914, pp. 11–12)

What further might we conclude about the real author of this recasting of Breuer's case? Are we to suppose that Eitingon was, after all, responsible for the revision, or that he formulated it for the 1909 seminar under Freud's close guidance?

Eitingon gave his paper during his second visit to Vienna to see Freud, the first having taken place in 1907 (Jones, 1955, pp. 35–6). We know from the minutes of the Vienna Psychoanalytic Society that Eitingon was present at the meetings of 12 and 20 October and also those of 3 and 10 November (Nunberg and Federn, 1967, pp. 276, 290, 303). In a letter to Sándor Ferenczi on 22 October Freud writes: 'Eitingon is here and goes for a walk with me twice a week before dinner, and has himself analyzed at the same time' (Freud and Ferenczi, 1992, p. 85). On 10 November in a further letter he wrote: 'Eitingon, who picked me up twice a week for an evening walk, where he had himself analyzed is coming on Friday for the last time and then is going to Berlin for a year' (p. 98). So during his stay in Vienna of at least a month Eitingon was in frequent contact with Freud, and given that he presented a paper on Anna O. at one of Freud's university seminars it is surely inconceivable that the two of them did not speak of the case in some detail outside the seminar itself. Since Eitingon put himself in the position of being a follower and pupil of Freud to the point of having himself analysed by him, it is also surely quite unlikely that he would propose any reinterpretation of the case in Freud's presence that was not in its major aspects in accordance with Freud's own views on the matter. This does not mean that all the key points of Eitingon's paper should be attributed to Freud, but that simply that a two-way influence on any one of them cannot as a matter of course be ruled out. Unfortunately there is no other clear evidence from the paper to indicate anything further that Freud may have contributed, directly or indirectly.[4]

Over the years after Eitingon's paper there accumulated further comments on the case by people who indicated that they had been privy to more information about the end of Anna's treatment than is given in the case history. Some of these are clearer than others, though none is straightforwardly and informatively reliable.

First of all in 1914 Poul Bjerre wrote enigmatically: '...I can add that the patient had to undergo a severe crisis in addition to what was given out in the description of the case' (Bjerre, 1920, p. 86, quotation taken from the revised edition of the English translation).

Then in a private seminar in 1925 Jung made some remarks about the case:

> Thus again, the famous first case that he had with Breuer, which has been so much spoken about as an example of a brilliant therapeutic success, was in reality nothing of the kind. Freud told me that he was

called in to see the woman the same night that Breuer had seen her for the last time, and that she was in a bad hysterical attack, due to the breaking off of the transference. This, then, was no cure at all in the sense in which it was originally presented, and yet it was a very interesting case, so interesting that there was no need to claim for it something that did not happen. But all of these things I did not know at that time. (Jung, 1989, p. 16)

In 1927 Marie Bonaparte wrote the following in her journal of her analysis with Freud:

> Freud told me the Breuer story. His wife tried to kill herself towards the end of the Anna = Bertha treatment. The rest is well known: Anna's relapse, her phantasy of pregnancy, Breuer's flight.
>
> Breuer's daughter questioned her father about it. He confessed everything that Freud had written in the *Selbstdarstellung*.
>
> Breuer to Freud: What have *you* got me into! (Bonaparte, cited in Borch-Jacobsen, 1996, p. 100)

Jung had further words to say on the case in an interview he gave on 29 August 1953 to Kurt R. Eissler. In the rough transcript of the interview we learn that the conversation went somewhat as follows:

J   […] and, for example: The … the … Breuer and Freud … the *Studies on Hysteria* – at the end it's said: She was cured, wasn't she – the one with the chimney sweeping?

E   Yes

J   It's said that she had been cured. Ah, but she was not *cured*! 'When she came into my hands, then she had … she immediately had – when Breuer discharged her as cured – then she had a great hysterical attack, where she … and then cried: "now Dr. Breuer's child is coming!"' We need the child, don't we!? Yes, but that belongs in the case history! (*he laughs*)

E   Yes

J   No?!

E   Yes

J   'Well,' he said, 'that makes a bad impression' and so on, 'doesn't it?'[5]

In each of these testimonies coming after Eitingon we should note one important point. Although they each appear to reveal something about the end of the treatment that had not been recounted by Breuer, and the last three clearly indicate that Breuer did not leave his patient in a state of health, none of them says anything about the fate of Bertha Pappenheim after Breuer left her or the nature of her eventual recovery. So Bjerre refers to the 'crisis' with which the treatment terminated, but says nothing about what happened afterwards. Jung justifies his statements that there was no brilliant therapeutic success and that the patient was not cured by revealing the 'bad hysterical attack', and his 1925 claim that this was no cure in the sense that it was originally presented is therefore a direct corollary of this climactic end to the treatment. Jung's declarations here in no way depend on Bertha's subsequent institutionalisation or any other assumed knowledge about her recovery or lack of it. Marie Bonaparte's journal note too carries the same implication, since the order in which she presents the events (relapse, pregnancy phantasy, flight) indicates that the 'relapse' she refers to occurred before Breuer's flight and is therefore manifested by the pregnancy phantasy itself, not a subsequent decline in Bertha's condition. In fact it is the problem with the transference and Breuer's response to it that is the primary focus of the testimony of all those other than Freud (apart from Jones) whose account appears to reveal something about the treatment that Breuer did not.

Otto Rank, for example, wrote of Anna O.: 'This patient had seemingly fallen in love with Breuer and imagined having a child by him – a phantasy which Breuer treated as a pathological hallucination' (Rank, 1958, pp. 276–7).

In the German edition of his book Borch-Jacobsen (1997, p. 44) cites another account by Rank:

> As Breuer one day revisited his patient, at that time almost recovered, he found her again in bed, in a state of excitement accompanied by violent convulsions whose meaning he had not long to look for. His patient cried out to him that she was now bringing forth the child begotten by him. This was enough to horrify any respectable doctor. Consequently he, so to speak, suddenly forgot his cue, took the matter personally, declared the patient insane, and arranged for her to be put in a mental hospital. There, after some time, this acute condition died away of its own accord. (Rank, 1996, p. 53)

A. A. Brill has his own even more distorted version:

> There was another and perhaps even more conclusive reason for Breuer's ultimate retreat. His famous patient, Anna O., kept coming

to see him for advice and assistance with her problems; and Breuer, following his custom, used to hypnotize her. One day the young woman came to him in a hysterical state, and while he was going through the hypnotizing formulas she suddenly grabbed him, kissed him, and announced that she had become pregnant by him. Of course the old man was shocked. He decided that the girl must be crazy, or, at all events, that the treatment had its dangers. The experience was too much for Breuer. He had not been able to brave the world of prudery to begin with, and this final incident was the climax. There and then he decided to separate from Freud. (Brill, 1948, p. 38)

The manifest confusion in Brill's account is an extreme example of comparable distortions in the other second-hand versions. Jung's 1925 account is plainly false in the respect that he has Freud himself attending the patient on the dramatic final evening and in his 1953 version too he has Freud witnessing the hysterical scene. Rank is clearly wrong in maintaining that Breuer declared his patient insane, and we have already noted the difficulties in Jones's rendering of the events, which will be considered further below. At the level of precise detail none of these versions is inherently trustworthy, yet they all clearly have as their nucleus the story of the end of the treatment as recounted by Freud privately in his letter to Stefan Zweig and as hinted at in some of his publications. The fact of the inaccuracies is in itself of no real account, since they could have arisen in some combination of the various forms in which the stories were received from Freud himself and the lapses of memory of the witnesses (including Freud). The only thing that is surely indubitably the case is that the accounts did originate at some point with Freud. Yet we must emphasise again one other thing that they have in common. None of them dwells in any detail or at any length on Anna O.'s subsequent spells of institutionalisation, and it is only Rank who even mentions her history after Breuer when he says that he placed her in a psychiatric clinic and that the acute state subsided of its own accord after a period of time. Jones's version is the only exception to this, but he is drawing on a completely different set of data to elaborate his point: the Freud family letters.

Freud does himself mention on two occasions the fact that Anna O. spent time in an institution after the treatment with Breuer concluded. The first is in the letter to Zweig, where he says that for months afterwards she struggled to regain her health in a sanatorium. The other occasion is in a letter to Arthur Tansley. In this letter Freud refers to the place in Breuer's chapter which alludes to the considerable time before the patient regained her mental balance entirely:

> Behind this is concealed the fact that, after Breuer's flight, she once again fell back into psychosis, and for a longish time – I think it was 3/4 of a year – had to be put in an institution some way from Vienna. Subsequently the disease had run its course, but it was a cure with a defect. (Forrester and Cameron, 1999, p. 930)

As with those who reported what Freud had told them, there is a problem with accuracy at the level of detail here. The reference to an institution distant (*fern*) from Vienna can only refer to Kreuzlingen and not Inzersdorf, but Bertha Pappenheim stayed here only three and a half months, not nine. The length of time that Freud tentatively suggests is more accurate if we include (as do Forrester and Cameron, p. 934) the five and a half months that she also spent in Inzersdorf on her first return there in 1883, but on the other hand this could hardly be counted as away from Vienna. We must also bear in mind a fact that we have already noted in our consideration of the contemporary documentation on the case. Bertha Pappenheim chose to end the treatment on 7 June 1882, left Vienna nearly two weeks later and it was not until 12 July that she arrived in Kreuzlingen after a stay in Karlsruhe with her relatives for about three weeks. There is no evidence at all here of any pressing psychotic emergency requiring immediate institutionalisation, as the tone of Freud's report tends to suggest. Of course there is every reason why this particular detail would be subject to distortion by Freud. We know that he did not hear anything about the case from Breuer until November 1882, the month after Bertha had left the Sanatorium Bellevue, and writing to Tansley a full fifty years after this, we would not expect absolute accuracy on such a small matter. Nevertheless, whichever accounts we consider we must accept the fact that they cannot constitute a reliable testament as to exactly what had happened at the end of Breuer's treatment of his patient. Moreover, leaving aside the inaccuracies, even in this case Freud constructs the institutionalisation not as the result of a generalised therapeutic failure but as immediately tied up with Breuer's 'flight', in other words, as a consequence of the badly negotiated transference relationship between the doctor and his patient. In all of Freud's accounts the failure of the case lies in Breuer's presumed failure to deal with the transference, not with any preceding problem in his method of removing immediately presenting symptoms.

So considering all these retrospective accounts together, and bearing in mind their common origin in Freud himself, what can we conclude about the end of the treatment, and particularly about the issue of the hysterical childbirth? There is no evidence from the period around the end of Breuer's treatment of Bertha Pappenheim to substantiate the story of a phantom pregnancy, any more than there is to support the notion that Bertha had to be immediately institutionalised as a direct consequence of anything occurring at this time. There is not even any direct evidence (beyond Freud's own testimony) of any kind of crisis at all at the end of the treatment. But in every example that we have from Freud himself – this includes the two published works of 1914 and 1925 as well as the letters to Zweig and Tansley – Freud alludes to the fact that his conclusion was nothing more than a surmise.[6] This conjecture was based on remarks that Breuer made in another connection and according to the letter to Zweig this only occurred after the break in their relations. Jones, for his part adds to the end of the Anna O. story an anecdote about how some ten years later Breuer had described to Freud the hysterical symptoms of another of his patients and how Freud had pointed out that they were typical products of a phantasy of pregnancy. This was too much for Breuer, who quickly left the house without saying a word (Jones, 1953, p. 248). The source of this improbable-sounding story is not given, and although Jones never says that this was the origin of Freud's supposition about the climactic end of the treatment of Bertha Pappenheim, the implication is fairly clear. Even if this supplementary tale has some foundation in fact, it is unlikely to be the sole source of Freud's false pregnancy hypothesis and we must accept that at this point we simply do not know what he was basing it on.

Given that in any case the contemporary evidence does not support such a sequence of events as Freud describes in his letter to Zweig, his most elaborated account, this seems to leave us with two possibilities. The whole story could be a pure concoction on Freud's part: 'sheer invention', as Borch-Jacobsen (1996, p. 33) would have it apropos the version given by Jones, and thus serve as a principal means of discrediting Breuer to those in his inner psychoanalytic circle. But it is surely a rather fantastic and over-elaborated narrative if it exists simply to achieve something that could have been done much more economically and, it has to be said, more plausibly. Why should Freud invent *this* particular fantasy? Why not a simple falling in love on Bertha's part, with Breuer unable to respond in the appropriately psychoanalytically detached manner? After all this would at least be thematically much more directly linked with the conventional notion of transference. (As we shall see later, it was also the version that Jones initially thought of offering to the world in the first volume of his biography). Just a modest amount of exaggeration would have clinched the ideological victory. But if we assume a simple fiction on Freud's part, then we appear to be left with an arbitrary fiction.[7] There is a further problem here. Freud went as far as he felt able in print in questioning the outcome of Breuer's treatment of his patient and never says anything about an hysterical crisis, but if his intention had been simply maliciously to discredit Breuer why would he have needed to gild the lily by concocting an elaborated version of events just for the benefit of psychoanalytic insiders? These after all were the very people who would need less convincing than anyone else of the shortcomings of Breuer's handling of the end of the treatment.

A second possible line of inquiry is that the whole account that Freud passed on to his followers is a mosaic of compressed and distorted fragments of memory and inference of which it may be possible to make some speculative kind of sense in the absence of any more secure forms of evidence. This kind of approach was taken by Christopher Reeves shortly after Ellenberger published his new data on Anna O., and he attempted to resolve the problem in a way which did not simply resort to the idea that Freud or his biographer had deliberately concocted a fictitious story (Reeves, 1982, p. 208). Reeves tackled the question by recognising that while they are fundamentally at variance with the known facts, it is necessary to take seriously the accounts given by Freud and Jones if we are to make sense of them. The first thing he notes is that the institution mentioned by Jones as 'Gross Enzersdorf' is very similar in name to 'Inzersdorf', where Bertha had been committed in June 1881. This suggests to Reeves that perhaps Freud or Jones had not only confused the name of the place to which she went at the end of her treatment with where she had been the year before, but had also attributed to the end of her treatment a sequence of events that had actually taken place at an earlier stage (ibid.)[8] This sequence of events that Reeves has in mind is the crisis in Breuer's treatment of Bertha. This particular line of inquiry is actually false, for we now know, as Reeves could not, that the confusion of 'Gross Enzersdorf' with 'Inzersdorf' originates in Freud's letters to his fiancée in 1883, and therefore from the time that Bertha Pappenheim actually was in the Inzersdorf sanatorium, so it was a simple error of nomenclature rather than of essential location. But leaving aside this erroneous premise, Reeves has other grounds for his idea that there may have been a false displacement from 1881 to 1882. For he next notes that as Breuer's daughter was born on 11 March 1882, she would have been conceived at more or less the time that Bertha was committed to Inzersdorf on 7 June 1881. Reeves observes that one of the main reasons for sending Bertha to Inzersdorf was Breuer's fear for her safety, given her suicidal impulses, and the fact that since her father's death she would take food from only Breuer. Breuer would have felt largely responsible for keeping his patient alive, and if his wife had been quietly jealous of the attention that her husband had been giving his patient then this period would have been one of great strain for Breuer and his family. Reeves is therefore surely right when he observes: 'Contrary to Jones, it makes much better sense to assume that this was the period of maximum strain than to attribute this to the same period a year later, when Anna O. from all accounts was no longer in a suicidal state and was on the way to at least partial recovery' (p. 209).

Reeves tries to account for the hysterical childbirth story by supposing that the date when the putative event occurred in 1882 (the anniversary of Bertha's committal to Inzersdorf) was also the anniversary (or thereabouts) of the conception of Breuer's daughter. Given that during the final period of her treatment Bertha was reliving the significant episodes of her life from one year earlier then it may be that she wanted her doctor to recognise that she had been marking events in his personal life as well as in her own. On this basis it may well be the case that Bertha Pappenheim uttered such words as 'now Dr Breuer's child is coming' in June 1882, but as a recapitulation of an observation made a year earlier that a child had been conceived, rather than as an expression of an immediately lived phantasy of childbirth. So Reeves holds that his idea of a displacement does not mean that there are grounds for believing in the existence of the phantom pregnancy and hysterical childbirth symptoms, rather: 'It seems more plausible to suppose that this reconstruction of what took place was based on Freud's faulty recollection of what Breuer had actually reported to him' (p. 210).

Reeves's interpretation of what may lie behind the story of the hysterical childbirth is a commendable attempt to make sense of something that on the face of it is plainly false, and yet which cannot be glibly dismissed without sacrificing any possible gains in understanding that might be obtained from an intelligent appraisal of the fragmentary data. Other interpretations of the same data are of course possible so it would perhaps be valuable to conclude this point by surveying the ground that Reeves's approach has opened up.

If we work on the assumption that Freud's letter to Zweig, as the most elaborated representative of all the extant accounts we have of his assumed ending of the treatment, is a compressed, distorted and

displaced conglomeration of fragments, then it is perhaps not too fanciful to postulate the following. We have no evidence of a severe crisis at
the end of Bertha Pappenheim's treatment in June 1882, but we do
know, as Reeves points out, that there was such an event a year earlier
when some two months after the death of her father she became impossible to manage safely in her own home and was forcibly removed to the
Inzersdorf sanatorium. There is no sign of Breuer completely abandon-
ing his patient at this point, but it was nonetheless clear that he did not
feel able to deal with her unaided. Here we should bear in mind Freud's
comment to Zweig about the birth of Breuer's youngest daughter and
Jones's more elaborated version about Breuer and his wife taking a second honeymoon in Venice, from which resulted the conception of the
daughter. Is it not possible that it was Bertha's crisis in June 1881 that
was followed the next month by the holiday away?[9] As Dora Breuer was
born on 11 March 1882, the conception does not exactly coincide with
a possible trip, but it would surely be close enough to it to be regarded
retrospectively in the same spirit of a tightening of the family ties in the
face of what Bertha Pappenheim could have come to represent to Breuer
and his wife.[10] Further possibilities open up if we take into account
Bertha's living one year in the past and proceed in the manner that
Reeves proposes. Bertha would not have known until some time later
that Mathilde Breuer had become pregnant during the summer of 1881,
but given that the treatment was to run for a further year it is quite likely
that some or other communication from patient to doctor on the topic
took place during that time. Whether there occurred odd pieces of
behaviour on Bertha's part connected with this, which Breuer may have
mentioned to Freud, cannot be ruled out: this may have been either in
June on the anniversary of the conception, as Reeves suggests, or could
even have been in March 1882, around the time of the birth, or a month
later on the anniversary of Bertha leaving her bed and the death of her
father.[11] While the possibilities are not endless they are certainly mani-
fold and one can construct several different ways in which Freud might
piece these fragments together. It must be borne in mind that he did not
hear about the details of the case until Breuer's treatment of his patient
had finished, and it would not be entirely surprising if events separated
in reality by a year, or many months, became compressed in Freud's
imaginative reconstructions, which we know he did not fit together
until the second half of the following decade at the very earliest.

While these speculations no doubt have their place, it is important
not to give undue influence to the problem of the hysterical birth in
reflections on Freud's stories of how Breuer's treatment ended. It is

certainly one event in some of the accounts where there is good reason to think that it did not occur in the way he described. Yet if we consider all of the extant reports that emanate ultimately from Freud it must be conceded that this is not the central point of his obviously intense preoccupation with what he thought was the unsatisfactory conclusion of the case. But in this respect it is comparable to Bertha's subsequent institutionalisation, which is also mentioned in a few of them in various forms, the only difference being that we know that Bertha actually *was* admitted to an institution after her treatment with Breuer finished. The fact, however, that one of these events did happen, while the other most likely did not, should not blind us to the recognition that neither of these features is pivotal to what Freud repeatedly seems to have put around about the end of the case. It is to this that we should now turn.

5
Defence and Sexuality

Wenn sie wüssten, wo das liegt, was sie suchen, so suchten sie ja nicht.[1]

J. W. von Goethe, *Maximen und Reflexionen* (Posth.)

The main feature of all of the subsequent accounts of the Anna O. case that we have been considering is the question of the transference. This is evidently clear from the context in which Freud develops his public position in 1914 and 1925, but it is also carried through into the supplementary narratives that he passed on privately. This matter is not simply a contingent issue of some details of the case that Freud thought had not been properly disposed of; it is the central principle of the dispute that divided him from Breuer, a key feature of the way psychoanalysis developed after Breuer and, as far as Freud was concerned, fundamental to its continuing existence. Having surveyed the source material on the case that originated after its publication, but still during Freud's own lifetime, we must now take a step back to reconsider in the light of this the immediate context of the case history as it was published in 1895. We need to examine more closely how the question of the transference came to be so important in the breakdown of Breuer and Freud's collaboration, and why it cannot be separated from the issues that drove them apart.

Even as early as 1883 the nature of the intense relationship between Bertha Pappenheim and her doctor had been a topic of discussion between Freud and his fiancée, as will shortly be explored further. Yet what was originally a potentially embarrassing problem of an emotional complication involving Breuer, his patient and his family was not at that stage, or for several years to come, a matter of theoretical importance in the understanding of the therapeutic process. Indeed the significance of this entanglement was not evident to Freud even at the maximum point of his collaboration with Breuer, but it was to become so before they published the *Studies on Hysteria* and it was to be the critical factor that drove them apart.

Freud puts this clearly enough in 1914 when he refers to the very intense suggestive rapport between Breuer and his patient, which served as a prototype of what by this time was known as the transference. Freud knew of some aspects of this transference (albeit not within the compass of this term) as early as 1883, after Breuer had told him both about the treatment and the effects on his wife, but what he did not attribute to it at that time, any more than did Breuer, was any sexual motivation. Neither of course could he think of it as playing any significant part in the outcome of the treatment of the patient. By 1914 he had come to believe that Breuer had inadvertently discovered this sexual motivation, but that his former partner had seen it all along only as an awkward occurrence and been unable to generalise from it.

From the point of view of the theoretical perspective on this phenomenon that Freud had developed by 1914, his comments on the Anna O. case are based on large quantities of judgement with hindsight. But not only was such a perspective impossible for Breuer at the time of the treatment, it was not available to Freud in 1883 nor even when he was embarking on his collaborative venture with Breuer. Not until after the working relationship had collapsed did he conceptualise the full implications of the Anna O. case, and only then as a result of particular theoretical developments. So when Freud pieces together, from various things that Breuer had said to him, a scenario for the end of the treatment, this final picture could not have emerged without the concept of the transference. And once Freud integrates this concept into his emergent system of explanation, then he is able to piece together what happened from the fragments presented by Breuer – possibly augmented by his memory of the emotional drama enacted between Breuer and his wife – on the basis that, given the implications of his theory, something like what he had managed to construct *must* have happened.

To understand why these issues were so important to Freud even at the point at which he was writing the *Studies on Hysteria* with Breuer, it is necessary to consider some of the developments in Freud's theory between the *Preliminary Communication* of 1893 and the final publication of the *Studies* in 1895. These developments have been well covered in the large secondary literature that deals with the theoretical differences between Freud and Breuer, but their connection with Anna O. has not always been sufficiently signalled.[2] For our present purposes these developments boil down to two significant conceptions: defence and sexuality.

Although there are hints of what was to become the theory of defence in a draft for the *Preliminary Communication* (Freud, 1892, p. 153), in the *Preliminary Communication* itself (Breuer and Freud, 1895, p. 10) and also in Freud's lecture of around the same time (Freud, 1893, p. 38), it is first outlined clearly in the middle of 1894 in Freud's paper, *The Neuro-Psychoses of Defence*. Here Freud sets out defence hysteria as an additional form of the illness to the hypnoid hysteria that appears in the *Preliminary Communication*. But this also occurs alongside a first, very visible divergence of views between Freud and Breuer. Describing first hypnoid hysteria, Freud writes:

> In contradistinction to Janet's view, which seems to me to admit of a great variety of objections, there is the view put forward by Breuer in our joint communication (Breuer and Freud, 1893). According to Breuer, 'the basis and *sine quâ non*' of hysteria is the occurrence of peculiar dream-like states of consciousness with a restricted capacity for association, for which he proposes the name 'hypnoid states'. (Freud, 1894, p. 46)[3]

There is no corresponding sign in the *Preliminary Communication* itself that this view was held only by Breuer, and the extent to which the question of defence was a matter of contention between the two authors even at that early stage is impossible to say. Moreover, wherever the concept of defence occurs (or is foreshadowed) before the 1894 paper it is subordinated to the trauma-based theory of the hypnoid state in the sense that the fending off of the unacceptable idea becomes itself the moment of trauma which precipitates the splitting of consciousness. The burden of the 1894 paper, however, is to break this subordination to a certain extent. When Freud now refers to the 'traumatic moment' (p. 50), he puts it in inverted commas, thus indicating, as Andersson (1962, p. 134) points out, that it now has more of a figurative meaning. It also gives the notion of trauma a different set of connotations, shifting away from the idea of the individual as a passive recipient of the traumatic experience to one where the subject is caught in the trauma of a psychic conflict and attempts actively to ward it off (p. 148).

But by extending the analysis to phobias, obsessions and hallucinatory psychoses, where the mechanism of defence is similar in each case, yet where the neurotic outcome varies depending on the disposition of the subject, the defining characteristic of hysteria no longer becomes the splitting of consciousness as such, but specifically the capacity for somatic conversion (Freud, 1894, p. 50). In this movement Freud not only broadens the scope of his analysis but shifts the centre of gravity away from Breuer's focus on hypnoid states and hysteria to the much broader concept of defence as a general category of explanation of a range of neurotic states.

The splitting of consciousness in defence hysteria is the unintended outcome of an act of will on the part of the patient in an attempt to fend off an idea or feeling that aroused a distressing affect (pp. 46–7). In the case of women these ideas arise 'chiefly on the soil of sexual experience and sensation' (p. 47). When it comes to cases of obsession Freud is equally clear about the extent of his commitment to the idea of the centrality of sexuality: 'In all the cases I have analysed it was the subject's *sexual life* that had given rise to a distressing affect of precisely the same quality as that attaching to his obsession. Theoretically, it is not impossible that this affect should sometimes arise in other fields; I can only report that so far I have not come across any other origin' (p. 52). So while sexuality is of marked significance to Freud he does not in this paper extend its role to that of the sole determinant of conflict in defence neuroses.

Yet it is almost certain that Freud actually did believe by this time that sexual factors were always to be found in the defence neuroses if one was prepared to search for them hard enough. This much is clear from his response in a letter of 7 February 1894 to Fliess's comments on his paper: 'You are right – the connection between obsessional neurosis and sexuality is not always all that obvious. I can assure you that in my case 2 (urinary urgency), it was not easy to find either; someone who had not searched for it as single-mindedly as I did would have overlooked it' (Freud, 1985, p. 66). By May Freud has taken his position one stage further. In a letter to Fliess written on 21 May 1894 Freud discusses obsessions again and sets out the basis of his classification of the neuroses. One of the categories, conflict, he glosses as follows: '*Conflict* coincides with my viewpoint of defence; it comprises the cases of acquired neuroses in persons who are not hereditarily abnormal. What is warded off is always sexuality' (p. 75).

These two major shifts in Freud's thinking could not help but place a strain on the collaboration with Breuer to the extent that the latter was not prepared to travel as far down the road in the direction that Freud was wanting him to go. By mid-1894 active cooperation between them had ceased (p. 86) and it is clear from some of the detail of the text of what they eventually published in the *Studies on Hysteria* the following year that they had agreed to differ on some points and compromise on others. On the question of hypnoid states and defence, Freud makes his own position and its difference from Breuer's quite clear:

> It was hypnoid hysteria which was the first of all to enter our field of study. I could not, indeed, find a better example of it than Breuer's first case, which stands at the head of our case histories. Breuer has put forward for such cases of hypnoid hysteria a psychical mechanism which is substantially different from that of defence by conversion. In this view what happens in hypnoid hysteria is that an idea becomes pathogenic because it has been received during a special psychical state and has from the first remained outside the ego. No psychical force has therefore been required in order to keep it apart from the ego and no resistance need be aroused if we introduce it into the ego with the help of mental activity during somnambulism. Anna O.'s case history in fact shows no sign of any such resistance.
>
> I regard this distinction as so important that, on the strength of it, I willingly adhere to the hypothesis of there being a hypnoid hysteria. Strangely enough, I have never in my own experience met with a genuine hypnoid hysteria. Any that I took in hand has turned into a defence hysteria. [...] In short, I am unable to suppress a suspicion that somewhere or other the roots of hypnoid and defence hysteria come together, and that there the primary factor is defence. But I can say nothing about this. (Breuer and Freud, 1895, pp. 285–6)

There is something of an odd logic about this. If one implication of the hypnoid state conception is that no resistance is encountered when the pathogenic idea is introduced during somnambulism, then this should be a way of distinguishing hypnoid hysterias from defence hysterias. Yet while Freud acknowledges the theoretical possibility of hypnoid hysterias, he claims never to have met one because every apparently hypnoid hysteria resolved itself eventually into a defence hysteria. But the corollary of this is must be that whereas there seemed at first to be no resistance to the pathogenic idea (hence making it appear a hypnoid hysteria), such resistance did eventually become manifest (thus bringing characteristics of a defence hysteria to light). This in turn means that the idea which first encountered no resistance could not have been the genuinely pathogenic idea at the root of the hysteria – this remained to be discovered by further work. This is of course an entirely theoretical, not an empirical argument. For if one encounters what might purport to be one of the hypnoid hysterias that Freud allows may well exist, one could never know whether this might not eventually raise elements of defence if only one were persistent enough in pursuing the chain of pathogenic recollections. There appears to be more than a little disingenuousness about Freud's concession to the existence of hypnoid hysterias, and this looks very much like a position that necessary compromise with Breuer had compelled him to adopt.

Having effectively dispatched hypnoid hysteria Freud proceeds to deal with retention hysteria, where there is also supposed to be no resistance, in a similar manner:

> I had a case which I looked upon as a typical retention hysteria and I rejoiced in the prospect of an easy and certain success. But this success did not occur, though the work was in fact easy. I therefore suspect, though once again subject to all the reserve which is proper to ignorance, that at the basis of retention hysteria, too, an element is to be found which has forced the whole process in the direction of hysteria. It is to be hoped that fresh observations will soon decide whether I am running the risk of falling into one-sidedness and error in thus favouring an extension of the concept of defence to the whole of hysteria. (p. 286)

These professions of modesty and tentativeness do little to allay the sense that Freud is writing this with a high degree of certainty that his convictions are correct. Breuer, on the other hand, shows equally little sign of relinquishing his hard-defended position that hypnoid states are the crucial determinant components of most hysterias. In a passage that is almost a direct counterpart to those of Freud's we have been discussing, Breuer embarks on a similar tactic, where concession to the other masks a firm defence of his own theory:

> Conversion – the ideogenic production of somatic phenomena – can also come about apart from hypnoid states. Freud has found in the deliberate amnesia of defence a second source, independent of hypnoid states, for the construction of ideational complexes which are excluded from associative contact. But, accepting this qualification, I am still of the opinion that hypnoid states are the cause and necessary condition of many, indeed of most, major and complex hysterias. (p. 216)

Again, after acknowledging that Freud had demonstrated that defence against distressing ideas can cause a splitting of the mind, he points out that this only happens in some cases, where it must be assumed that there is some kind of mental idiosyncrasy:

> I only venture to suggest that the assistance of the hypnoid state is necessary if defence is to result not merely in single converted ideas being made into unconscious ones, but in a genuine splitting of the mind. Auto-hypnosis has, so to speak, created the space or region of unconscious psychical activity into which the ideas that are fended off are driven. (pp. 235–6)

Kenneth Levin notes that Breuer ascribes to the concept of defence much the same status that Freud accords to the theory of hypnoid states: 'Each insists in *Studies of Hysteria* that, while the other's formula possesses some validity, his own model is the more fundamental one and the one which is the key to the pathogenesis of hysteria' (Levin, 1978, p. 117).

If there is an effective standoff between the two writers on the question of defence, the same is true on the issue of the aetiological significance of sexuality. As has often been noted, Breuer was by no means ill-disposed towards the idea that sexual factors can play a significant part in the genesis of hysteria, nor even to the possibility that they do so in the majority of cases. But as Levin again has pointed out (p. 112–4), Breuer offers explanations of the prominence of sexual factors in the aetiology of hysteria that differ from those of Freud in having nothing to do with defence against sexuality. For example, he suggests that being in love, like sick-nursing, can produce prolonged reveries charged with affect, which are then apt to develop into auto-hypnotic states where the splitting of consciousness can occur. Similarly, because the sexual instinct is a major source of increases in nervous excitation, this nervous energy is a prime candidate for hysterical conversion if the affects cannot be successfully disposed of. So while Breuer was quite prepared to acknowledge sexual factors in the aetiology of hysteria he did so in the service of a quite different explanatory mechanism than the theory of defence advocated by Freud.

Just as important as the difference in mechanism, however, is that fact that while Breuer was prepared to recognise even the preponderance of sexual factors in hysteria he was not willing to go so far as Freud and make them the exclusively determining factor. Towards the end of his theoretical chapter in the *Studies on Hysteria* Breuer comes very close indeed to Freud's own position on sexuality and defence, yet he always manages to qualify this with a reservation. So for example, after writing that: 'I do not think I am exaggerating when I assert that *the great majority of severe neuroses in women have their origin in the marriage bed*' (Breuer and Freud, 1895, p. 246, emphasis in original), he follows it a couple of sentences later with: 'It is self-evident and it is also sufficiently proved by our observations that the non-sexual affects of fright, anxiety and anger lead to the development of hysterical phenomena' (ibid.) Again, towards the end of the same paragraph he says: 'The sexual needs of hysterical patients are no doubt just as variable in degree from individual to individual as in healthy people and are no stronger than in most of them; but the former fall ill from them, and, for the most part, precisely owing to struggling against them, owing to their *defence* against sexuality' (p. 247, emphasis in original). But he then immediately writes: 'Alongside sexual hysteria we must at this point recall hysteria due to fright – traumatic hysteria proper – which constitutes one of the best known and recognized forms of hysteria' (ibid.)

So the crucial difference between Freud and Breuer resides in the fact that whereas Freud's tendency was to place exclusive emphasis on defence as the key aetiological factor in hysteria and the other neuroses and to make sexuality the sole factor in pathological defence, Breuer was not similarly inclined. Although he would acknowledge the significance of these two aspects, he would never concede that they necessarily excluded others. He himself summarised his own position some years later in 1907 in a letter to August Forel:

> Freud is wholly responsible for the 'conversion of affective excitation', for the theory of the 'neuroses of defence' and for the enormous importance of 'defence' in the formation of ideational complexes 'inadmissible to consciousness' from which the splitting of the psyche (*double conscience*) arises. In comparison with this, the pathological effects of the 'hypnoid states' seemed to him negligible – which was not, I think, to the benefit of his theory.
>
> Together with Freud I was also able to observe the prominent place assumed by sexuality, and I can give an assurance that this arose from no inclination towards the subject but from the findings – to a large extent most unexpected – of our medical experience.
>
> Freud is a man given to absolute and exclusive formulations: this is a psychical need which, in my opinion, leads to excessive generalisation. There may in addition be a desire *d'épater le bourgeois*. (Breuer, cited in Cranefield, 1958, p. 320)

That the difference between Freud and Breuer came down not to sexuality as such, but to its role in the aetiology of neurosis is by no means a novel conclusion, and those familiar with the standard secondary literature will know that it has long been established there. Jones (1953, p. 279) is an obvious example, but others could be cited. It seems necessary to emphasise the point anew, however, because in a number of more recent writings the exact role of sexuality in the disagreement between Freud and Breuer is misunderstood because of Breuer's manifest willingness in principle to attribute an aetiological significance to it in some particular cases, as though this signifies that he and Freud were essentially in agreement on the matter. This notion will be examined further below. Confusions on this key point are to some extent understandable when one considers the way Freud himself on occasions publicly recorded his separation from Breuer. In 1914, for example, after describing how Breuer failed to recognise that the sexual nature of Anna O.'s transference was a universal occurrence, and then broke off all further exploration as a result, he continues:

> When I later began more and more resolutely to put forward the significance of sexuality in the aetiology of neuroses, he was the first to show the reaction of distaste and repudiation which was later to become so familiar to me, but which at that time I had not yet learnt to recognize as my inevitable fate. (Freud, 1914, p. 12)

This representation is certainly consistent with the idea that Breuer had a characteristically Victorian aversion to sexuality as such, but given that Breuer was not entirely without justice in his judgement of Freud being given to absolute and exclusive formulations it is also compatible with the more subtle scenario of Breuer reacting unfavourably to Freud's assertion of it as an aetiological factor to the exclusion of all others. When such passages are read on the basis of an image of Freud as waging a one-man war on Victorian aversion to sexuality this easily steers their interpretation in one direction rather than the other. One reads in Rank for example:

> When Freud incidentally among friends spoke of Breuer's part in Psychoanalysis, he betrayed very deep understanding, which likewise appears in the most personal of his works, *The History of the Psychoanalytic Movement* (1914), where he states that Breuer finally fled from the consequences of this discovery, as from an *untoward event*, because he did not want to recognize the sexual factor, the courageous recognition of which helped Freud himself much later to the understanding of his teacher's reaction. (Rank, 1973, pp. 183–4)

Strictly this is a misreading of course, because Freud states not that it was the sexual factor that Breuer failed to perceive, but rather the general nature of the sexual motivation of the transference. It is nevertheless understandable how such representations of Freud's position could arise when the subtleties of his and Breuer's positions in the 1890s are over-looked, and indeed one may wonder how much Freud himself may have contributed to them, since it seems from Rank's account that he quite commonly spoke to friends of Breuer's part in psychoanalysis. Back in the 1890s it is apparent that matters were a little more complicated.

The theoretical differences that brought the relationship between Breuer and Freud to crisis point by 1895 had not been so marked at the time of the *Preliminary Communication* back at the beginning of 1893, and in almost every respect they were the results of Freud's having changed his position. From his point of view the *Studies on Hysteria* taken as a whole were already out of date by the time they came to be published: as early as a year before this he had already disassociated himself from Breuer's the-oretical chapter (Freud, 1985, p. 83) and been frustrated because he was under constraints not to reveal the sexual factor (p. 74). Even Freud's own case histories predated the full extent of the development of his views on defence and sexuality by the time they were published, although this does not prevent him from retrospectively reconsidering the cases and specu-lating on where sexual factors may have been involved (Breuer and Freud, 1895, pp. 259–260). But while Freud was convinced that in his own cases there had in fact been sexual factors at work that he had simply been unprepared to seek out, Anna O. presented a rather different problem. Freud's 'official' position is as follows:

> Breuer's patient, Anna O., seems to contradict my opinion [that hysteria is not an independent clinical entity] and to be an example of a pure hysterical disorder. This case, however, which has been so fruitful for our knowledge of hysteria, was not considered at all by its observer from the point of view of a sexual neurosis, and is now quite useless for this purpose. (p. 259)

But given everything we know about Freud's theories at this time and everything that he knew about Bertha Pappenheim's illness, it is incon-ceivable that Freud would not have thought that this case too could have been regarded as a case of defence hysteria with a sexual aetiology. As we have seen, Freud formally concedes on the basis of the Anna O. case that there may be such a thing as a genuine hypnoid hysteria (p. 286) but there can be little doubt that he did not actually regard this case as one of them. However, while it was one thing to revise publicly his own cases in the light of his new theories, it would have been quite another to do the same to the case of his radically dissenting colleague in a work in which he was supposed to be, at least in some respects, co-author. Yet if Freud and Breuer had been involved in a prolonged tussle about the issues of sexuality and defence in the period leading up to publication, the Anna O. case will necessarily have been brought into their disagreement, with Breuer maintaining that this was a hypnoid hysteria with no trace of sexuality or neurotic defence against it. This much may be gleaned from a further passage in Breuer's 1907 letter to Forel: 'The case of Anna O., which was the germ-cell of the whole of psycho-analysis, proves that a fairly severe case of hysteria can develop, flourish and resolve itself without having a sexual basis' (Breuer, cited in Cranefield, 1958, p. 320).[4] Breuer will surely have said as much to Freud in 1895.

By this time, however, Freud will have accumulated enough evidence to convince himself that Breuer was wrong. We know from Freud's correspondence with his fiancée in 1883 that there had already been something of an entanglement between Breuer and his wife because of Bertha's ability to preoccupy Breuer's attention and his own failure to see clearly what was happening in his own domestic setting. Breuer's refusal to budge on the general question of the sexual aetiology of the neuroses, which Freud found so infuriating, will for him have been inextricably tied to the question of the nature of Bertha Pappenheim's illness and treatment. While Breuer always maintained that her illness had a non-sexual basis, he did concede in the same letter to Forel: 'I confess that plunging into sexuality in theory and practice is not to my taste. But what have my taste and my feeling about what is seemly and what is unseemly to do with the question of what is true?' (ibid.) There is an honest ambivalence here, which, if it was evident to Freud at the time of their dispute, can only have fuelled his exasperation with his erstwhile colleague. From his point of view Breuer's taste and feeling in relation to matters sexual will have had everything to do with his attitude towards Anna O. and will have prevented him not only from confronting Bertha's transference at the time that it occurred, but also from acknowledging it even years afterwards. Such reflections on the character of his colleague would become inseparable from Freud's view of the implications of the Anna O. case in the succeeding years.

6
Transference and the Faustian Imperative

> Was nicht originell ist, daran ist nichts gelegen, und
> was originell ist, trägt immer die Gebrechen des
> Individuums an sich.[1]
>
> J. W. von Goethe, *Maximen und Reflexionen* (Posth.)

The key issue for Freud about the Anna O. case that continued to resonate with him for years after the publication of the *Studies on Hysteria* had very little to do with the subsequent fate of the patient, Bertha Pappenheim, and everything to do with how Breuer had dealt with the manifestations of his patient's transference. The theoretical preconditions for the development of the concept of the transference in its specifically Freudian sense had been laid down by Freud in his theory of sexuality and defence, and the very last section of his contribution to the *Studies on Hysteria* is devoted to a discussion of the phenomenon. By comparison with what he was later to write on the subject it is quite an undeveloped outline of some of the problems of resistance caused when the patient transfers onto the person of the doctor distressing ideas that arise in the course of the analysis. At this point, the development of such a 'false connection'[2] is seen by Freud as a difficulty that will arise in the course of every serious analysis, rather than as an essential mechanism of the treatment itself, but the examples he gives of this are all to do with the patient becoming over-dependent on or sexually attracted to the physician. He says that the way to deal with this is simply to draw attention to it and treat it as one more symptom that will dissolve with the end of the analysis. But right at the end of this section Freud adds a cautionary note about what may ensue if this is not properly confronted:

> I believe, however, that if I had neglected to make the nature of the
> 'obstacle' clear to them I should simply have given them a new

hysterical symptom – though, it is true, a milder one – in exchange for another which had been generated spontaneously. (Breuer and Freud, 1895, p. 304)

Of course, as we first learnt from the account of correspondence between Freud and his fiancée in Jones's biography (Jones, 1953, p. 247), from as early as 1883 Freud knew of the extent of Bertha Pappenheim's demands on her doctor and had grounds for believing that such a transfer of affection on her part may have occurred. He also knew that Breuer had failed to see this developing when it happened, but he also thought that Breuer was not prepared to confront it for what it was. Freud is surely gently suggesting at this point that this affection itself was a part of the dynamic of the illness – an hysterical symptom – and that Breuer left this in place at the end of the treatment. Subsequently 'transference' was to become a key concept of the psychoanalytic vocabulary and as it did so, Freud's perception will have been that Breuer's failure to recognise the significance of its emergence in the Anna O. case became ever greater in its implications than simply the incomplete resolution of one patient's hysteria. Freud publicly drew attention to what he had assumed had been the nature of Breuer's lapse in his 1914 account, *On the History of the Psychoanalytic Movement*, and here characterised his stumbling on the transference as an 'unwelcome discovery' which prompted him to give up the whole work (Freud, 1914, p. 17).[3] In a technical paper, *Observations on Transference Love*, written shortly afterwards, Freud threw any remaining discretionary caution to the winds in declaring that the emergence of the transference situation of a woman falling in love with the doctor analysing her had held back the development of psychoanalytic therapy during its first decade and he made a direct allusion to what he had published about Breuer and Anna O. in his work of the previous year (Freud, 1915, p. 159).

At this point we should recall how Freud was later to characterise Breuer's failing to Stefan Zweig in 1932:

At this moment he had in his hand the key that would have opened the way to the Mothers, but he let it drop. With all his great intellectual gifts he had nothing Faustian in him. Seized by conventional horror he took flight and abandoned the patient to a colleague. (Freud, 1961, p. 409, translation modified.)

The reference here is to the first act of Part 2 of Goethe's *Faust*, where Faust has promised to the Emperor that he would conjure up the spirits of Helen of Troy and Paris. In order to gain the power to do this he has to descend to the mysterious realm of the Mothers and touch a burning tripod with a key given to him by Mephistopheles. Later in the same 1915 paper on transference love that opens with the reference to Breuer, the image of the Faustian undertaking and its perils recurs when Freud raises the question of whether an analyst confronted by an erotic transference in one of his patients should make her give up her desires in the name of social morality before proceeding with the analysis:

> To urge the patient to suppress, renounce or sublimate her instincts the moment she has admitted her erotic transference would be, not an analytic way of dealing with them, but a senseless one. It would be just as though, after summoning up a spirit from the underworld by cunning spells, one were to send him down again without having asked him a single question. One would have brought the repressed into consciousness, only to repress it once more in a fright. Nor should we deceive ourselves about the success of any such proceeding. As we know, the passions are little affected by sublime speeches. The patient will feel only the humiliation, and she will not fail to take her revenge for it. (Freud, 1915, p. 164)

This was a compelling metaphor for Freud and he resorts to it again in a similar context eleven years later in *The Question of Lay Analysis*:

> It would be folly to attempt to evade the difficulties by suppressing or neglecting the transference; whatever else had been done in the treatment, it would not deserve the name of an analysis. To send the patient away as soon as the inconveniences of his transference-neurosis make their appearance would be no more sensible, and would moreover be cowardly. It would be as though one had conjured up spirits and run away from them as soon as they appeared. Sometimes, it is true, nothing else is possible. There are cases in which one cannot master the unleashed transference and the analysis has to be broken off; but one must at least have struggled with the evil spirits to the best of one's strength. (Freud, 1926, p. 227)

The Faustian venture of engaging with the forces of the transference is not a theme that emerges only relatively late in the development of psychoanalysis. Ten years after the publication of the *Studies on Hysteria* Freud evokes a similar scenario in describing how he had grappled with his own failure to deal adequately with transference issues in the case of

Dora. Pondering on the circumstances of Dora's unanticipated discontinuation of her analysis, he writes:

> Her breaking off so unexpectedly, just when my hopes of a successful treatment were at their highest, and her thus bringing those hopes to nothing – this was an unmistakable act of vengeance on her part. Her purpose of self-injury also profited by this action. No one who, like me, conjures up the most evil of those half-tamed demons that inhabit the human breast, and seeks to wrestle with them, can expect to come through the struggle unscathed. (Freud, 1905a, p. 109)

This was the struggle that Freud thought Breuer had so significantly refused to undertake in the case of Bertha Pappenheim. But in the way that Freud described it to Zweig, Breuer's failure was not just an intellectual one – an inability to see what was before his eyes – it was a failure of moral courage, compounded when he persisted even afterwards in denying the significance of the erotic transference, which in 1882 had given him the priceless opportunity to announce a new scientific triumph to the world. As far as Freud was concerned, not only did Breuer waste that opportunity, but he was now in the *Studies on Hysteria* complicit in helping deny the same to Freud himself as a result of his own 'taste and feeling' masquerading as scientific caution. Later, in the postscript of the Dora case study, there is a further passage that is quite striking when seen against the background of the Anna O. case:

> I have been obliged to speak of transference, for it is only by means of this factor that I can elucidate the peculiarities of Dora's analysis. Its great merit, namely, the unusual clarity which makes it seem so suitable as a first introductory publication, is closely bound up with its great defect, which led to its being broken off prematurely. I did not succeed in mastering the transference in good time. Owing to the readiness with which Dora put one part of the pathogenic material at my disposal during the treatment, I neglected the precaution of looking out for the first signs of transference, which was being prepared in connection with another part of the same material – a part of which I was in ignorance. At the beginning it was clear that I was replacing her father in her imagination, which was not unlikely, in view of the difference between our ages. (Freud, 1905a, p. 118)

Apart from the fact that if the name of 'Anna' were substituted for 'Dora' this passage could read exactly as a retrospective commentary on

Breuer's case, even down to the theme of the father replacement, there is something of a peculiarity in the way in which Freud alludes to the case as a 'first introductory publication'. Given that four of the case studies in the *Studies on Hysteria* were Freud's own, the Dora case was hardly his first. But of course Freud is setting those cases behind him and marking a break with the past.[4] In this sense the Dora case is *his* first case study in the same way that Anna O. was Breuer's. And the message to Breuer is quite clear: there is no disgrace in failing to negotiate at the outset all the complications of a path-breaking new form of psychotherapy as long as one is prepared to recognise where things go wrong and to learn lessons from it. The Dora case is an example of how victory can be snatched from defeat: even here, where there was a manifest failure leading to the publication of only a fragment of a case, he, Freud, was able not only to demonstrate the intricate structure of a neurotic disorder and the determination of its symptoms but also to shed light on the circumstances that brought about the treatment's premature ending. All this, Breuer should have done with *his* first patient, Anna O.[5]

Freud's frustration with Breuer and the sense of bitterness that it left him with was long lasting. It is revealed very clearly in a letter that Freud wrote to the philosopher and sexual reformer, Christian von Ehrenfels in 1904. Ehrenfels had written to Breuer to try to enlist his support for his reform movement, which argued against the constrictive effects of monogamy and in recognition of the merits of a more polygamous sexual ethic. Breuer replied with an emphatic refusal, which Ehrenfels then forwarded to Freud. Part of Freud's response runs as follows:

> I can disclose to you that this letter was written in a great excitement, indeed indignation: he would never otherwise have resolved upon such a decisive refusal. The same indignation used to turn against me when I had communicated to him a novelty by which 'Throne and Altar' appeared threatened. It then came back each time as an accompanying sentiment and preamble when he had to admit to a validation of it. You have, in fact, assaulted precisely that which enjoys with him precisely the greatest innermost estimation: monogamous marriage. It will indeed not have escaped you that then there is a buckling in the argument where he deals with his personal attitude to the problem.

> What he communicates of himself can be believed without qualification. He could content himself with saying: I am one of the lucky ones whose moderated and well-directed sexual drive has spared them the struggle against the temptation that you have drawn into

account. But I do not wish for that reason to deny the fact that it is different with most other people, but to give to your achievements all the interest required by the fact that this conflict is so widespread. Instead of this, we have the not-completely-open suggestion that the appetites that struggled out over marriage simply issued from a wicked mode of life in younger years, and a badly concealed inclination to make his individual case a paradigm for the majority. Thereby, a deep-seated bitterness which knows how to make its mark in place of the proclaimed indifference. That fits with what I have always assumed about him: that he is in no way less polygamously disposed than others, but that by leave of a weak sexual executive and by means of a great moral exaltation he has instituted a highly energetic suppression of his superfluous desires into work, but which he must defend against every assault. With this suppression is lost to him – as he very well knows – a large piece of his strength of will and judgement (so far as judgements are based on decision and not on understanding), to the great detriment of science and his success in life. (Letter of 13 March 1904 in Ehrenfels, 2006)

It is against the background of these perceptions and this way of looking at Breuer's handling of the Anna O. case, that we must understand Freud's repeated return to it, more or less obliquely in his published writings, and more fully in conversations and correspondence with his followers. One of the consequences of this is that the issue of Anna O.'s cure becomes more marginal to the complex of issues that concerns Freud, and entirely subordinate to the question of the transference. For Freud, the indication of a successful treatment here was not only the alleviation of the manifest symptoms, but the successful negotiation and resolution of the transference. This is not just a technical point about handling the patient at the conclusion of the treatment. The whole point about the transference is that it is based in the patient's sexual instincts and a transfer of their sexual drives onto the figure of the doctor. As such it is simply one of the consequences that Freud drew from his theory of the sexual aetiology of neurosis, and as the ramifications of the theory of sexuality developed in the years immediately succeeding the publication of the *Studies*, so did the importance of the transference. In Freud's view Breuer had been unable to see any of this because of the inadequacy of his ability to confront the implications of his own sexual drives, as described so graphically in the letter to Ehrenfels. Freud could no more allow Breuer to demur on the question of the transference than he could on the theory of sexuality: both of them were right at the heart of psychoanalysis. Considered in this way, the fate of Bertha Pappenheim in respect of her original complaints immediately after the end of the treatment was more or less irrelevant. If, as is maintained here, Breuer's treatment of Anna O. could have been deemed a success in terms of conventional criteria of hysterical symptom resolution, this does not mean that Freud would have considered the case any more satisfactory as far as the transference relation was concerned. Even allowing for the success of the therapeutic method, about which Freud was never in any doubt, the case represented at least a partial failure on Breuer's part. Breuer is indeed quite candid that even though the presenting disturbances had cleared up it was a considerable time before she regained her mental balance, which Freud could no doubt have persuaded himself was at least in part a direct consequence of the lack of transference resolution when the treatment ended. But once we move onto the terrain of the transference, the very index of a successful cure is displaced and transformed compared with the kind of criteria that would have been in play in 1882, or even 1895.

At the end of his section of the *Studies on Hysteria* Freud describes the consequence of not resolving the transference as simply replacing an original hysterical symptom with a new one (Breuer and Freud, 1895, p. 304). This tactic immediately enlarges the range of what is considered to be a part of the illness. If Breuer had indeed been confronted with an emotional involvement on the part of his patient during the treatment, he would have regarded it as a complicating and personally troublesome factor, but not necessarily as a vicissitude of the neurosis. Under such circumstances he could quite easily have distinguished between the alleviation of the hysterical symptoms to the point where he considered his patient effectively recovered, and what could be construed as accompanying difficulties of emotional over-dependence on the doctor. Psychoanalysis renders such a clean separation impossible to sustain. In fact Freud is eventually able in the case of Anna O. to blur the boundaries even more and to extend the effects of a transference that has never been confronted way into the patient's life after the treatment. The unresolved sexual dynamic has a determining effect on character and achievement. After reporting (as we have noted, somewhat inaccurately) to Tansley in 1932 that after Breuer's flight Anna lapsed back into psychosis and was institutionalised for three quarters of a year, he continues:

> Subsequently the disease had run its course, but it was a cure with a defect. Today she is over 70, has never married, and, as Breuer said, which I remember well, has not had any sexual relations. On condition

of the renunciation of the entire sexual function she was able to remain healthy. Breuer's treatment, so to speak, helped her over her mourning. It is of interest that, as long as she was active, she devoted herself to her principal concern, the struggle against white slavery. (Freud, quoted in Forrester and Cameron, 1999, p. 930)

Whether this is a justified inference or not, its principle radically questions the standard notion of the 'cure'. Once the disease had run its course, then in the conventional sense she was cured and the symptoms were resolved, but the defect consists in the fact that the complete renunciation of sexuality was required because this aspect of her psychology had never been satisfactorily explored and confronted in so far as Breuer had always denied its existence. Ostensibly 'normal' functioning is here effectively pathologised, as lines of continuity are drawn between neurotic processes at the height of the illness and their residual traces in 'character', in this case a renunciation of sexuality, even many years later. Freud's criticism of Breuer's negotiation of the end of the treatment is independent of whether Anna O. continued to be 'ill' in the conventional sense. Even if Breuer had been able to maintain that after the final session his patient showed no residual difficulties whatsoever and had immediately functioned as an effective and autonomous individual, this would not have satisfied Freud as long as he could argue that the transference had neither been faced up to nor resolved.[6]

Approaching the problem in this way we can perhaps appreciate more clearly exactly what Freud had objected to in what Stefan Zweig had written, and what prompted him to relate the anecdote of the phantom childbirth. In Zweig's description of the Anna O. case we find the following:

In the hypnotic state, when shame was in abeyance, the girl told Breuer that beside her father's sickbed she had had certain feelings which she had been ashamed to acknowledge to her doctor and even to herself. The feelings had been repressed from consciousness on moral grounds, but had by deflexion given rise to the morbid symptoms from which she suffered. For whenever, under hypnosis, she avowed these feelings, the hysterical trouble, a substitute manifestation, vanished for the time. Breuer, therefore, continued the hypnotic treatment systematically. As by degrees the patient grew aware, even in the waking state, of the previously suppressed feelings which had been the cause of her illness, the illness disappeared even in that state. Hypnosis was no longer needed. After some months she was cured. (Zweig, 1933, pp. 285–6)

Zweig's account gives the impression that Anna O. became conscious of the sexual motivation for her illness, first in hypnosis, and then without it, and that this increased awareness was the mechanism of the resolution of her symptoms. Zweig had certainly not based his version of the treatment on anything like a close reading of Breuer's case study,[7] but it was to this specific point of the revelation of the sexual basis of the hysteria that Freud objected when he read Zweig's essay in an Italian translation:

> If things had been as your text maintains, then everything else would have taken a different turn. I would not have been surprised by the discovery of sexual aetiology, Breuer would have found it more difficult to contradict this theory, and if hypnosis could obtain such candid confessions, I probably would never have abandoned it. (Freud, 1961, p. 408, translation modified)

Freud then proceeds immediately[8] to recount what 'really' happened with Breuer's patient, how he had pieced together his reconstruction, the story of the hysterical childbirth and Breuer's flight. Freud's objection does not concern any lack of success of Breuer's method, nor any issue about whether the patient was 'really' cured or not. It was solely about the point at which the sexual aetiology of the neurosis became apparent, and to whom, along with consequences of its non-recognition at the time of the original treatment.

The general point here is that in all the examples that have so far been found of Freud's later references to Anna O., his primary focus is not whether she was 'cured' after the ending of Breuer's treatment, but how far the transference was recognised and dealt with. The empirical fact that the patient was institutionalised within weeks of the treatment ending will have done his case no harm in the use he was able to put it to, and we have noted how, when he draws in this fact, he reports it with varying degrees of accuracy. But this is essentially subordinate to the main point about the transferential crisis that Freud draws attention to in all of his retrospective statements. If we wish to use these statements by Freud as independent evidence of the radical failure of Breuer's treatment, then we must pay the price for this by accepting Freud's inference that Breuer's inability to confront and deal with the transference was both the reason for the failure and what defined its character. However, this involves redefining the concept of therapeutic failure away from conventional ideas of the resolution of presenting symptoms and in the direction of some kind of terminal transferential crisis, perhaps with longer-term character residues. This is no doubt a price that many psychoanalytically minded critics will be prepared to pay, although it does not sit at all well with the contemporary evidence from the 1880s about the aftermath of the treatment. Others must recognise that if we do not accept Freud's inviolable linking of the outcome of the treatment to the resolution of the transference, then his retrospective observations, which are focused almost exclusively on this one aspect of the therapy, have very little bearing on the question of whether the patient's immediate hysterical symptoms were resolved and therefore whether Breuer's new therapeutic method was effective. Since Freud's retrospective observations provide no reliable evidence on that question they cannot be adduced to support the claim that Breuer's treatment of Anna O. was, by the standards of the time, unsuccessful.

Part II The Evolution of the Legend

Ein schäbiges Kamel trägt immer noch die Lasten vieler Esel.
(Even a shabby camel can carry the loads of many donkeys.)

J. W. von Goethe, *Maximen und Reflexionen* (Posth.)

7
The Birth of the Legend:
Ernest Jones

> Man geht nie weiter, als wenn man nicht mehr weiß,
> wohin man geht.[1]
>
> J. W. von Goethe, *Maximen und Reflexionen* (Posth.)

We now find ourselves in a curious position. The argument so far about the Anna O. case has been predicated on a close examination of the available evidence. Considering first the documents contemporaneous with her treatment by Breuer it appears that in his view the underlying illness that she suffered from passed more or less spontaneously, but that the hysterical symptoms grounded in the illness were susceptible to the new method of treatment that he developed in working with his patient. By the time Bertha decided to end the treatment on 7 June 1882, both the illness itself and the concomitant hysterical symptoms had considerably subsided. After a brief trip to stay with relatives, she went to the Sanatorium Bellevue for just over three months to convalesce and to try to be rid of a morphine dependence which had developed as a consequence of an acute facial neuralgia. At the end of her stay at the sanatorium, however, she still required the morphine, although it appears that apart from a brief loss of her ability to use her native language each evening, her hysterical symptoms were still in abatement. This residual symptom too declined over the months following, though it is possible that she sometimes still suffered from her absences, which, in Breuer's view, though not hysterical symptoms themselves had been the ground on which the hysteria had taken root. In the succeeding months Bertha's facial neuralgia still continued to plague her, but there is no sign that she suffered from the hysterical symptoms that had been the object of Breuer's therapeutic intervention and the treatment of which later came to mark the case as particularly novel and distinctive.

When the case study came to be published in 1895 the claims for what had been achieved by Breuer were quite circumscribed. He had not found a radical cure for hysteria but a means of removing persistent remaining symptoms once the acute phase of the illness had passed. By this time, however, Freud had developed a new theory of hysteria based on the idea that all neurosis results from a defensive reaction to sexual impulses. This meant that the Anna O. case had to be understood rather differently from the way Breuer still approached it, as he regarded the apparently asexual Anna O. as susceptible to the development of hysterical symptoms when she was taken by the hypnoid states which regularly dogged her and which originated when she was nursing her father. The fact that Breuer refused to accept the universality of Freud's sexual theory of neurosis meant that as far as Freud was concerned he had also failed to appreciate the significance of the transference of aspects of the illness onto the figure of the doctor, and this would have become the key component of the form that the disagreement about defence and sexuality took in the specific context of the Anna O. case. Among Freud and his followers the perils of the supposedly unresolved transference constituted the central problem of the case, particularly as Freud himself had shown in his Dora case study that lessons could nevertheless still be learnt from a prematurely ended treatment. Given that Freud only developed this position after his collaboration with Breuer had collapsed, this aspect of his reconstruction of what had transpired in the case was pieced together from a collection of fragments of evidence and assumptions about what must have happened, until eventually this took in his mind the form of a full-blown transferential crisis on Bertha's part in the shape of an hysterical childbirth, despite the fact that there is no contemporaneous evidence that such an event ever occurred. It does not appear that Bertha's period at the Sanatorium Bellevue, or even her subsequent stays in the sanatorium at Inzersdorf were ever an important factor in the evaluation of the case by psychoanalytic insiders. While in respect of the transference Freud constructed the case as something of a failure, there is no evidence that this affected his view of it in other aspects as a successful therapeutic venture and one which provided the first foothold for psychoanalysis.

So why does this leave us in a curious position? The answer is plain. The summary of the ground traversed in the first part of this book that has just been set out is based for the most part on no new evidence. Almost all the material discussed so far is in the public domain, and although some has not been there for very long, there is nothing in this new material which should radically affect the way the case has been viewed. However, the customary representation of Anna O.'s treatment and recovery as it has been constructed over the last 50 years differs markedly from the reading of the history given here. How can a single and by no means small body of evidence be subject to such varied interpretation? Can it really be that so many people have got it so wrong? Surely, the sceptic will persist, there must be some truth in the findings of modern scholarship, for as more and more evidence has come to light it would be very odd indeed to maintain that for all of this work we actually know less now than we did 50 years ago. That is indeed the implication of what has been argued here, and if we examine some key moments in the creation of the modern story of the Anna O. case it is possible to see how each layer of accretion has incorporated and passed on the distortions of the previous one before adding its own.

The story of Anna O. as it is usually told today operates most often to the detriment of Freud, and in recent times the case is commonly in the forefront of the attack by those fervently opposed to the psychoanalytic movement. It is a curious irony therefore that the unwitting person most responsible for inaugurating the modern fable of Anna O. was one of Freud's most loyal disciples, Ernest Jones. The starting point of the modern myth was the first volume of Jones's semi-official biography of Freud, first published in 1953, where his presentation of the Anna O. case seems at first sight to be straightforward. It comprises eight paragraphs, some details of which have already been noted in passing. He begins with a brief, two-paragraph exposition of the case history, before a third paragraph, which relates what further Jones claimed he had learnt from Freud about the case, beyond what was published in his writings. This consists, in sequence, of Breuer's counter-transference reaction to his patient, his breaking off of the treatment, his return in the evening to witness the hysterical childbirth and his calming down of his patient before leaving on a second honeymoon the next day. The fourth paragraph of Jones's version is a 'confirmation' of this, found in the 1883 letters between Freud and his fiancée in their exchange of remarks about the complications arising between Breuer, his wife and his patient. The fifth gives an account of Bertha's subsequent institutionalisation back in Vienna in the year after the treatment finished and of her subsequent sufferings, and a sixth recounts biographical material about her and her later career. The seventh relates a later incidence of an apparently phantasy pregnancy that Freud and Breuer encountered together and that Breuer again was unable to cope with, and in the final paragraph we are told of Charcot's lack of interest in the case when Freud raised it with him during his stay in Paris. Although this was the version that was published by Jones in 1953 (pp. 245–8) it was not the way he originally conceived the text. In an early handwritten draft, preserved in the Institute of Psychoanalysis in London, the account of the Anna O. case is not only significantly shorter but it also differs in crucial respects from the published version in ways which allow us to surmise the status of some of his sources and their reliability.

After the first two expository paragraphs in the early, handwritten account, which correspond very closely to the published version, there are only two more. One gives a rendering of what Freud told Jones about the case, which differs appreciably from the published version of the same paragraph, and the final one deals with Charcot's lack of interest in the matter in substantially the same form as the final paragraph of the published account. In summary therefore, the published version compared with the early draft has a considerably rewritten third paragraph and four completely new paragraphs interposed between the third and the final one.

In the third paragraph, concerning what Jones had supposedly learnt from Freud, there is in the early draft no mention of any countertransference on Breuer's part, no reference to him breaking off the treatment, nothing about the hysterical childbirth or about calming down his patient before leaving. Instead, we find something quite different:

> F has related to me a fuller account than he described in his writings of the peculiar circumstances surrounding the end of this novel treatment. It is quite true that all the symptoms vanished, after which the patient returned to Frankfurt and – let us hope – lived happy ever after. But in the night after B had bad [sic] farewell to her, highly satisfied with his success, he was fetched back to find her in a greatly excited state, apparently as ill as ever. The patient who, according to him, appeared an asexual being and had never made any allusion to such a forbidden topic throughout the treatment, now declared a passionate love for him and made unmistakable erotic advances. Like a proper Victorian he was profoundly shocked and fled the house. The next day he and his wife left for Venice to spend a second honeymoon, which resulted in the conception of a daughter.

There is clearly a problem here in relation to exactly what Freud had told Jones, for this story is not only different from the one in the published version, but it is also hardly compatible with it. Either Bertha declared passionate love and made erotic advances or she underwent an hysterical childbirth; it is difficult to imagine that she did both, or that

Jones could see them as effectively equivalent versions of the same set of events. But what is also here, though not in the published account, is the claim that all of the patient's symptoms vanished.

How do we make sense of the major discrepancies between the two versions? Let us approach this by way of the four added paragraphs. They suggest that in some form or another Jones gained access to material that had not been available to him when he wrote his first draft, which he then later considered needed amending in the light of the new information. The first new source is fairly obvious: the betrothal letters between Freud and his fiancée. In Jones's first version, not only is there no reference to these letters, but also there is no reference to any information that could be gleaned only from that correspondence. In fact in the final paragraph of the published version he amended a detail to bring it into line with what he had learnt from the correspondence. In the handwritten draft we read that: 'Freud was greatly interested in hearing of this case, which he did soon after the termination in June 1882, or possibly still earlier.' The last phrase was changed later to: 'to be exact, on November 18' (p. 248) a date he ascertained from the betrothal letters.[2] It was not until quite late in the day in the writing of the first volume of his biography that Jones was given access to these letters. Freud's widow had died in November 1951, and the following March Jones received a letter from Anna Freud indicating that she and her sister, Mathilde, were opposed to releasing the letters to Jones, while among the brothers, Ernst was in favour, with Martin wavering. But by the end of the month, Mathilde had changed her position and Anna Freud also assented.[3] Access to these letters meant that not only was Jones now able to add additional chapters to his book, but he was more or less obliged to embark upon a rewrite of some chapters that were notionally complete.

Two of the four new paragraphs in the Anna O. section are clearly derived directly from these letters because Jones cites them explicitly in his footnotes. The first concerns Martha's expression of concern that she herself might end up in the same predicament as Breuer's wife, and Freud's attempt to allay her fears on that count. This is where Jones uses the letters to 'confirm' the account he has just given that there was something untoward about the end of Bertha Pappenheim's treatment with Breuer. We shall return to this paragraph shortly, but the second of the new paragraphs concerns the fate of Bertha Pappenheim back in Vienna, her further institutionalisation in Inzersdorf and the continuing symptoms of illness. This information is derived solely from the family correspondence between August 1883 and May 1887 and we can therefore reliably assume that they gave him data he had not previously been aware of.

On the basis of this new information Jones concludes that 'The poor patient did not fare so well as one might gather from Breuer's published account' (p. 247). These letters were therefore undoubtedly what prompted him to drop the assertion from the third paragraph of his first draft that all the patient's symptoms vanished at the end of the treatment. This is important because it suggests that Jones's only source for his new assertion that the patient did not fare so well as one might think from Breuer's account is these betrothal letters. We should also note in passing that he knew nothing of Bertha's stay in Kreuzlingen after her treatment ended, for the correspondence makes no mention of this. But given that he was so willing to drop it, the claim in the handwritten draft that all the patient's symptoms vanished has no specific evidential value whatever in relation to what really was the state of affairs at the end of the treatment, nor can it even be assumed that this claim derived from Freud's direct personal testimony as Jones suggests. It is much more likely that Jones simply derived this from the standard readings of the Anna O. case itself.

Having said that, what is surely implied is that the notion that the symptoms disappeared was quite compatible with the general picture of the Anna O. case that Freud was putting about informally in various forms among his followers, including presumably Jones. If Freud had been denigrating Breuer's treatment on the specific count of the persistence of the illness, why would Jones not include this in his original draft? In fact he only began to doubt the success of the cure as conventionally conceived when he read the family letters. This is consistent with the earlier conclusion that whatever Freud may have been saying in private about Breuer's failure to conclude the treatment in a satisfactory manner because of his inability to handle the transference, the idea that the treatment was not a therapeutic success was not part of it. Indeed while Jung seems to have been the first person to question the claim of therapeutic effectiveness in the case, he did so purely on the grounds of Freud's tale about the transferential crisis at the end of the treatment, not because he knew anything of Bertha's subsequent history. Jones, on the other hand, seems to have been the first person to challenge Breuer's (and implicitly therefore Freud's) declaration of therapeutic success on the basis of what he thought was independent evidence pointing in this direction. It is merely unfortunate that he did not contextualise the details of the betrothal letters, but simply assumed, wrongly, that they necessarily related to hysterical symptoms that the treatment did not succeed in clearing up, rather than a non-hysterical neuralgia and an accompanying narcotic dependence, as the evidence now actually suggests. But then, unlike many of his successors, Jones did not have the advantage of seeing Breuer's original report of the case, the report written at the end of her stay at the Sanatorium Bellevue, nor the follow-up correspondence.

Once we begin to appreciate the extent to which some of the distinctive features of Jones's version of the case are derived solely from these new sources, and not from what he already knew, we can suddenly see that there is another feature of his 'fuller account' that now immediately seems not to stem from Freud directly, but from the betrothal letters. This is the set of remarks about Breuer's counter-transference. In the published version of the book, he begins this paragraph with the following:

> Freud has related to me a fuller account than he described in his writings of the peculiar circumstances surrounding the end of this novel treatment. It would seem that Breuer had developed what we should nowadays call a strong counter-transference to his interesting patient. At all events he was so engrossed that his wife became bored at listening to no other topic, and before long jealous. She did not display this openly, but became unhappy and morose. It was long before Breuer, with his thoughts elsewhere, divined the meaning of her state of mind. It provoked a violent reaction in him, perhaps compounded of love and guilt, and he decided to bring the treatment to an end. He announced this to Anna O., who was by now much better, and bade her good-bye. (pp. 246–7)

In the next paragraph, the first of those added to what he had written in the earlier draft, Jones cites in support the letter that Freud wrote to his fiancée on 31 October 1883, but he does not quote from it. Compare what Jones wrote with the following passage from the letter, which has since been published in part:

> The poor wife could not bear it that he devoted himself so exclusively to a woman, about whom he obviously spoke with much interest, and was certainly jealous of nothing else but the engrossment of her husband by a stranger. Not in the ugly, tormenting way, but in the quietly resigned manner. She fell ill, lost her spirits, until it dawned on him and he learned the reason for it, which of course was a command for him to withdraw completely from his activity as a physician of B.P. (Cited in Borch-Jacobsen, 1996, p. 41)[4]

These two passages are surely not so dissimilar as to preclude all possibility that the first is a paraphrase of the second, albeit that Jones might simply have used the letter to flesh out the detail of something that Freud had remarked to him at one time or another. Jones will certainly have known that Freud considered Breuer to have been unable to handle the manifestations of Bertha Pappenheim's transference, since this was well established by this time as a part of psychoanalysis's construction of its own history, and indeed Jones gave a version of this in his first-draft account of the ending of the treatment in the form of Breuer's 'Victorian' flight when confronted with Bertha's declaration of love. What seems most likely though is that when he came across the allusions in the betrothal letters to Breuer's domestic entanglement because of his patient, Jones jumped to the conclusion that these referred directly to the stories of the dramatic episodes surrounding the end of the treatment that had been swirling around in psychoanalytic circles since Freud launched them decades earlier. They therefore apparently corroborated something that Jones thought that he already knew the gist of, so he inserted the story of Breuer's counter-transference, including its effects on his marriage and his decision to end the treatment, and then simply 'confirmed' this new version by citing the betrothal letters which had prompted him to amend his account in the first place. In the course of this it was obviously necessary for him to drop his claim that when Breuer said farewell to the patient he was 'highly satisfied with his success', since this would have implied that the treatment was not ended prematurely because of Breuer's need to placate his wife and it would also have contradicted his later claim that the treatment was not the therapeutic success that Breuer had made out.

If this was indeed the way that Jones's manufacture of this point proceeded, then there are two principal implications for the evidential status of his text. First of all its manifest circularity means that the story of Breuer's counter-transference as Jones gives it has no independent validity outside his own inference that the betrothal letters point inevitably to this particular version of the end of the treatment. In fact the dramatic end of the treatment was a retrospective construction of Freud's years afterwards, and bears no direct relation to the matters he was discussing with his fiancée in 1883. We shall return to this point below. Secondly, it therefore follows that despite the opening sentence of his paragraph, this particular version of events was not part of the fuller account of the ending of the case that he had learnt directly from Freud. Indeed there is no independent evidence for Jones's report of the course and consequences of Breuer's counter-transference beyond the evidence from the betrothal letters. But if they do not in fact support his conclusion, then Jones's account must be completely discarded.

So just how reliable is Jones's own construction here? One of the reasons why the question of its accuracy is so important lies in the assertion that Breuer decided to bring the treatment to an end and then announced this to his patient, thus prompting her hysterical crisis of termination: 'He announced this to Anna O., who was by now much better, and bade her goodbye' (Jones, 1953, pp. 246–7). This stands in stark contradiction to Breuer's claim in the published case that it was Bertha Pappenheim herself who determined that the treatment should end by 7 June, the anniversary of her removal to Inzersdorf (Breuer and Freud, 1895, p. 40). Either one or other of the accounts must be false. And if Jones is dependent entirely on the betrothal letters at this point we must confront the fact that here Freud clearly states that Breuer felt under a command to withdraw completely from his activity as a physician of Bertha Pappenheim, which does indeed seem to clash with Breuer's statement that it was the patient herself who decided when the treatment should end.

Or does it? Let us assume that what Freud writes to Martha in October 1883 is broadly true, and that Breuer was motivated to withdraw completely from Bertha's treatment. What evidence do we have to tie this to the beginning of June 1882 rather than sometime later? There is nothing about this in the letter to Martha itself. Here it is necessary to go back a year to the time that Bertha Pappenheim was still in the Sanatorium Bellevue in Kreuzlingen. In a letter of 7 October 1882, Bertha's mother, Recha Pappenheim, writes to Robert Binswanger at Bellevue concerning Bertha's future. She has received a report from Binswanger that Bertha's withdrawal from morphine has not been successful and that this has 'cut across our plans and left our expectations in the lurch' (Hirschmüller, 1989, p. 303). However, Bertha's mother also knows that her daughter is not willing to stay any longer at Bellevue and that a change of residence is inevitable. She continues: 'Like you, I am of the opinion that B[ertha] must be transferred from the care of one doctor into the charge of another so that the ground we have gained so far is not soon forfeited again. It is equally clear that, as things stand, all so-called travel plans must be abandoned and a place accepted somewhere, for a few months at least' (ibid.) Later in the letter, when considering the prospect that Bertha might return immediately to Vienna, she notes simply that 'Dr Breuer is unable to take over the treatment' (p. 304).

These passages are quite revealing. They indicate first that Bertha's period at the sanatorium was longer than had been anticipated and that she only stayed as long as she did because of the morphine problem. Secondly, it is clear that it had not by any means been taken for granted at the outset that continuing medical treatment would be necessary: this only comes about because of the failure of the morphine withdrawal. Thirdly, we can assume from this that when Bertha and Breuer parted in June, he would have had no reason to presume automatically that he had an immediate continuing responsibility for his patient. This issue only arises again now, in October 1882, given the lack of progress that Bertha has made. It is therefore entirely possible that both versions of the story of the end of the treatment are true: it was Bertha herself who decided that her direct treatment by Breuer would be finished by 7 June, but it was only when, a few months later, Recha Pappenheim was exploring the various possibilities for Bertha's continuing treatment in the light of the failed morphine withdrawal that Breuer was compelled to indicate that he wished to have no further involvement with her at all, and this quite possibly for the reasons indicated by Freud to Martha a year later. At any rate, this is not a scenario that is inconsistent with the contemporary evidence, and it has the merit of resolving the glaring contradiction posed by Breuer's quite specific statement about Bertha herself choosing to end the treatment by 7 June. By making this stark claim, the detail of which was quite unnecessary in the context, Breuer would have been leaving himself open to immediate contradiction by anyone who was familiar with the case, were it not true. In summary therefore, Jones was in error to assume that the context of the discussion between Freud and Martha in the autumn of 1883 was the dramatic end to the treatment over a year earlier that Freud, years afterwards, was to reconstruct as having transpired. The correspondence could just as easily have been about something that happened some months after Bertha finished her treatment with Breuer.

There is another aspect of Jones's construction here that is worth further consideration, to do with the exact nature of the dynamic between Breuer, his patient and his wife at the end of the treatment. Both in the unpublished draft and in the published version of the episode Jones discusses what, in psychoanalytic terms, may be characterised as transference and counter-transference issues, albeit that they appear in rather different forms in each account. In the unpublished version, there is no hint of an emotional aspect to Breuer's attitude to his patient during the course of the treatment. It is Bertha who, at the end, is overwhelmed by her transference, and Breuer's unsatisfactory response – in this case attributed to his 'Victorian' character, rather than a counter-transference – arises only in relation to this. In the published version, however, it is Breuer's counter-transference, his preoccupation with his patient at the expense of his wife, that comes first, before we are given the account of Bertha's transferential pseudocyesis, followed again by Breuer's flight, the only common factor in the two versions of events. Nevertheless, whatever the exact form of the story that had trickled down from Freud, it contained both of these two elements. But was Jones justified in seeing evidence of transference and counter-transference in the betrothal correspondence?

For in the opening sentence of his next paragraph in the published version he cites Freud's letter of 31 October 1883 in support of his narrative: 'Confirmation of this account may be found in a contemporary letter Freud wrote to Martha which contains substantially the same story' (Jones, 1953, p. 247). Now of course this is not true as regards the bare facts: there is nothing in the letter about the hysterical childbirth or Breuer's flight from this or his second honeymoon. Moreover the likelihood has already been established that, rather than just confirming to Jones the details about Breuer's problems with his wife, it was the letter that provided him with them in the first place. But Jones continues by paraphrasing some of the exchange between Freud and Martha: 'She at once identified herself with Breuer's wife, and hoped that the same thing would not ever happen to her, whereupon Freud reproved her vanity in supposing that other women would fall in love with *her* husband: "For that to happen one has to be a Breuer."' (ibid.) Jones's emphasis in this paraphrase is clearly on the emotional response of the patient in falling in love with her doctor, but this does not capture the entirety of what Martha wrote about Bertha. What Martha had actually written was:

> It is remarkable that another man has never come closer to poor Bertha than her physician of the moment; ah, as a healthy person she would sure enough have had the ability to turn the head of the most sensible of men – what a misfortune for the girl. You will surely laugh at me dearest but the story scarcely let me sleep last night; I put myself so vividly in the position of the silent Frau Mathilde until, half waking, I felt and half dreamt of being in her place and in the situation that you wrote of yesterday, which brought me to such an excitement that I felt a burning longing for you [...]'[5]

In this passage there are two quite distinct ideas, and it is only the second that Jones alludes to. The first is to do with Bertha's misfortune that her illness has tended to preclude active interest on the part of potential suitors, with the effect that the only people who come close to her are her doctors. This is in response to Freud having written that a colleague of his who knew Bertha in Inzersdorf was quite enraptured with her, and had he not as a psychiatrist been aware of the problems stemming from a disposition to severe hysterical illness then Freud believed he would have fallen in love with her (letter cited in Borch-Jacobsen, 1996, pp. 40–1). Martha's comment implies that whereas he had been deterred from following his inclinations because of Bertha's illness, had she been healthy he would surely have been unable to resist her charms. While it is true that in the epithet of Bertha having the ability to turn the heads of men there is slightly implied an active engagement on her part, the clear implication is that because of her malady all that she can hope for in the way of men's attention is what may legitimately and properly be expected from her doctors.

It is the following sentence that Jones refers to directly, and here Martha moves to a different focus as she imagines herself in the position of neglect experienced by Breuer's wife, with her future husband monopolised by the demands of a stranger. It is clear, however, that Martha infers no impropriety on the part of either Breuer or his patient, nor had Freud at this point given her cause to, for as he had written in his previous letter, urging Martha to be discreet about what he was telling her: 'It is nothing dishonourable, but rather something very intimate and that one keeps to oneself and one's beloved' (p. 41).

Freud's response to Martha's expression of her apprehension is playfully direct:

> You were right to expect that I would laugh at you. I do so with great gusto. Are you really so vain as to believe that people are going to contest your right to your lover or later to your husband? Oh no, he remains entirely yours, and your only comfort will have to be that he himself would not wish it any other way. To suffer Frau Mathilde's fate one has to be the wife of a Breuer, isn't that so? But when you are quite fond of me I am immensely glad; I need no other favour than yours. (Partly cited in Forrester, 1990, pp. 19–20)[6]

So Freud denies that anyone else would actively want to make such demands on him as Bertha made on Breuer, but reassures Martha that in any case he would not wish to attract such interest because he is devoted to her. The reference that immediately follows to being the wife of a Breuer is tantalisingly ambiguous when taken in isolation: either Breuer was so attractive as to make women want to monopolise his attention (which Freud modestly denies would be so in his own case) or he, unlike Freud, was the kind of person to respond to such interest. Jones resolves this ambiguity in the direction of the first alternative and puts the matter in terms of the woman's emotional desire, rather than the man's, when he refers to the possibility of another woman falling in love with Freud. However, Freud himself in his final sentence seems to resolve this more in the way of a comment on Breuer's susceptibility to distraction, in contrast to his own imperviousness to such an enticement, given Martha's own affection for him.

The concept of the transference is sufficiently flexible to cover the emotional aspect of most kinds of relational circumstance, if one is of a mind to use it in this way. Nevertheless it is difficult on the whole to see the passage from Freud's letter that Jones paraphrases, when put into its full context and examined in detail, as justifying a reading in terms of the most patent transferential features often ascribed to the Anna O. case. Still less could it be the basis for Freud's later construction as to how the treatment ended. Jones is surely approaching this correspondence already inclined to look for evidence of transference and its correlates by what he already thinks he knows about the Anna O. case. But considered without the support of such a predisposition the exchange between Freud and his fiancée appears to suggest that Breuer's failing consisted of little more than the overlooking of his wife's sense of neglect in the face of overweening demands from a patient on his time and attention, and it says nothing direct at all about any emotional ties to Breuer on the part of Bertha Pappenheim.

The point here is that Freud's published writings on the Anna O. case, particularly those of 1914 and 1925, are pitched in general terms of transference and counter-transference, but without revealing the detail of exactly what he thought had happened. Judging by the various accounts that are to be found in the testimonies of other people, including Jones's own two versions, there was no great clarity even in Freud's lifetime about exactly what had transpired or when, although how much Freud himself was responsible for this lack of precision remains an open question. But Jones over-interprets what he will have seen in the letters as the new data on transference and counter-transference in the light of what had been passed down to him about the dramatic end of the treatment and assumes that it is one and the same event that is the common reference point. If thus forging two sources about two possibly quite separate occasions into a single mythical incident was something of a speculative enterprise it was perhaps not an entirely unreasonable one, given what Jones may have presumed he knew about the terminal crisis of the treatment. But now that we have access to the correspondence between Bertha's mother and her doctor, suggesting that it was some months after the ending of the treatment that Breuer declined to become involved again, there is no need for us to prolong the flight of fancy since we can provide an alternative explanation that is consistent with all the available data.

If Jones is somewhat careless in confusing the end of Anna O.'s treatment with the topic under discussion in the betrothal letters, things are not much clearer for readers of his chapter as regards the link between these matters and Bertha's subsequent fate. In the two new paragraphs that derive solely from the Freud family correspondence, Jones relates first the engaged couple's comments about Breuer's domestic problems, and then in the next paragraph he gives details about Bertha's subsequent institutionalisation and her continuing suffering. But it is important to note that Jones makes no explicit connection between the story of how the treatment concluded and Bertha's later progress: they are two separate narratives. The uninformed reader could be excused for linking the two, given the sequence of Jones's text, and Jones certainly does not make it clear exactly what was the nature of Bertha's problems in the years succeeding her treatment with Breuer. He was not, of course, in any position to do this since he had not seen any of the Kreuzlingen reports nor the ensuing correspondence concerning the case, which might have made it clearer to him that the evidence that these problems had anything to do with Bertha's hysterical symptoms was exceedingly thin. The construction of Jones's text therefore seems to weld into a single continuous narrative of failure and complication what are in fact a series of relatively independent episodes with quite diverse evidential bases. In sequence we are presented with a number of elements: Breuer's counter-transference; his breaking of the treatment; Anna O.'s relapse and Breuer's flight; confirmation of the counter-transference; Anna O's subsequent suffering. In fact the first two refer to domestic complications and their results, which probably have no relation at all to the termination of the treatment in June 1882; the third is a retrospective construction of Freud's from years later; the fourth simply restates the first element in its original form, while the fifth is actually referring to a set of symptoms that were not substantially the subject of Breuer's treatment of his patient in the first place.

What then of the hysterical childbirth? How are we to account for the fact that this only appears in the published version of Jones's work, while a different story is given in the early draft? Was this too a case of Jones learning something from a new source that he had not known when he wrote his first draft? Apart from Jones's own account, and leaving aside Eitingon's 1909 paper where he attributes to her a pregnancy phantasy ostensibly on the grounds of the internal evidence of the case, we currently have four different references to the idea that Anna O. thought she had become pregnant by Breuer: those of Marie Bonaparte, Rank, Brill and of course Freud himself. Only two of these (Rank and Freud's letter to Zweig) mention an actual hysterical birth. Leaving aside the question of the accuracy of some of the versions, there is no doubt that this was a story in one form or another that Freud himself told at least some of his followers. Why did Jones not mention this in his first draft? Among the leaves of the handwritten draft of his book there exists a separate sheet of paper containing the following passage, including the indications at the beginning and end to indicate where it should be placed in the existing text:

> ...throughout, was now in the throes of an hysterical childbirth, the logical termination of a phantom pregnancy that had been invisibly developing in response to Breuer's treatment. Though profoundly shocked, he managed to calm her down by hypnotising her, and then hurriedly left the house in a cold sweat. The next...

This is substantially the same as what was to appear in the published text and it represents the interpolation in its earliest form, displacing the statement that Anna O. made erotic advances towards Breuer. This is so different from Jones's first version that it seems doubtful that he knew this story all along, and more likely that he learnt it from a source which, at the very least, confirmed its authenticity as far as he was concerned. Among the likely candidates, Marie Bonaparte seems on the face of it a possibility. However, it appears that she did not provide Jones with notes abstracted from the journal of her analysis with Freud until June 1954 (see Borch-Jacobsen, 1996, p. 102), and even here she does not mention a phantom birth, though the possibility that she had provided Jones with details of what Freud had told her about Anna O. before this time cannot entirely be ruled out. Anna Freud is another possible source who also cannot be discounted.[7]

Correspondence between Jones and Strachey preserves the possibility that Jones had known about hysterical childbirth story for some time. Late in 1951, Jones had sent a draft of the chapter relating the Anna O. narrative to Strachey. Strachey wrote on 24 October 1951 in his responding notes that he himself had been told the same story by Freud, but had always wondered whether this might just be Freud's construction:

> Breuer's adventure. Freud told me the same story with a great deal of dramatic business. I remember very well his saying: 'So he took up

his hat and rushed from the house.' – But I've always been in some doubt of whether this was a story that Breuer told Freud or whether it was what he inferred – a 'construction' in fact. (Strachey, cited in Borch-Jacobsen, 1996, p. 39)

His notes continue: 'My doubts were confirmed by a sentence in the *Selbstdarstellung* [...]' and he then goes on to quote the key passages from Freud's 1925 *Autobiographical Study* which refer to the obscurity surrounding the end of the treatment and his own reconstruction of events. Strachey's phrasing thus implies here that he had been told this 'same story' by Freud in the early 1920s, before the publication of the *Autobiographical Study*. He continues: 'But you seem on p. 20 to have further evidence on the subject. Were Freud's published remarks put in that form for reasons of discretion?' (letter in the Jones Archives at the Institute of Psychoanalysis). Jones unfortunately did not respond directly to Strachey's implied question about further evidence. He replied on 27 October:

> Freud gave me two versions of the Breuer story. The theatrical one about his grabbing his hat, and then the true one that Breuer hypnotised Anna and calmed her before leaving. I have left out the hat; 'rushed from the house' seems to me legitimate; since it conveys the spirit of the situation. (Cited in Borch-Jacobsen, 1996, p. 39)

What is not totally clear is what exactly Jones had sent to Strachey for comment and therefore what the 'same story' that the latter had heard really was. In 1951 the betrothal correspondence had still not been released to Jones, so Strachey certainly did not see the version that Jones eventually published. But given the probability that Jones will have sent a typescript copy, this will surely postdate his longhand notes and therefore incorporate his handwritten interpolation about the hysterical childbirth. The detail about Breuer hypnotising his patient appears only in the published version, not in the manuscript draft, so what he sent to Strachey seems on the face of it to be a relatively late draft of this chapter, though obviously not the final one. Neither Strachey's comment in his letter, nor his own footnote to Breuer's chapter of the *Studies* is explicit about the details of what he thought had happened, although in the latter he does refer to Jones's biography for the whole story (Breuer and Freud, 1895, pp. 40–1) thus apparently endorsing Jones's account. No doubt Jones thought that he had sufficient evidence to print the hysterical pregnancy story, though whether he had adequately distinguished between direct corroboration of the events as related by Freud from further evidence of their second-hand transmission to other parties remains doubtful.

In any event, the uncertainty about the source of the published version of Jones's account and the difference between this and the earlier draft are sufficient to indicate the vagueness of the stories that were circulating among Freud's closest followers about exactly how the treatment of Anna O. had ended. Freud no doubt gave variant accounts of this at different times to different people, and the extent of the ensuing corruption of the narrative as it passed through different hands is difficult to gauge. Clearly none of the second-hand accounts gives the story any more validity as a description of what actually happened between Breuer and his patient than Freud's own tale. Freud may or may not have had good reasons for his retrospective construction, but in the manner that it has been cited as an indicator of the extent of Breuer's therapeutic failure with his patient it carries no weight at all.

What then of the significance of another of the paragraphs that Jones added to his account when it came to publication? Does not the anecdote of the case of phantasy pregnancy that Freud and Breuer came across together some ten years later add credence to the equivalent part of the Anna O. story? Here too Breuer manifested the same reaction of flight (Jones, 1953, p. 248). Borch-Jacobsen wonders whether this was the incident that gave rise to the Anna O. pregnancy story in the first place (Borch-Jacobsen, 1996, p. 44) but perhaps more likely is that this story of supposedly ten years afterwards is a corrupted variant of Freud's Anna O. reconstruction.

For in the Bernfeld section of the Sigmund Freud Archives in the Library of Congress in Washington is an essay of memoirs written by Ludwig Jekels. In this essay is the following passage:

In public discussions Freud was backed up by Breuer. Privately, however, there were occasionally some differences of opinion between the two of them. One such episode related to me by Freud is worth mentioning in this context. Freud had come to the home of one of Breuer's patients for a consultation. Breuer described at length the symptoms of the patient – a woman. Freud thereupon attempted to make it clear to Breuer that quite obviously the content of the patient's symptoms were pregnancy fantasies. Breuer was shocked; without a word he rose, took his hat and stick and left the house.

It is not clear for whom this essay was written, but it is instructive to compare it with the passage in Jones's book, for surely it is the source of Jones's anecdote:

> Some ten years later, at a time when Breuer and Freud were studying cases together, Breuer called him into consultation about the case of an hysterical patient. Before going into see her he described her symptoms, whereupon Freud pointed out that they were typical products of a phantasy of pregnancy. The recurrence of the old situation was too much for Breuer. Without saying a word he took up his hat and stick and hurriedly left the house. (Jones, 1953, p. 248)

In the Jekels version there is no reference to the incident occurring ten years afterwards, and no supposition that this was a recurrence of a previous situation. What seems most likely is that Jekels has rendered a corrupted version of what he had been told by Freud about Breuer and Anna O. and that Jones has unwittingly taken this as referring to a separate occasion and reinforced this in his own representation of the story. If this is so then of course it completely undermines the status of the event as Jones recounts it.[8]

   When we look at Jones's account of the Anna O. story as a whole, we therefore find not a coherent and reliably sourced narrative but a mosaic of fragments of unclear origin, questionable interpretation and doubtful, third-party hearsay. Although his version of events has been questioned on specific details, particularly on the matter of the hysterical childbirth and its repercussions for Breuer, there can be no doubt that it set the pattern for subsequent revisions of the Bertha Pappenheim case history and legitimated the birth of the legend: not only was the treatment broken off abruptly, prematurely and for dubious reasons before her hysteria had been in any way resolved, but she continued to suffer from her hysterical affliction for some years to come, a fact that both Breuer and Freud had an interest in suppressing. As the legend developed from infancy to maturity it grew in size and complexity, voraciously incorporating all the evidence on the case that subsequently came to light and turning it to its own ends. At no point has this evidence been looked at afresh to see if it sanctions the story perceived in Jones's account; rather, the tenor of the Jones account and the implication that the Anna O. case was essentially a failure has dominated the last 50 years of the case's history, shifting and mutating to assimilate new details and possibilities as successor historians of psychoanalysis have followed in Jones's footsteps.

8
The Development of the Legend: Henri Ellenberger

> Wer das erste Knopfloch verfehlt, kommt mit dem
> Zuknöpfen nicht zu Rande.[1]
> J. W. von Goethe, *Maximen und Reflexionen* (Posth.)

A fine example of the process of incorporation of further evidence and the consequent enlargement of the myth can be seen in Henri Ellenberger's several discussions of the Anna O. case. Henri Ellenberger is best known for his massive study of the development of dynamic psychiatry, the fruits of which he published in 1970 as *The Discovery of the Unconscious*. Central to this project was the attempt to demonstrate that theories of the unconscious, and dynamic psychologies in general, did not begin or end with Sigmund Freud. Ellenberger's examination of Freud's work, the first significant general biographical incursion into Freud's life since Jones – and arguably still the best – presented many fresh insights and interpretations based on a mass of new research by its author undertaken over many years. A re-examination of the Anna O. case formed a key part of Ellenberger's attempts to revise the accepted depiction of Freud and his work, although the extent to which his research would contribute to a wholesale alteration of way the case has been regarded was perhaps not anticipated by him at the outset.

In 1966 Ellenberger published a review of a book consisting of a selection of Bertha Pappenheim's more informal writings accompanied by a short biography compiled by Dora Edinger (1963), and he used this to air his evaluation of the competing accounts of her treatment by Breuer and others. This was before he made his discovery of the Kreuzlingen documents and therefore even before he knew that Bertha had spent time at the Sanatorium Bellevue. As he saw it at the time

111

there were two versions of the story. The first was the one given by Breuer in 1895:

> In that account, the illness is said to have started in the summer of 1880, to have been treated by Breuer from December of the same year, and to have become worse after the father's death in April 1881, necessitating the patient to remain in a sanitarium from June 1881 to June 1882; this was the point which the patient had fixed in advance for her recovery, after which she left for a vacation. (Ellenberger, 1966, p. 95)

But this is a misreading of Breuer, who is quite explicit in his case study that although Bertha was indeed institutionalised in June 1881, she returned to Vienna in the autumn of the same year (Breuer and Freud, 1895, p. 32). Ellenberger seems to be under the illusion that the whole of the last period of her treatment by Breuer took place in a sanatorium. This might seem at first to be a trivial slip, but as we shall see, its consequences in Ellenberger's later argument are quite significant.

Ellenberger continues with a summary of the second account, the alternative to Breuer:

> According to the other account the story is more complex. In a Seminar given in Zurich in 1925, Jung had already revealed that Freud told him that the patient had actually not been cured. In 1953, Ernest Jones said that on the alleged terminal point, far from being cured, the patient was in the throes of a hysterical childbirth, terminating a phantom pregnancy, and that Breuer hypnotized her, whereupon he fled the house in a cold sweat, and left for Venice the next day 'to spend a second honeymoon which resulted in the conception of a daughter'. The patient had to be removed to an institution in Gross Enzersdorf, and she remained sick for several years. (Ellenberger, 1966, p. 95)

We should recall first of all that Jung's testimony concerns the absence of a cure only to the extent that this is evidenced by the supposed hysterical attack produced by the breaking of the transference: it does not refer to the later fate of Anna O. in the years afterwards or any reference to time spent in any institution. Moreover, this means that the origin and reference point of what Jung had said are identical to those of Jones's story, so that what appear here at first sight to be two different sources for an alternative to Breuer's account in fact have as their common origin only Freud's construction of what had happened at the end of the treatment.

The last sentence of Ellenberger's summary of Jones is particularly important. Its first clause is almost a direct quotation from Jones, but it does not come from his account of the end of Bertha's treatment by Breuer in June 1882 as Ellenberger implies. It is based on the second part of Jones's revision, where he draws on the Freud family correspondence to chart details of Bertha's subsequent history. In Jones, the sequence is as follows: first the story of the hysterical childbirth; next the alleged confirmation of the emotional entanglement between Breuer and his patient based on the engagement correspondence between Freud and Martha; finally the snippets drawn from the Freud family correspondence of the succeeding years up to 1887, culminating in the reference from that year to Bertha still suffering from 'hallucinatory states' (Jones, 1953, p. 247). Jones prefaces this last part with the following: 'The poor patient did not fare so well as one might gather from Breuer's published account. Relapses took place, and she was removed to an institution in Gross Enzersdorf' (ibid.) Taken by itself, Ellenberger's sentence is a reasonable representation of what Jones had written: Bertha was removed to an institution and Jones thought she remained sick for several years. But while Jones does not reveal exactly when this institutionalisation took place, Ellenberger's summary misleadingly suggests that events at the ending of the treatment resulted directly and immediately in an institutional outcome, followed by several years of continuing sickness. Whereas Jones's version relates events supposedly occurring at the end of the treatment in June 1882 and then refers to 'relapses', which did not actually occur until the following year, Ellenberger erroneously collapses this into a single sequence of events: crisis at the end of the treatment followed by immediate institutionalisation.

Ellenberger then immediately sets out why he considers the Jones account to be 'fraught with impossibilities': Breuer's daughter was born in March 1882 and therefore could not have been conceived after the treatment finished in June 1882 as Jones states; there was no sanatorium at Gross Enzersdorf; although there was a sanatorium at Inzersdorf, the most likely alternative, no case details could be found in its archives. 'Finally it will be noticed that both accounts, of Breuer and Jones, are in contradiction with the biographical notice which states that Bertha Pappenheim left for Frankfurt in 1881' (Ellenberger, 1966, pp. 95–6).

The biographical notice in question is one that was published at the time of Bertha Pappenheim's death in 1936, which Ellenberger had referred to earlier in his review: 'In the biographical notices of 1936, nothing was said of a nervous illness which she suffered in her youth. It was reported that one year after her father's death, she left Vienna with her mother in 1881 to settle in Frankfurt, where she gradually became concerned with social work' (p. 94). This should immediately have made Ellenberger suspicious of the source, for of course Bertha Pappenheim's father only died in April 1881, as Breuer reveals in the case study and as Ellenberger will no doubt have verified[2], so leaving Vienna a year after that would make it at least 1882, and therefore there would be no contradiction on this point with Breuer's account. In fact what now turns out to be an erroneous piece of information represents the *only* piece of apparent evidence in this review that Ellenberger brings against Breuer's account of the case, as opposed to the alternative one set out in Jones's biography. In the light of this, the strength of his indictment of Breuer that follows seems rather exaggerated:

> What will objective research now reveal about the true story? Almost nothing, save that it throws the greatest doubt upon both Breuer's and Jones' versions. (p. 96)

But having indicted Breuer on the thinnest of grounds (which we know now to be completely spurious) he then almost seems to try to absolve him of any deliberate falsehood by reminding us that psychiatrists often went to great lengths to disguise their patients' identities, which would include altering dates. Moreover: 'it is obvious that Breuer's case history is a reconstruction from memory, written thirteen or fourteen years later, and – as he says himself – "from incomplete notes". Obviously, too, Breuer published it half-heartedly and to please Freud' (ibid.) This appears perhaps to be not so much of an exoneration as a broad-brush attempt to represent the whole case history as unreliable in principle.

As for the alternative account, it is curious that Ellenberger should not even consider the possibility that Jones might be right, or at least that there might be some grain of truth, however distorted, in what Jones had written. In fact in only one respect is the array of data that Jones presents, and which Ellenberger considers to be 'fraught with impossibilities', really substantially incorrect: the details about Dora Breuer's birth.[3] In the other cases Jones turned out to be basically right, and Ellenberger wrong, since the trivial slip of placing the sanatorium at Gross Enzersdorf, rather than Inzersdorf was Freud's own, and in fact, as Hirschmüller was later to discover, there were indeed case details of Bertha Pappenheim in the Inzersdorf records. Moreover, the biographical detail that Jones reported about Bertha not returning to Frankfurt until the late 1880s was also correct.

This brief review by Ellenberger is not a very careful piece of writing. In the space of just three pages he manages to misread Breuer on the length of Anna O.'s institutionalisation, significantly misrepresent Jones's revision of the Anna O. story and dismiss Breuer's account solely on the basis of a manifestly spurious piece of biographical data. Ordinarily one might leave aside such a slight work from an appraisal of Ellenberger's contribution to the debates about Anna O., for it is, after all, hardly a well-known article. But it was to form the basis of his much more accessible and widely read discussion of the case in his 1970 book *The Discovery of the Unconscious*, and large parts of it are reproduced in the later work almost word for word. However not only does Ellenberger carry forward the worst of his earlier errors, in some cases he compounds them.

After giving some biographical data about Bertha Pappenheim and a more extended summary of Breuer's version than in the earlier paper,[4] Ellenberger moves on to the Jones account. He presents a slightly changed version of the paragraph he had written in 1966, although he again begins with the reference to what Jung had revealed in 1925. But there is still no evaluation of Jung's statement or its implications, and because the reference is unelaborated in both of Ellenberger's discussions neither do we learn in 1970, any more than in 1966, that the Jung and Jones accounts are essentially referring to the same hysterical-crisis incident as related by Freud and that both therefore have their origin in the same problematic source.

Ellenberger again compresses both parts of Jones's revision into a single continuous narrative, as if the institutionalisation in Vienna followed immediately from the ending of the treatment, but he concludes with the following:

> The patient Anna O. was admitted to an institution in Gross Enzersdorf, where she remained ill for several years. Jones's version indicates that Breuer had been fooled by the patient, and that the supposed 'prototype of a cathartic cure' was not a cure at all. (Ellenberger, 1970, p. 483)

By changing the 'and she remained sick' of the 1966 paper to 'where she remained ill', Ellenberger has now distorted Jones even more by implying that he reported not only that Bertha had been removed to an institution immediately after the conclusion of Breuer's treatment, but also that she remained there for several years.

Moreover, the status of Ellenberger's conclusion about the prototype of the cathartic cure not being a cure at all is strangely ambiguous. On the one hand it seems to follow quite naturally from his exposition of Jones's revelations, and in fact it is more or less repeated on the following page: 'It is ironic that Anna O.'s unsuccessful treatment should have become, for posterity, the prototype of a cathartic cure' (p. 484). On the other hand Ellenberger of course no more accepts the accuracy of Jones's account now in 1970 than he had in 1966, so the implication it carries of the failure of the cure ought properly to be doubted by Ellenberger because he sees Jones's testimony as so generally unreliable. Given that Jones's revelations are the principal grounds that Ellenberger has for thinking that Breuer's treatment was unsuccessful, it is curious that he should treat them as so untrustworthy while nevertheless accepting as a conclusion their principal implication.

Ellenberger then raises again the supposed biographical data that supposedly contradicts both the Breuer and Jones accounts:

> Comparing Bertha Pappenheim's biography with the two versions of the story of Anna O., one notes that, in the former, Bertha left Vienna for Frankfurt in 1881, whereas Anna remained in the Viennese sanitarium until June 1882 according to Breuer, and much longer according to Jones. (ibid.)

This single sentence contains three separate errors. First, the biographical data. In his 1966 review this consisted of a patently unreliable report dating from the time of Bertha Pappenheim's death that she had left Vienna for Frankfurt in 1881, a year after her father's death. Four years later in 1970 Ellenberger not only cites the German edition of the book by Dora Edinger that he had previously reviewed, but he also gives a reference to the English edition, which had been published in 1968[5] (p. 560, n.267). If he had read this edition as carefully as he cited it, he would have seen that when Edinger refers to the memorial journal issue published when Bertha Pappenheim died she writes the following:

> It contains errors. The most serious one has puzzled all later students of Bertha Pappenheim's life. It gives the date of her move from Vienna to Frankfurt as 188*1*. Actually the date was November, 1888. The 'Meldeschein' is still preserved in the city archives of Frankfurt. Hannah Karminski must have taken literally Bertha Pappenheim's casual remarks that she came to Frankfurt after her father's death. (Edinger, 1968, p. 13, emphases in original)

And referring to the treatment with Breuer:

> Bertha Pappenheim never mentioned this period of her life, not even to her most intimate friend, Hannah Karminski, for Hannah believed

that Bertha Pappenheim had come to Frankfurt in 1881 when, according to the case study published by Breuer, she was in Vienna being treated by him. (p. 15)

So although he cites evidence that directly contradicts it, Ellenberger still gives credence to the false notion that Bertha was not in Vienna in 1881. And even if he did not look at the book he refers to, he reveals in a footnote to the very sentence where he depends on it that he knew this data was flawed:

Mrs Dora Edinger informed the author that according to a document (*Meldezettel*) recently found in the Frankfurt City Archive, Bertha Pappenheim and her mother moved to that city in November 1888. It has not been possible to find out where they lived between 1882 and 1888. (Ellenberger, 1970, p. 561, n. 272)

The sudden reference to 1882 here seems to imply that Ellenberger accepted after all Breuer's word that the treatment ended in this year, but at any rate he now knew that the 1881 date for the removal to Frankfurt was untenable and should instantly have recognised that this eliminated at a stroke the only reason he had given for doubting Breuer's account of the treatment. But Ellenberger does not amend the argument in the main body of the text and leaves intact its implied, but spurious, subversion of Breuer's case history.

The second error of course relates to the fanciful idea that Breuer recounts that Anna O. was institutionalised until 1882. This merely rolls forward the misreading of Breuer that Ellenberger had perpetrated in his 1966 review, which extended Bertha's stay in the sanatorium to a full year from June 1881 to June 1882. The third error is to repeat the inflation of Jones's account from earlier in the text, whereby Bertha's remaining ill for years suddenly becomes remaining ill and in an institution for years, which has no basis at all in what Jones actually wrote. At this point therefore Ellenberger is relying on non-existent evidence to call into question claims of both Breuer and Jones which are equally non-existent.

Ellenberger next discounts further evidence which he himself has produced with his important reference to a photograph first published in Dora Edinger's biography:

A still stranger fact is that the photograph of Bertha (the original of which the author has seen) bears the date 1882 embossed by the photographer and shows a healthy-looking, sporting woman in a riding habit, in sharp contrast to Breuer's portrait of a home-bound young lady who had no outlet for her physical and mental energies. (Ellenberger, 1970, p. 483).

The conclusion that Ellenberger draws from this is odd, for of course on Breuer's account it does not at all follow that a photograph of his patient in 1882 would be of a semi-invalid. The whole point of the published case history is that Bertha had been relieved of her hysterical symptoms by June 1882, and such a photograph, if taken after this point, would reflect that fact. Ellenberger arbitrarily turns what could possibly be regarded as a primary vindication of Breuer into a piece of evidence against him.[6]

The rest of Ellenberger's evaluation of the case repeats arguments made in his earlier review. Once again he excuses Breuer by pleading necessary disguise of case details, reconstruction from memory and half-hearted publication to please Freud. This is followed by his legitimate objection to the Jones account, that the birthdate of Breuer's daughter is inconsistent with it and that there was no sanatorium at Gross Enzersdorf: 'Jones's version, published more than seventy years after the event, is based on hearsay and should be considered with caution' (pp. 483–4).

Two years later, and in the light of the newly discovered Kreuzlingen documents, Ellenberger was to revise fundamentally his assessment of the whole case in a short but important paper which presented his new findings. In the introductory sections of his article, and before revealing this new data, Ellenberger provides a new summary of Breuer's outline of the case[7] and some of his earlier commentary that he had published just two years before. On one crucial point he tells more of what he had previously only briefly alluded to. In 1970 he had written: 'In a seminar given in Zurich in 1925, Jung revealed that Freud had told him that the patient had actually not been cured' (Ellenberger, 1970, p. 483). Now, he elaborates this:

> In a seminar given in Zurich in 1925, Jung revealed that Freud had told him that the patient had not actually been cured. Jung stated that this famous first case 'so much spoken about as an example of a brilliant therapeutic success, was in reality nothing of the kind... There was no cure at all in the sense of which it was originally presented.' And yet, Jung added, 'the case was so interesting that there was no need to claim for it something that did not happen.' (Ellenberger, 1972, p. 270, ellipsis in Ellenberger's original.)

There then follows a retelling of Jones's story of the hysterical childbirth, Breuer's second honeymoon and his resulting daughter, the patient being removed to Gross Enzersdorf and remaining very sick for several years, but Ellenberger still concludes that 'Jones's version is in many points incompatible with that of Breuer' although he does not now detail what these points are (ibid.). However, while he continues to reject Jones's particular revision of the story, the discovery of Bertha's stay at the Sanatorium Bellevue and the associated case reports enable Ellenberger to shift his position on what he had previously taken to be the logical consequence of Jones's account: that the prototypical cathartic cure was in fact no such thing. In his earlier work Ellenberger had rejected Jones's account and by implication therefore also its inherent consequence that there had been no cathartic cure. The clear suggestion now is that Jones had reached the right conclusion, but for the wrong reasons. This is surely why Ellenberger now allows himself to reveal a little more of what Jung had said in 1925. In the 1966 and 1970 accounts, the reference to Jung had been drafted in as a mere prelude to the Jones story of the hysterical childbirth, and as its apparently independent corroboration, with the common origin of the two narratives in Freud's own account being disguised through the omission of what Jung had actually said. But now Jung is allowed a greater voice because his testimony serves a different purpose. Here Jung is revealing what Ellenberger himself is about to demonstrate through the production of the Kreuzlingen documents: that Breuer's treatment was not the success that had been claimed because Bertha Pappenheim continued to suffer from her illness for some time afterwards.

Ellenberger is only able to produce this effect because of a quite tendentious piece of editing of what Jung had said, for the ellipsis in his quotation hides the following: 'Freud told me that he was called in to see the woman the same night that Breuer had seen her for the last time, and that she was in a bad hysterical attack, due to the breaking off of the transference' (Jung, 1989, p. 16). Ellenberger conceals the fact that Jung's claim that Anna O. had not been cured was based solely on the presumed crisis at the end of the treatment, and not because of any privileged knowledge of her subsequent fate. Ellenberger, as we shall see, has not been the only one to perpetrate such a manœuvre.

Further curious features reveal themselves when Ellenberger's 1972 account is compared with the earlier ones. In the two earlier versions he is inclined to doubt aspects of what Breuer wrote in the case study for three reasons: he thought he had evidence that Bertha was in Frankfurt by 1881, not in a Viennese sanatorium until June 1882 as Breuer relates;

he had a photograph of Bertha dated from 1882 showing her as more healthy than Breuer would have had us believe she should have been; the fact that Breuer wrote the case from memory makes such lapses on Breuer's part understandable. As we have seen, none of these considerations should have contributed much weight to the drift of Ellenberger's argument even at its earlier stages, but by 1972 two of them have visibly collapsed by virtue of his new discovery alone. Because of his find, Ellenberger now has documentary evidence that Bertha was, after all, in Vienna and Kreuzlingen in 1882, not in Frankfurt, and he also concedes: 'We know, now, that when Breuer published Anna O's story in 1895 he had under his eyes a previous report he had written in 1882 (whole lines are sometimes identical)' (Ellenberger, 1972, p. 278). The only intact piece of evidence from his 1970 discussion which might have caused him to doubt what he inferred from Breuer's account is the photograph, but here he simply repeats his unaccountable puzzlement of two years earlier: 'This discovery led to the question: What was Bertha doing in riding habit in Konstanz, Germany, at the time when she was supposed to be severely sick in a sanitarium near Vienna?' (pp. 273–4).

Ellenberger persists in his disavowal of this evidence. In his earlier argument it supposedly contradicted Breuer's portrait of a homebound young lady with no outlet for her energies, but now it is also in conflict with the idea that the patient could be severely sick in a sanatorium near Vienna. Breuer of course never maintained either of these two things in such a way that they could be construed as being undermined by the content of the 1882 photograph that Ellenberger now confronts his readers with. For Breuer never said anything in the case history that would lead one to suppose that Bertha was somehow unlikely to be appearing as a healthy looking, sporting woman in a riding habit in Konstanz after the treatment was completed, nor was she at any point in 1882 in a sanatorium near Vienna.[8] In fact the very impression given by the photograph is something that Ellenberger recognises, but whose implications he does not face: Bertha Pappenheim was indeed not as disabled by continuing illness after the completion of her treatment with Breuer as he is inclined to suggest. But the evidence of the photograph that Bertha was indeed in 1882 a 'healthy-looking, sporting woman' is never allowed to contaminate Ellenberger's conclusion that she was, after all, still an institutionalised invalid after the conclusion of Breuer's treatment.[9]

In his earlier accounts Ellenberger seems to have the problem of being pulled in two different directions. His reliance on such thin evidence about Bertha's whereabouts, along with his patent misreading of what

Breuer actually states about this, suggests that he is deeply sceptical about Breuer's published version of the case and is inclined to push in the direction of discrediting Breuer by any means available. Jones's 1953 story should therefore have been something of a gift for Ellenberger, at least in the way that he reads it. But this posed a problem in its appearing to be so manifestly wrong on a number of points. Having already in 1970 compressed together the two quite separate issues of the conclusion of Bertha's treatment and her progress in the subsequent years, Ellenberger is now, two years later, already working on prepared ground when he turns his Kreuzlingen discovery to the purpose of doubting Breuer's testimony, and is presented with the opportunity to do so on a basis that is different from that of the unreliable Jones.

His treatment of the photograph is not the only occasion on which Ellenberger presents an accurate descriptive summary of newly discovered evidence while at the same time expressing conclusions that are not warranted by the exposition. A further example of this can be seen in his synopsis of the reports that he discovered in Kreuzlingen. He makes a prefatory comment on the new material: 'The time has not yet come for a publication of the complete document, but we will give a cursory view of the early case history, stressing the points where it gives new information or differs from the 1895 report' (p. 274). But this does not fit with what follows, for he then very fairly summarises the main points of the Breuer report, with very little in the way of his own evaluation or commentary, but everything that he presents is 'new information'; there is not one single instance where he notes a presumed discrepancy between the 1882 report and Breuer's 1895 version.

When it comes to the summary of the follow-up report by the Bellevue doctor, he regarded it as both instructive and yet disappointing.

Someone who would know of Anna O only what Breuer related in the *Studies in Hysteria* would hardly guess that it is a follow-up of the same patient after she had undergone Breuer's 'cathartic cure.' This follow-up consists of a long enumeration of medications given to the patient on account of a severe facial neuralgia. We learn that the facial neuralgia had been exacerbated during the past six months (that is, the 'fourth period' of her illness) and that during that period high amounts of chloral and morphine had been prescribed. On her admission the amount of morphine was reduced to 7 to 8 centigrams of morphine in two daily injections. But the pains were at times so intolerable that one had to give her 10 centigrams. When she left the sanitarium, she still received injections amounting to a total of 7 to 10 centigrams *pro die*. (p. 277)

There is no sign in this report, even for Ellenberger, of the features that made this, in its published version, such a striking case. Although there is a brief mention of some of the patient's hysterical features, including the fact that she was regularly for a period each evening unable to understand the German language, Ellenberger's view is that here 'the patient is depicted as a neurological case of a rather unpleasant person showing some hysterical features' (p. 279).

Again, this is a very fair and balanced summary of the doctor's account, but Ellenberger avoids drawing from it the obvious conclusion: if the patient depicted in the follow-up report seems to bear little resemblance to Breuer's severely hysterical patient, this is quite possibly because there *was* very little similarity. Ellenberger is so predisposed to believe that Bertha Pappenheim was essentially in the same condition when she was in Kreuzlingen as she had been when treated by Breuer, that he cannot quite conceal his regret when there is little evidence of this in the final Kreuzlingen report. So although the report is instructive, Ellenberger also finds it 'disappointing' because it consists mainly of a catalogue of neurological symptoms and the fruitless attempts to treat them.[10]

In the final section of his commentary, Ellenberger delivers his coup de grâce:

Thus, the newly discovered documents confirm what Freud, according to Jung, had told him: the patient had not been cured. Indeed the famed 'prototype of a cathartic cure' was neither a cure nor a catharsis. Anna O had become a severe morphinist and had kept a part of her most conspicuous symptoms (in Bellevue she could no longer speak German as soon as she had put her head on the pillow). Jones's version of the false pregnancy and hysterical birth throes cannot be confirmed and does not fit into the chronology of the case. (ibid.)

This conclusion is not at all justified by the evidence that Ellenberger has produced. As we have already noted, Jung's claim that the patient had not been cured relates solely to the hysterical attack that was supposed to have taken place at the end of her treatment by Breuer; there is no reference to what may or may not have happened subsequently. The Kreuzlingen documents that Ellenberger discovered do not support the notion that Bertha Pappenheim was still suffering from the array of symptoms that she had presented to Breuer, and the fact that she was a severe morphinist was unrelated to her hysterical condition. It is true that the one hysterical symptom that the final report from Kreuzlingen alludes to and that Ellenberger refers to here was still present in an attenuated form, but this by itself hardly justifies the sweeping judgement that there had been neither a cure nor a catharsis. Finally, it is again asserted that Jones's version of the hysterical birth is not confirmed, but if this is then to be discarded as unreliable, so too must the evidence deriving from Jung from which Ellenberger draws support, since it too is predicated on the same source: Freud's account of a transferential crisis at the end of the treatment.

It is something of an irony that the historian whose monumental work has contributed so much to the recent rewriting of the history of dynamic psychology and who placed such an explicit emphasis on the importance of accuracy should have played such a significant part in the wholesale distortion of the Anna O. case by other modern historians of psychoanalysis. Mark Micale has noted with justification about Ellenberger's summary rejection of the cathartic cure that he 'does not pursue the matter further, allowing readers to draw their own conclusions; but the interpretive implications are seriously subversive' (Micale, in Ellenberger, 1993, p. 67). And there has certainly been no shortage of people rushing in to provide these conclusions on the basis of what they have no doubt considered to be firm foundations.

For all that Ellenberger was highly critical of Jones's 1953 account of the Anna O. case, his own version of the story has combined with it in a curiously contradictory manner to produce a highly resilient depiction of the course of Breuer's treatment and its aftermath. This has not only been resistant to substantial modification, but it has also provided a stable enough platform for further elaboration in the secondary literature. The myths established by both Jones and Ellenberger have been consolidated and developed in writings by others to the point where their original conclusions are not fundamentally questioned but rather taken as a starting point for supplementary hypotheses and theories. In now looking at some of these in detail we shall come to see how the fable of Anna O. has become so apparently impregnable.

9
The Maturation of the Legend: The Derivative Literature

Mancher klopft mit dem Hammer an der Wand herum
und glaubt, er treffe jedesmal den Nagel auf den Kopf.[1]
J. W. von Goethe, *Maximen und Reflexionen* (Posth.)

It is not intended as a slight to classify the secondary literature to be considered in this chapter as derivative, for it is indeed remarkable the extent to which recent accounts of the Anna O. case have taken first Jones's and then Ellenberger's reshaping of the story as both their foundation and their inspiration. However, while Jones has been repeatedly criticised along the lines that Ellenberger first pursued, it has largely gone unremarked that he himself set out a view of the Anna O. case that is implicitly critical of Breuer, and by extension (though to a lesser extent) of Freud himself, for in recent years this strain in Jones's argument has been completely overshadowed by Ellenberger's own commentary. While Ellenberger's classic work *The Discovery of the Unconscious* has certainly not been immune to criticism, it has not been possible to find in the published literature any critical examination at all of his specific study of Anna O. Even those most sympathetic to the psychoanalytic project have tended to take Ellenberger's work for granted, and where they have not simply ignored it, they have felt compelled to bend to its claims.

Almost two decades separate Jones's publication from Ellenberger's key discovery of the Kreuzlingen files, and during this time most of the reaction to Jones's version of the end of the treatment and its aftermath came from those broadly sympathetic to psychoanalysis, a fact which is also visible in the character of their response. Karpe (1961), for example, took for granted the veracity of Jones's account and simply elaborated from it a view of Bertha Pappenheim's eventual professional career in terms of her libidinal developments and conflicts subsequent to their first dramatic manifestation at the climax of the treatment with Breuer. Karpe retells the Jones version and concludes, albeit with a slight hint of scepticism, but not wholly unreasonably: 'This sounds dramatic and, if it is true, proves a sexual fantasy in Bertha Pappenheim' (p. 14). Noting that Breuer always denied that there was a sexual element in his patient's case, Karpe then asks whether perhaps Freud and Jones made unwarranted conclusions to the contrary because of their psychoanalytic bias (ibid.) But in their support he suggests that Bertha Pappenheim's preoccupation with sex later expressed itself in her fight against immorality and the sexual exploitation of women, not only in her work but also in her writings. Effectively therefore: 'Breuer's conviction that, because his patient showed no overt interest in sex, hysteria has no sexual etiology was disproved when Bertha Pappenheim, in her middle age, made the fight against illegitimate sexuality the main concern of her life' (p. 24). Such a stark conclusion is fairly much in line with Freud's own theory of sexuality and its vicissitudes, but whether it is entirely defensible need not concern us here. Freud, of course, did not need such evidence to reach his conclusion from 1894 onwards that hysteria had a sexual aetiology and that Bertha Pappenheim's case would have been no exception to this. Karpe is surely right to the extent that her subsequent career could not be said to undermine Freud's argument. For our purposes, however, his paper does not expand our understanding of the historical material unless one accepts unquestioningly the veracity of Jones's account and the implications of orthodox psychoanalytic theory.

A similar position, but with a slightly different inflection, may be discerned in the earliest of a series of articles about the Anna O. case by George H. Pollock (1968). Rather than concentrating on Anna O., Pollock shifts the focus to Breuer to try to understand his reaction to his patient. He prefaces his discussion by quoting at length from Jones's account of events and Freud's letter to Zweig in order to establish the empirical starting-point for his analysis (pp. 713–6). Pollock regards Breuer as essentially ambivalent about the role of sexuality because while he was willing to see it as a potent source of neuroses, he was nevertheless unable to confront this factor in the case of Anna O. and her eminently sexual phantasy of pregnancy. These oscillations, and Breuer's eventual flight from sexuality in its psychoanalytic form, Pollock attributes to the fact that Breuer suffered the loss of his mother at an early age when he was at the height of his oedipal period between the ages of three and four. His ability to confront and capitalise on the implications of his own discovery was therefore vitiated by his intra-psychic conflicts.

Pollock's thesis is crucially dependent on three factors. First, the empirical veracity of the Anna O. story as portrayed in the combined versions of Jones's biography and Freud's letter to Zweig. These we have already established as being somewhat less than wholly reliable as a literal narrative of events. Secondly, he is dependent on historical data about Breuer's age when he lost his mother. Pollock states as a fact that Breuer was between three and four when his mother died (p. 718), although he does not give an exact source for this, nor the date of the death. The diligent Hirschmüller was unable to ascertain the date of Bertha Breuer's death (1989, p. 327) so it is likely that Pollock was less secure about Breuer's age when this happened than his text implies. In fact Breuer's mother is buried in the Währinger Friedhof in Vienna, and a list of burial entries for this cemetery in the Rathaus in Vienna gives the night of 7–8 August 1843 as the date of her death at the age of 26. This was just over two months after the birth of her son, Adolf, on 1 June 1843. Breuer would therefore have been just over 17 months old when she died, not the three to four years that Pollock's oedipal hypothesis requires. Given this empirical collapse of his case, then his dependence on orthodox psychoanalytic theory to elucidate historical events (the third crucial ingredient of his analysis) becomes somewhat beside the point.

Pollock was subsequently among the first to use Ellenberger's discovery of the Kreuzlingen documents as a basis for further speculation about the Anna O. case. Having in the meantime (1972) developed the psychoanalytic thesis that Bertha Pappenheim's illness can be elucidated by the recognition that the death of her father reawakened pathological and unresolved mourning for her two sisters who had died in childhood, Pollock uses this notion to interpret further the data discovered by Ellenberger. He regards the symptoms that Bertha suffered from during her stay at Bellevue and which were described in the follow-up report of October 1882 – specifically the facial neuralgia – as a re-emergence of symptoms brought about by the termination of the treatment in June. Although she was relatively well when the treatment ended, the loss of Breuer exacerbated the original symptoms and those of the pathological mourning that had been there earlier. In fact the medication on which she became dependent had been prescribed to alleviate these symptoms, and given that she was normally opposed to medical prescription she was therefore 'iatrogenically addicted' (Pollock, 1973, p. 331), for Breuer did not know as we do today about mourning work or about the return of symptoms at the end of a period of treatment. To sustain this theory Pollock has to regard the facial neuralgia as part of the original set of hysterical symptoms, and the period of institutionalisation after the end of Breuer's treatment as a period of mourning marked by a continuation of the hysteria, but necessary to her eventual full recovery. This is not well sustained by a close examination of the contemporary evidence, but this is just one variant in the secondary literature that tries to make sense of the Kreuzlingen symptoms in relation to those occurring earlier. Other writers perceive other possibilities, as we shall see.

The most lengthy consideration of the newly discovered evidence after Ellenberger is to be found in Hirschmüller's biography of Breuer, where he publishes the documents in full. Hirschmüller undertakes a close comparison of the 1882 report and the published case study, and his description of the former in particular is the best general explication of the document so far published. It is sensitive to its subtleties, to the changing nature of some of the diagnostic categories (recognising in particular the distinction between mental illness and hysteria) and also to the way that a formal publication would naturally differ from a private report to a professional colleague (Hirschmüller, 1989, pp. 107ff.). Hirschmüller tries to be as fair to Breuer as he can, yet he is nevertheless still under the sway of the construction that Ellenberger put on the documents he discovered. He records the differences in what was revealed to be the patient's problems in the Kreuzlingen report compared with what was related in the public version, specifically in respect of the trigeminal neuralgia, convulsions, drug dependency and the intermittent loss of her mother tongue. Hirschmüller concludes from this that: 'What is certain is that the impression he [Breuer] gives in *Studies on Hysteria* that the patient was completely cured does not square with the facts' (pp. 106–7). This idea of 'complete cure' is exactly what is not promised or heralded by Breuer of course, and it is curious that Hirschmüller does not recognise this at this point, given that he goes to great pains in his exposition of Breuer's 1882 report to note the reference to the 'unknown cerebral disease' (p. 110) and the general complexity of Bertha's condition besides the hysterical symptoms. In relation to the other problems he concludes, somewhat reluctantly: 'If we are not to impute base motives to Breuer, the only feasible explanation to my mind is that he saw no connection between the severe neuralgia and the rest of the symptoms, and therefore assumed that he had been completely successful in eliminating that element in the hysteria which was accessible to psychotherapy' (p. 116). This is a far from unbalanced summing up of the situation, though why Hirschmüller arrives at it so grudgingly is not entirely clear, for the rest of his analysis of the documents is both accurate and fair to Breuer. Indeed, elsewhere he writes: 'Breuer assumed that Bertha's illness arose from a disposition which was partly hereditary and partly due to her upbringing, and which was not susceptible to treatment. His treatment, in consequence, was designed purely to combat symptoms [...]' (p. 132). Again, this is an entirely reasonable summary of Breuer's position, although it jars somewhat with his harsh judgement that Breuer, at the end of the case history, gave the impression of a 'complete cure'. This impression only follows if one divorces individual passages from Breuer's case history from their immediate context and from the overall picture of Anna O.'s illness and its susceptibility to treatment by the new method that Breuer discovered with her.

Nine years after Hirschmüller's biography first appeared, there emerged another substantial account of the Anna O. case in the form of Fritz Schweighofer's (1987) book-length treatment of the story. Despite the detail of Schweighofer's analysis and the seriousness with which he presents his data and arguments, his book has received very little attention in the other literature on the Anna O. case and to that extent it is almost completely unknown. No doubt this is mainly due to the fact that the book has not been translated into English, but also in part to the principal thesis of the book, entirely alien to mainstream psycho-analytic schools, namely that Bertha Pappenheim largely simulated her symptoms. At root this means that Schweighofer's book is in large part just one more exercise in retrospective rediagnosis – an attempt to show what was 'really' wrong with Anna O. – for the charge of simulation is itself a statement that the patient was not in fact suffering from hysteria and that Breuer's diagnosis was essentially incorrect.

If Schweighofer's book amounted to no more than a speculative rediagnosis, then it would not need to concern us here. But his analysis of the case includes a number of acute observations about the historical evidence which have a lasting value in any attempt to understand it, notwithstanding that fact that these insights have largely been ignored by subsequent historians. Writing in the late 1980s, Schweighofer had at his disposal both Ellenberger's reappraisal of the case in the light of the evidence he discovered, and also Hirschmüller's comprehensive discussion and evaluation, but it has to be acknowledged that Schweighofer makes curious use of these sources. On the one hand he is quite uncritical about Freud's story of the phantom pregnancy, accepting it as having occurred exactly in the way Freud describes it in his letter to Zweig (Schweighofer, 1987, pp. 60–1). This is despite the very severe cautions on this score issued by both Ellenberger and

Hirschmüller, and Schweighofer pays no attention at all to their reservations. Indeed he uses the phantasy of pregnancy as evidence that Breuer and Bertha Pappenheim had actually had a sexual relationship and gives it as the reason for Breuer abruptly breaking off the treatment (p. 132).

On the other hand, Schweighofer takes an independent view of the documentary evidence unearthed by Ellenberger in that he largely disregards the latter's own commentary and views the findings as supporting his own independent hypothesis of simulation. Schweighofer's diagnosis of Bertha Pappenheim's afflictions focuses to a much greater extent than does the rest of the literature on her facial neuralgia, which he sees as being key to the case. He argues that many of the patient's complaints stemmed initially from a severe somatic condition and that this accounts for several of the sensory and motor peculiarities considered by Breuer to be hysterical in origin. The patient's upper jaw was the focus of this somatic complaint: 'Since already in the spring of 1880 symptoms of a facial neuralgia had appeared, it is to be supposed that Bertha had suffered for a long time – certainly at least 2–3 years – from an ulceration of the left upper jaw, which had probably implicated the nerves leading to the left cerebral hemisphere' (p. 66). Schweighofer concludes that this affliction could in this way have been indirectly responsible for Bertha's disturbances of vision, movement and speech, but that these genuine symptoms then became the basis for a complicated pattern of simulation, first with the motive of relieving her from her nursing duties for her sick father, and later as a consequence of her emotional entanglement with Breuer, as a means of holding his attention and affection (pp. 66–7, 100). We know that Bertha Pappenheim underwent a dental operation on the jaw in February 1882 (Hirschmüller, 1989, p. 302) and Schweighofer supposes that it was the success of this that brought about the eventual recovery from her afflictions. Schweighofer's thesis, in short, is as follows:

In the history of medicine no case history has certainly ever excited so much of a sensation and brought about so much as that of Bertha Pappenheim. All the more surprising is the paradox that this one, which was to found a new branch of psychopathology, describes at its core a dentistry case. The first causes of the pains were – if one sets aside a certain susceptibility to nervous states – not the alleged psychic traumas, but it was the ulceration of the left upper jaw which evoked the disturbances of function in the left cerebral hemisphere. The various 'neuralgias' and 'aphasias' were therefore not cured by the cathartic method, but by the operative removal of the focus of the illness. (Schweighofer, 1987, p. 149)

This is a rather nice, if somewhat eccentric thesis, but it is underpinned by some fairly dubious neurology. It is true that affections of the trigeminal nerve can be linked to dental problems – and we shall return to this issue shortly – but it is not so clear that such affections can so readily be assumed to have invoked functional aberrations of the left cerebral hemisphere. Schweighofer's downgrading of Anna O.'s iconic status within the world of psychotherapy by turning her into a complicated dental patient, if correct, would probably be counterbalanced by making her something of a celebrity within the world of dentistry, for she must surely be unique in being rescued from such severe problems of vision, movement and language through the simple expedient of a dental operation.[2] But even leaving aside the extravagance of Schweighofer's rediagnosis of the whole panoply of symptoms as essentially the result of toothache plus simulation, there are problems with the assumptions that he makes about the place of the dental procedure.

The principal merit of Schweighofer's analysis of the case is that it gives Bertha's neuralgia its proper due, for this is a factor that has been relatively neglected by all other commentators. The facial pains began in the spring of 1880, and the patient underwent a dental operation in February 1882, but beyond this we know little more than that her sufferings after this point were quite severe. There are, however, a number of possibilities about how these details fit together. In the first place it is not clear what Schweighofer means by 'ulceration' or 'suppuration' (*Vereiterung*) of the upper jaw, for this is just his term, and not one given in the contemporary documents. All we know is that Bertha underwent a 'dental operation' in February 1882, but again, its nature and the reason for it are not known. If one presents with facial pains to a doctor today, it is important to rule out dental problems before considering as a possibility facial neuralgia, which still has no clear diagnostic test; moreover the trigeminal nerve does indeed innervate teeth in the upper jaw, so it is perhaps possible on the basis of the medical knowledge then obtaining that Bertha's neuralgic pain was misdiagnosed as an affliction curable through dental treatment. But on balance it seems rather unlikely that there was a connection between Bertha's facial pains and any dental problem, since Binswanger would surely not have contemplated surgical treatment for the neuralgia (Hirschmüller, 1989, p. 301) if there was the merest hint of a possibility that the root cause could be dealt with by a dentist. If there is a link then it is more likely that

Bertha's dental operation in February 1882 triggered a severe worsening of the trigeminal neuralgia. Even this, though, is perhaps improbable because Bertha's mother makes it clear that the pain of the neuralgia did not become persistent and excruciating until mid-March, the month after the dental operation was performed (ibid.) Most telling of all is that she herself makes no connection at all between the neuralgia and the incidence of the dental treatment. It would seem that both in terms of how the ailment was perceived at the time, and even with the benefit of retrospective diagnosis, there was no relationship between Bertha's facial pains and the dental treatment (or the cause of it) that she underwent in February 1882.

But if Schweighofer's fanciful thesis of a dental cause for Bertha's malady cannot be sustained, this does not undermine his perceptive comments on the Kreuzlingen documents. He is able to make these because he is largely uncluttered by the notions persisting to this day in the secondary literature that Bertha's condition remained largely unchanged or had even worsened after her admission, and that the documents reveal this lack of improvement. We have already noted Schweighofer's (1987, p. 65) observation that the sanatorium treatment concentrated on combating the facial neuralgia and the narcotic dependence, but he also comments that it is striking that the hypnoid states that had occupied so much of her existence during her treatment by Breuer stopped after the end of the treatment and after the beginning of the period in Kreuzlingen (p. 96). The absences and disturbances of speech only lasted for a few moments on going to bed, and they were only barely mentioned in the report, with all the signs that the staff paid them very little regard (p. 97). There were also no disturbances of movement (p. 101) nor of vision (p. 103). These observations are marshalled to support Schweighofer's general thesis that while Bertha's original problems were due to an ulcerated jaw, Breuer's experience of her was governed by her simulation of a range of symptoms. Therefore once Breuer had broken off the treatment as a reaction to becoming too enmeshed in a relationship that had got out of hand, there was no reason for her to sustain the pretence of illness. All that remained was for the neuralgia and the narcotic addiction to be dealt with, and this was the purpose of the stay at Kreuzlingen. While Schweighofer perhaps exaggerates the extent to which the residues of Bertha's putative hysterical state had completely disappeared during her stay in Bellevue, there is no doubt that he is able to take a more balanced view than most other commentators of Bertha's dominant affliction during this period. Once the significance of the neuralgia and the narcotic dependence is fully recognised, this not only affects how we regard

Bertha's general state when the treatment with Breuer was concluded in June, but it also sheds a rather different light on the undoubted suffering that she still experienced in the period during which Freud is commenting on her state in his letters to his fiancée. It is generally recognised today that trigeminal neuralgia is one of the most painful afflictions known to humankind, and it is not uncommon for acute sufferers to regard death as a preferable alternative. If Bertha was tormented by such a complaint it is no wonder that she condemned science for its inability to combat her suffering (Hirschmüller, 1989, p. 291), that she would be quite unhinged by it or even perhaps that Breuer himself would wish that she could die so she could be relieved of it (Jones, 1953, p. 247).

From the point of view of Breuer's case study, it is the relative insignificance of any clearly hysterical complaint that marks Bertha's stay at Bellevue, and Schweighofer's study has the merit of pointing this out. But if we remain faithful to the views of her illness portrayed in the contemporary documentation, declining to follow Schweighofer in his diagnosis of simulation, then we also have no reason to depart from the implications of Breuer's own account of the end of the treatment. If trigeminal neuralgia and the related narcotic dependence were Bertha's dominant problems, then there is little evidence of failure on Breuer's part in relation to her hysterical symptoms, and little sign that the stay in Kreuzlingen was the result of a disastrous treatment outcome that Breuer, and following him Freud, subsequently did their best to conceal. But Schweighofer's work has gone mostly unnoticed in the secondary literature and it stands quite outside the snowballing effect of mainstream commentary on the Anna O. case, which has largely uncritically taken Jones and particularly Ellenberger as its inspiration in the story it tells. The extent to which this has been the case is apparent from a survey of the work that came after Schweighofer.

John Forrester was the first to publish extracts from the correspondence between Freud and his fiancée that Jones had alluded to in the second part of his own commentary on the case. As we have seen, these date from Bertha's later periods of institutionalisation, from 1883 to 1887, but Forrester assumes that Bertha's suffering from this period was a direct continuation of the problems that were the subject of Breuer's case history and of those which resulted in her 1882 stay at Kreuzlingen. In forging these links from the later material without interrogating the possible reasons for further institutional care, Forrester is directly dependent on the impression created by Ellenberger that 'Breuer's treatment of Anna O. was in large part a medical disaster' (Forrester, 1990, p. 26). As with Pollock and Hirschmüller, the additional symptoms described in the Kreuzlingen documents are run into one with the hysterical symptoms: 'What Breuer did not say in his case history was how the treatment had not come to such an idyllic end, but had, over the prior few months, run out of control. Bertha had become addicted to the chloral she was prescribed for her sleep, had undergone severe intermittent convulsions linked to her level of drug use, and was suffering from facial pain so acute that it necessitated injections of morphine, to which she was also, in June 1882, addicted' (Appignanesi and Forrester, 1992, pp. 76–7). If it were the case that Breuer's case history had claimed that the new method of treatment was a breakthrough cure for every aspect of Anna O.'s affliction, then this charge might have been justified. Once it is recognised that what is at stake is the alleviation of a number of severe, but residual, hysterical symptoms, then the matter has to be seen in a different light.

As might be expected to be the case with secondary literature, as the years go by and each new fragment of interpretation is forced into an apparently coherent picture, the differences between these fragments, their diverse origins and statuses, become gradually elided and the cracks are smoothed over.[3] It eventually becomes possible to give quite a short account of what is supposed to have happened in the years after Breuer's treatment by relying directly on what has been claimed by the previous commentators and without paying further attention to the evidence that they themselves invoked. In this way the story receives its own inflationary character with each retelling. A good example of this is Malcolm Macmillan's brief synopses of the outcome of the case. His first extensive excursion into this area occurs in a 1977 paper, which therefore predates the publication of the full case notes by Hirschmüller in 1978 and is entirely dependent on Ellenberger's own summary of them in his 1972 work which announced their discovery. In recounting the end of Breuer's treatment Macmillan summarily judges that: 'According to the 1895 account she was now cured' (Macmillan, 1977, p. 110) thus eliminating at a stroke the myriad of problems lying behind this simple formula.[4] He continues:

> Within 5 weeks, however, she had relapsed, and a fifth period, not described in Breuer's later account, commenced. [...] Although Breuer's original notes had claimed a 'great alleviation,' much pathology was still present during her stay at the Bellevue. Hysterical features, speech disorders, alternations of consciousness, and a facial neuralgia described only in the original case notes, were still present. [...] Her symptoms were apparently unchanged on discharge. (pp. 110–1)

What Macmillan was not to know (because he had not seen the original notes) was that the 'great alleviation' claimed by Breuer pertains only to the end of the third period of the illness, not to the whole treatment,[5] and that the 'hysterical features' in the follow-up report by the Bellevue doctor refer only to the patient's unmotivated fluctuations in her moods. On this precarious basis Macmillan goes so far as to construct a 'fifth period' to the illness.

By the time Macmillan revisits the case for his large work *Freud Evaluated: the Completed Arc*, first published in 1991, some details have changed to take account of the publication of the case notes. So the references to an imagined 'fifth stage' of the illness and Breuer's claim of a 'great alleviation' of the symptoms have disappeared, but the false sense of continuity between the treatment by Breuer and Bertha's institutionalisation is, if anything, reinforced by its extension to Bertha's subsequent stays in Inzersdorf up to 1887. Macmillan writes:

> Breuer himself was wrong in implying that Anna O. was cured. Although neither described in his published account nor referred to publicly by him or Freud, within five weeks of the close of treatment Anna O. had the first of four relapses. On July 12, 1882, she was admitted to the Sanatorium Bellevue, Kreuzlingen, Switzerland, where she remained until October 29, 1882. [...] Many symptoms remained: the hysterical features, speech disorders, alterations of consciousness, and the facial neuralgia. (Macmillan, 1997, p. 9)

The inflationary twist that is common to both of Macmillan's slightly variant accounts, however, is the idea of a 'relapse', which we first met with in Jones. Whereas Hirschmüller and Forrester both tend to depict the stay in Kreuzlingen as a continuation of the treatment of the same illness by other means, after Breuer had effectively given up, Macmillan, on the basis of the same evidence, sees the subsequent institutionalisations as repeated returns of the illness after partial recoveries. Neither of these views is explicitly articulated by Ellenberger himself, nor can they be read directly from the evidence he presented. What is clear from the contemporary documents is that the stay in Kreuzlingen was neither a different treatment of the same illness, nor a response to a relapse, but a convalescence and a means of withdrawal from narcotics that had been planned ahead from the very ending of the treatment with Breuer (Hirschmüller, 1989, pp. 293–6).

Han Israëls (1999) discusses the Anna O. case as part of a broader project of indictment of Freud and psychoanalysis, most of the details of which do not concern us here. But a central part of his thesis in relation to the development of Freud's theory of the sexual aetiology of hysteria is crucially reliant on the assumption that Anna O. was not cured, and that Freud knew this, but betrayed the truth to only a few followers. To shore up this view he repeats the Ellenberger conclusion about there being neither a catharsis nor a cure, and for good measure adds Hirschmüller's comment about the deceptive nature of the impression given by Breuer that his patient was cured (Israëls, 1999, pp. 145–6).

Israëls turns this standard repetition of the Anna O. story to a new purpose, for he wishes to establish that the main offence at the heart of the history of the case within Freud's lifetime was not Breuer's but Freud's own. Israëls claims that when Freud in 1925 said that he had never been able to understand why Breuer had kept secret for so long his invaluable discovery, this was a mere affectation. In fact Freud knew there was a very good reason: 'Namely that the treatment of Anna O. had in no way led to a cure' (p. 154). Freud eventually came to explain Breuer's delay in publishing in terms of his resistance to sexuality, but this was also disingenuous, Israëls argues, because it is quite evident from the *Studies on Hysteria* that Breuer was perfectly able to acknowledge the frequent importance of sexual factors in the production of hysteria. When Freud later returned to the topic of Anna O. he gave out that he had managed to piece together years afterwards that the exact reason for the breaking off of the treatment was that Anna O. had fallen in love with her doctor and that Breuer had been unable to deal with this. This version of events was presented in its most developed form in the 1932 letter to Zweig, which contains the account of the hysterical childbirth, and in the version given by Jones in his biography.

Even though it has been established that some of the details Freud presented could not be true, particularly in the version as given by Jones, Israëls is resistant to the idea that the whole story is nothing other than a fantasy. For Israëls also quotes from those parts of the 1883 correspondence between Freud and his fiancée that Jones had alluded to, but which had in the meantime, in 1986, at least in part been published. In these letters, Freud and Martha are quite explicit about the domestic entanglement that Breuer drifted into as a result of his over-preoccupation with his patient. This demonstrates to Israëls that the story of the end of Anna O.'s treatment had surely not, after all, been completely retrospectively fantasised by Freud (p. 160), for we can see from the betrothal correspondence that the story has a grounding in reality. In this sense Israëls approaches these letters in the same spirit as Jones: predisposed by what Freud said about the ending of the treatment to discover in the letters more evidence of its precise emotional complexion. But here we come to a particularly inventive twist in Israëls's argument, as he remarks on two key differences between the 1883 correspondence and the accounts of the end of the treatment given by both Jones and Freud himself. The first is that in the correspondence it was Breuer who was showing too much interest in his patient, whereas in the later versions by Freud and Jones the emphasis has shifted to what the patient felt for her doctor. The second discrepancy lies in the fact that in Freud's own retrospective accounts, but not in the correspondence nor in Jones's version, the episode is accounted for as a retrospective reconstruction by Freud. Why, Israëls asks, did Jones omit this detail? Answer: because he knew that the idea of a mere 'reconstruction' was contradicted by the fact that the kernel of the whole story was to be found in the betrothal correspondence. There is a further implication:

> This thus means that Freud has furnished a not unimportant piece of false information in his later representation of the course of events: in his publications he always maintained that he had for years no knowledge of the true context, which he had only very much later been in a position to reconstruct; in reality Freud knew from the beginning why Breuer had broken off the treatment. (p. 161)

Why should Freud do this? Why, should he give the impression in his later accounts that his version of events was less credible, through being a 'reconstruction', than was actually the case? Israëls's answer is that there was a distinct advantage in being able to present his account as a retrospective reconstruction years after the events because he could then change some of the details of the story to suit his own depiction of himself and Breuer:

> In his later retrospective views Freud wrote that Breuer had delayed considerably with regard to the publication of the case history of Anna O., a delay that to him, Freud, appeared for a long time to be incomprehensible. As concerns the last point, Freud undoubtedly told an untruth. Breuer's delay must even have been very understandable, not only in consideration of the less than satisfactory therapeutic course of the treatment, about which Freud was informed, but in particular because of the affective complication between doctor and patient, about which Freud was equally in the picture. (p. 162)

Because Israëls is in no doubt that Freud knew all along about the circumstances of the ending of the treatment, he is able to charge Freud with falsely casting himself as an innocent victim of Breuer's dishonesty. This meant that Freud was able to maintain that only *after* the collaboration with Breuer did he become aware of the significance of sexuality, the implication being that it was Breuer's resistance to the fact and his lack of openness that had thrown him off the track. In fact Freud's whole retrospective emphasis on the key role of sexuality in his dispute with Breuer is little more than a smokescreen, Israëls implies, to disguise the real reason for Breuer's reluctance to publish: the Anna O. case had not been a success and it had caused him considerable personal and domestic disturbance.

In summary therefore, Israëls's case is as follows. In his retrospective accounts of the *Studies on Hysteria* Freud falsely claims first that he never understood why Breuer had delayed in publishing the Anna O. case, and secondly, that he later surmised it was because of his resistance to recognising the aetiological role of sexuality. This latter factor both inhibited his own theoretical progress and became the grounds on which he eventually broke with Breuer. We know that both parts of this claim are false. First of all, Breuer's acknowledgement of the importance of sexuality is quite evident from the *Studies* themselves, so we know that resistance to the aetiological significance of sexuality cannot have been in play in the way Freud suggests. Secondly, we also know that one of the real reasons for Breuer's disinclination to publish was the fact that the case had not been successful, and that this had been known by Freud all along; there can never have been any question of his not understanding Breuer's reluctance. As evidenced by the correspondence with his fiancée, Freud had been familiar as early as 1883 with the other main reason, the emotional entanglement that had arisen with Anna O. Freud's denial of his knowledge of these two factors allows him to suppress them in the interests of reconstructing a history more favourable to his own version of events, namely that the significance of sexuality had only emerged after the break with Breuer and that he, Freud, had been prevented from developing this insight earlier because of Breuer's own lack of straightforwardness in acknowledging the role of sexuality in the case of Anna O.

There can be little doubt about Israëls's originality in using the Anna O. case in a creative manner to cast doubt on Freud's own accounts of the history of the *Studies on Hysteria* and his collaboration with Breuer. But there are three major areas where Israëls's thesis presents difficulties. The first is his presupposition drawn directly from Ellenberger that the outcome of the Anna O. case was problematic in terms of its therapeutic results. Leaving aside the issue of the claim of a 'cure', which we have already dealt with at length, Israëls is in several respects dependent on Ellenberger's work, and in just those respects misled by it. He quotes Ellenberger's citation of Jung's 1925 seminar statement claiming that Anna O. had not been cured, but without revealing (presumably because he did not check the original source) that this claim was linked solely to the supposed hysterical attack due to the breaking of the transference, not to any particular knowledge of her history after the treatment ended. He then relies in the conventional manner on the Jones account of the Inzersdorf treatments and on the correspondence between Freud and Martha from 1883 in respect of Bertha's continued misery, and is thereby misled into concluding that the researches made possible by Jones's revealing of Anna O.'s real identity 'confirmed to a full extent what Freud told Jung and had made evident in his personal correspondence' (Israëls, 1999, p. 145). This is not so: Ellenberger's discovery of the Bellevue files bears no relation at all to what Freud told Jung, nor to what Freud had written to Martha about Breuer's wish that Bertha could be relieved of her suffering.

The second area where Israëls's thesis goes astray concerns the dispute between Breuer and Freud about the sexual aetiology of hysteria. Israëls supposes that because he can demonstrate that Breuer was fully prepared to acknowledge sexual factors as a frequent cause of hysteria then he has falsified Freud's claim that this was a prime issue of contention between Breuer and himself. But the issue that was at the heart of the dispute was not whether sexual factors were sometimes present, but whether they were *always* to be found. This more radical thesis was a 'late' discovery for Freud in the sense that when he treated the four patients that feature as his four cases in the *Studies* he had not reached this conclusion, and so they were not investigated or written up as exemplifications of his argument: this is quite evident from Freud's brief retrospective commentary in the cases in the final chapter of the book (Breuer and Freud, 1895, pp. 259–60). So while Freud does indeed announce his thesis of the universal sexual aetiology of hysteria in the final chapter (p. 257), the thesis that had first seen the light of day at the beginning of 1894 (Freud, 1894), there is a real sense in which this theory is not supported by the case studies, nor was there ever any intention that it should be so. The most that could emerge as a joint view at the end of the project as a rough compromise between their opposing views was what was enunciated in the *Preface to the First Edition*, that sexuality played a principal part (*Hauptrolle*) in the pathogenesis of hysteria (Breuer and Freud, 1895,

p. xxix). It was only towards the end of his collaboration with Breuer that Freud developed his own theory of the indispensable part played by sexuality, and therefore only towards the end that the issue of sexuality in the Anna O. case could have emerged as a vital matter of dispute. Israëls sees discrepancies in Freud's retrospective versions of the publication of the *Studies* only because he misrecognises what the real issue of disagreement was between Breuer and Freud. Breuer's letter to August Forel in 1907 makes the matter quite clear: he objected not to sexuality as such, but to Freud's emphasis on sexuality to the absolute exclusion of all other factors (Breuer, cited in Cranefield, 1958, p. 320). Israëls ignores this vital piece of evidence and nowhere mentions this important document.

The third major flaw is less significant for Israëls's overall thesis, but important as a commentary on the relationship between Breuer and Anna O. Israëls claims that Freud knew all along of the emotional complication that had developed, and that he was therefore being less than honest in passing it off in later years as a 'reconstruction'. Yet at the same time Israëls points out a significant discrepancy between the 1883 letters and Freud's later reconstruction of events. In the first it is a matter of Breuer's over-involvement with his patient, while later on the issue was represented as one of Breuer's flight in the face of his patient's over-attachment to her doctor. According to Israëls, Freud therefore not only falsely claimed that he knew no reason for Breuer's reluctance to publish, but even distorted the details of what he did know when he presented it years afterwards as a surmised reconstruction. But these two parts of Israëls's argument are in considerable tension with one another. When he points out a *difference* between what was said in 1883 and what Freud says he constructed years later, this is hardly supportive of a contention that Freud knew all along what had happened. Moreover, it merely compounds the logical fallacy to argue on the basis of this difference that it simply shows that once again Freud was at fault for distorting what he (secretly) knew. Israëls is surely right about the character of the 1883 correspondence: there is nothing here about any emotional over-involvement with Breuer on the part of Bertha Pappenheim, and he is also correct to criticise Jones for including the notion of a patient falling in love with the doctor in his own summary of the letter, when this does not actually occur in what Freud and Martha wrote (Israëls, 1999, p. 160). Yet is it precisely for this reason that this correspondence cannot be seen as evidence that when in his later accounts he stresses Anna O.'s dramatic transference, Freud knew of this all along: the letters simply do not say anything about it. It may be that in later years Freud recalled what he had learnt from Breuer about his wife's jealousy of his patient's demands, and that this was one of the fragments that contributed to his reconstruction of the ending of the case as something of an emotional mêlée. But at this earlier point not only did Freud not have the theoretical means or inclination to think in terms of Bertha's 'transference' onto her doctor, there is no evidence that he had any idea that anything resembling such a turn of events had actually transpired. Freud's later point was always geared towards emphasising the general theoretical and practical significance of the patient's transference, and this involved a hypothetical reconstruction of what *must* have been the case with Anna O., supported by odd scraps of detail that he had put together from things said by Breuer. There is no reason at all for supposing that Freud's later version was a direct and deliberate distortion of something that he had known all along since 1883.[6]

Furthermore Israëls persistently assumes that the emotional entanglement was not only responsible for Breuer's reluctance to publish, but that it was instrumental in causing the treatment to be broken off prematurely. But as is evident from the case study, it was the patient herself, not Breuer who determined that the treatment should end on 7 June 1882. There is no evidence at all that Breuer decided this. The idea that Breuer broke off the treatment comes solely from Freud's own reconstruction, and while it may have some basis in fact in a possible refusal by Breuer to resume treatment after the stay at Kreuzlingen or even be a distorted echo of Anna O.'s original institutionalisation in 1881, it cannot be linked to the termination of the treatment in June 1882, shortly before she was to go to Kreuzlingen.[7]

Israëls's extended discussion of the Anna O. case and its place in the *Studies on Hysteria* therefore recycles some long-standing misconceptions about the case and shares characteristics with the other secondary literature in basing itself in an over-dependent fashion on the flawed arguments of Ellenberger, but at the same time it elaborates these into a new version of Freud's use of the case which is no more secure in its conclusions than those proffered elsewhere.

Three years after the appearance of Israëls's work in its original Dutch version, Mikkel Borch-Jacobsen published in a similar spirit a book-length treatment of the Anna O. case (1996). Borch-Jacobsen presents his work as a critical examination of a myth: the myth that establishes Anna O. as the original, founding patient of psychoanalysis and around whom the psychoanalytic literature in all its varieties has ever since woven its own version of how her treatment with Breuer managed to rid her of her symptoms. But if this myth was founded one hundred years ago, the basis for its debunking was first revealed by Jones in 1953 when he showed, says Borch-Jacobsen, that Breuer's treatment did not, after all, remove the symptoms. Although Borch-Jacobsen is of the view that this revelation has been thoroughly corroborated by a number of historians since, nevertheless the myth refuses to die and persists to this day in the pervasive idea of the 'redemptive value of recollection and narration' (p. 10). Borch-Jacobsen intends that his book should effect a forcible confrontation between the bearers of that myth of origins and the essential facts of the case: the true story of Anna O. Yet this is just a means to a rather different end, for Borch-Jacobsen contends that myths are impervious to history, since the means of their validation is simply repetition, which has nothing at all to do with historical critique (ibid.) His main goal is to show that the myth of the origins does not, after all, mark an essential foundation or an absolute beginning, but is itself a repetition: 'The real crime of lese-myth consists in demonstrating that the narration of this particular myth repeats other myths, which in turn repeat others' (p. 13).

Borch-Jacobsen's enterprise therefore aims to show that not only did Breuer's treatment of Anna O. not attain what has commonly been claimed for it, but that the treatment itself was predicated on and indeed constituted by emulations of other models. So he argues that the doctor and patient engaged in a kind of non-intentional and mutually deluding conspiracy of activity which spiralled to create not only the majority of the symptoms themselves but the very method of treatment of those symptoms. Breuer brought to the treatment of his patient a prior knowledge of hypnosis, given impetus by the performances of the stage hypnotist, Carl Hansen, in Vienna shortly before the treatment started and which could have shaped Bertha Pappenheim's own performance in her cure process. Breuer's approach to hypnosis could well have been mediated too by the work of his colleague, Moriz Benedikt, who lectured on the subject in the aftermath of the sensation caused by Hansen. So if Bertha Pappenheim copied the post-hypnotic symptoms elicited by Hansen and the magnetisers of old, Breuer's increasing stress on the importance of remembering as the treatment progressed was probably a direct result of an interest in hypnotic hypermnesia derived from Benedikt (pp. 63–75). Bertha Pappenheim was a gifted simulator who managed to actualise her symptoms, to make them 'real', and in so doing was also able to fool the gullible Breuer with whom she engaged in a childish game of illness and cure, whose rules the two of them made up as they went along (p. 92). This, in a nutshell, is Borch-Jacobsen's pre-history of the Anna O. myth of origination.

Yet there is a sense in which Borch-Jacobsen's discussion of the mythic status of the Anna O. story soon becomes something of a side issue, for his book is not in fact dedicated to analysing its status and function as an 'origin-myth' so much as trying to subvert the myth itself, paradoxically, by means of that very historical critique to which he thinks myths are impervious. By attempting to reveal that the mythical events commonly described had their own sources in other myths, Borch-Jacobsen is simply analysing received history and trying to tell a different story about what 'really' happened. Whether Bertha really produced her symptoms in emulation of Hansen's subjects, whether Breuer really shaped his approach to her under the influence of Benedikt, whether Bertha was really a simulator and Breuer really so gullible are all matters for discussion that are outside the scope of the present work, for they mainly concern the origins, nature and course of the treatment – in themselves certainly very interesting issues – rather than the particular circumstances of its ending and the aftermath, which are the primary focuses here. But Borch-Jacobsen has much to say too about these aspects, for of course they are just as much part of the so-called myth of Anna O.'s treatment as ideas about its genesis and real nature.

The chapters of Borch-Jacobsen's book that deal with this part of the story present the evidence collated by those who over the last 50 years have provided the possibility of subverting the received version set in motion by Breuer and Freud, but they add more to it, mainly from sources which, while not all unpublished, have not before been set alongside one another. Yet ironically the framework of this re-presentation duplicates the mythic structures and processes of the Anna O. case that Borch-Jacobsen is so sceptical about. For in so far as his presentation of evidence is a re-presentation, it is a re-presentation that is gripped firmly by the structures of the narrative as told by its originators, especially Ellenberger. If the story of Anna O. has been related for a century, the new story that reveals the original to be a myth is itself all of 50 years old, and since Ellenberger gave it his own twist some 20 years after Jones it has been repeated incessantly and, it seems, ever more frequently. But of course, in common with all myths, this new story loses nothing in the re-telling; in fact it thrives, grows and complicates on the basis of it.

The first main element of the myth, and the part that in its published form stems first from Jones, concerns the essential failure of the treatment, but when he embarks on his own re-telling of this particular tale Borch-Jacobsen skips over this first source and runs straight to Ellenberger and the Kreuzlingen documents. In common with some other commentators Borch-Jacobsen makes Bertha's trigeminal neuralgia continuous with her other symptoms and thus sees the resulting morphine dependence as well as a sign of Breuer's failure. What is more curious though is that Borch-Jacobsen does this while at the same time perceptively recognising the essential difference between Bertha's neuralgia and her hysteria. So we are told:

> This facial neuralgia, which Breuer mentions nowhere in the *Studies on Hysteria* (he likewise refrains from any mention of Bertha's embarrassing morphine addiction), appeared briefly in the spring of 1880 and played only a 'quite subordinate role' in Bertha's illness until 'the middle of March' 1882, when, quite possibly as a result of surgery performed in February on the patient's upper left jaw, the pain became 'persistent and very excruciating.' (p. 22)

But in a related footnote Borch-Jacobsen also tells us that:

> The role that this apparently bungled dental surgery played in Bertha's facial neuralgia has been pointed out by Fritz Schweighofer, who quite rightly deduces (as Breuer himself also seems to have done) that these pains were not hysterical in nature, even if Bertha did immediately integrate them into the panoply of her other symptoms. (ibid.)[8]

But if the neuralgia had nothing to do with the hysteria, why should Breuer mention it in the case study, which was solely to do with the alleviation of hysterical symptoms? And if the morphine dependence was brought about by this neuralgia, as Borch-Jacobsen concedes, why should it be 'embarrassing' for Breuer, since it too was unrelated to Bertha's hysteria? There is no indication at all that Breuer used morphine as a means of treating Bertha for her hysterical condition. Moreover, Borch-Jacobsen cites no evidence for his notion that Bertha somehow integrated her neuralgic pains into the panoply of her other symptoms, whatever this might mean.

Borch-Jacobsen's assimilation of a somatic complaint to the hysterical symptoms for which Bertha was being treated by Breuer is characteristic of his technique of exposition. For in his attempt to demonstrate that what Breuer said was not true, it seems that every possible nuance of difficulty (and sometimes even of recovery) implied in Bertha Pappenheim's history is separated from its context and turned into evidence of Breuer's failure. For example, he refers to information from Dr Laupus's report at the end of Bertha's stay in Kreuzlingen about '"dramatic" enactments of her "private theatre"' as though this were evidence that had been perceived as 'genuine signs of hysteria' (pp. 22–3). What Laupus had in fact written was: 'She frequently allowed her phantasies to range freely in escapist dreams, though her presence returned immediately to a summons and she would reproduce her fairy tale-like dreams (private theatre!) with good humour and vivid, dramatic diction' (Hirschmüller, 1989, p. 292). This hardly constitutes evidence of hysteria, nor does Laupus construe it as such.

Similarly, Borch-Jacobsen cites the report written by Bertha at the Sanatorium Bellevue, 'in which she complains of periods of "timemissing"' (Borch-Jacobsen, 1996, p. 23). In fact what Bertha had written was: 'In the first 2 months of my sejourn here, I had shorter or longer absences, which I could observe myself by a strange feeling of "timemissing"; (…) but since some weeks there have been none' (Hirschmüller, 1989, p. 297). So contrary to what Borch-Jacobsen implies, at the time she wrote about these periods of 'timemissing' they had actually lifted.

Again, Borch-Jacobsen charges that while on the one hand the published case study states that at the point when she returned from her first stay in a sanatorium in the autumn of 1881 the talking cure had rendered Anna O.'s condition bearable, both physically and mentally, newly discovered documents actually reveal that Breuer had written a letter at the beginning of November indicating that the attempt to acclimatise the patient to her family would probably fail and that it would be 'best to prepare her for immediate hospitalization' (Borch-Jacobsen, 1996, p. 23). This implied contradiction between the published case history and what really happened dissolves when one looks closely at the evidence. What Breuer actually writes in the published version is:

> When, in the autumn, the patient returned to Vienna [...] her condition was bearable, both physically and mentally; for very few of her experiences – in fact only her more striking ones – were made into psychical stimuli in a pathological manner. I was hoping for a continuous and increasing improvement, provided that the permanent burdening of her mind with fresh stimuli could be prevented by her giving regular verbal expression to them. (Breuer and Freud, 1895, p. 32)

This optimistic strain is quite consistent with what Breuer had written with reference to the autumn period in his 1882 report, which was probably the direct source of the later version:

> She now processes only comparatively few events of the day pathologically, converting them into psychical stimuli which must be got

rid of in the evening. This continues to happen, however, with particularly radical experiences. [...] At the beginning of November she came to live with her mother in the city, and I thought that her largely unchanged position would gradually improve if I were able to prevent any lasting stress by means of the psychic stimulus of daily 'talking cures'. (Hirschmüller, 1989, p. 289)

While Bertha was certainly not well, there is no doubt that Breuer entertained a degree of hopefulness around this time that his patient's improvement could be sustained, but he is quite candid in the case study that this was not borne out, since he was immediately disappointed, and then in December there came a marked deterioration of her condition (Breuer and Freud, 1895, p. 32). The letter that Borch-Jacobsen sees as contradicting the public version of events in fact does no such thing. Breuer there reports that: 'An attempt is being made at this very moment to acclimatize the patient to her family: she is – or at least was – undergoing crucial convalescence. The attempt will probably fail' (Hirschmüller, 1989, p. 292). Yet, while relations with her family were clearly fragile, Breuer notes in the very same letter that her general condition had 'started to improve' (p. 293). At this point then, Breuer's discussions about Bertha's potential stay in Bellevue were precipitated not so much by her poor general state of health but by an expectation that it would be necessary for her to continue her convalescence away from her family. Moreover Borch-Jacobsen's dramatic statement that Breuer thought it would be 'best to prepare her for immediate hospitalization' is misleading in another sense. The Sanatorium Bellevue was not a 'hospital' (*Krankenhaus*) in either the late-nineteenth-century or the present-day sense. It was a private clinic or 'cure facility' (*Kuranstalt*) specialising in nervous and mental illness where Bertha would be expected to convalesce, as indeed she finally did the following summer.[9]

Furthermore, Borch-Jacobsen even supplements his elaborated version of Ellenberger's story with non-existent evidence. We are told that we know from unpublished letters from Freud to his fiancée that 'Breuer first spoke to Freud about Bertha Pappenheim on November 18, 1882, making no attempt to conceal the disastrous outcome of the treatment...' (p. 25). Borch-Jacobsen's alleged source for this is Jones's citation of a letter from Freud to Martha, but all that Jones reports is the simple fact of the date on which Breuer spoke to Freud (Jones, 1953, p. 248). There is no mention at all about his not concealing any disastrous outcome of the treatment either in the original letter (now available in the Library of Congress in Washington) or Jones's citation of it on which Borch-Jacobsen depends.[10]

Building on his idea of the essential fraudulence of the Anna O. case history, Borch-Jacobsen plays out the logic of his case in the following chapter with a gripping and racy account of what happened to the scandalous story of the failed treatment within the inner circles of psychoanalysis: 'The Pappenheim affair, carefully concealed from the public, seems nevertheless to have been an open secret among psychoanalytic insiders' (p. 29). There then follows a catalogue of Bjerre's early reference to Anna O.'s 'severe crisis', Jung's 1925 claim that the case was not a 'brilliant therapeutic success', Marie Bonaparte's journal note that the Breuer story was well known and Jones's revelation of the 'skeleton in the psychoanalytic closet' in 1953. But according to Borch-Jacobsen, Jones's disclosure was 'conveniently' drowned out by the even more sensational story (also conveyed by Marie Bonaparte) about Breuer's counter-transference, the hysterical childbirth and Breuer's flight. This story of course is rejected as spurious by Borch-Jacobsen on the usual grounds that are well charted in the other secondary literature and which need no further repetition at this point. But also in common with much of the rest of the literature is Borch-Jacobsen's failure to point out that the sources of the story he dismisses as 'a spiteful piece of slander' (p. 34) are the same as those he relies on for the idea that Breuer's treatment was a disaster.

In the case of the testimony from Jung, for example, we have already noted that only by suppressing a key part of what Jung had actually said does Ellenberger manage to present matters as though Jung had privileged knowledge of the fact that Anna O.'s treatment had not been a success. In fact this notion of Jung's was crucially dependent on his having been told by Freud about the putative hysterical attack of the patient resulting from the breaking of the transference, the very story that Ellenberger repeatedly repudiates in the version as told by Jones. Borch-Jacobsen executes a comparable manipulation of the quotation from Jung. At the point in his text where he wishes to show how the disastrous treatment had been an open secret among psychoanalytic insiders Borch-Jacobsen quotes the first part of what Jung had said: '"Thus again, the famous first case that he [Freud] had with Breuer, which has been so much spoken about as an example of a brilliant therapeutic success, was in reality nothing of the kind."' (pp. 29–30) Several pages further on he again quotes Jung, but this time he gives the continuation, the very next sentence, of the quotation begun earlier:

> To Jung, whose account is far too often overlooked, Freud was soon confiding that he himself had witnessed Bertha's transferential

delirium: 'Freud told me that he was called in to see the woman the same night that Breuer had seen her for the last time, and that she was in a bad hysterical attack, due to the breaking off of the transference.' We know this isn't true, of course [...] (p. 45)

Borch-Jacobsen swoops to the precarious conclusion that Freud actually did tell Jung that he had been there on the night of Anna O's hysterical attack, though his reasons for this manœuvre are not very plain apart from enabling him to discredit Freud by attributing to him personally, rather than to a lapse in Jung's memory, a statement that is patently false. Yet this statement, to which Borch-Jacobsen rightly gives no credence, is nothing more than Jung's substantiation of the point made in his previous sentence that the case of Anna O. was in reality not a brilliant therapeutic success, and which Borch-Jacobsen depends on to carry his accusation against Breuer and Freud. Whereas Ellenberger's citation of Jung suppresses this part of the quotation entirely, Borch-Jacobsen divides Jung's testimony and as a result conjures for the unwary reader the impression that the two fragments relate to two different contexts.

Everything in Borch-Jacobsen's account of the Anna O. case points in the same direction: if Breuer was gullible, then Freud was culpable. Borch-Jacobsen is hardly alone today in furthering this kind of notion, but then his book is notable not because of any new evidence or thesis it announces, but because in many ways it stands as a typical summary of the state of play of the secondary literature on the Anna O. case. It is true that not all the secondary literature bears such a marked animus against all things Freudian but the book is quite exemplary as a digest of the general knowledge of the case in today's literature, even augmented as it is by significant examples of unfounded speculation, quoting out of context, tampering with evidence, fragmentation of quotation and a general tendentiousness of argument against its historical subject matter that rather removes it from the terrain of dispassionately scholarly study.

But this kind of literature spawns its own imitations, for a summary of the Anna O. case which is parasitic on Borch-Jacobsen's work and created entirely within its spirit forms the opening of Todd Dufresne's rather grotesquely titled book, *Killing Freud: Twentieth-Century Culture and the Death of Psychoanalysis* (2003). This work is mentioned here for the sake of completeness, rather than for any positive addition it makes to the canon of writings on Anna O., for as a piece of historical writing it adds nothing new of value to the debate. Also tapping the same vein of this new orthodoxy is the brief descriptive article by Robert Kaplan (2004), which for the most part repeats points lifted piecemeal from Ellenberger and Borch-Jacobsen, adding only a few minor historical errors of its own.

With hindsight it was perhaps inevitable that this trend in the treatment of the case should culminate in its mode of appearance in the modern-day *Malleus Maleficarum* of psychoanalysis, *Le Livre noir de la psychanalyse* (Meyer, 2005), a leviathan of a book dedicated to an evangelistic attempt to bring Anglo-American standards of science, rationality and clinical psychology to a benighted French nation subjected for too long to the stifling tyranny of psychoanalytic ideology. Part of the philosopher Frank Cioffi's contribution to this most recent French enlightenment is to reduce within the confines of one paragraph the whole of the Anna O. case to a single, almost aphoristically simple contradiction that demonstrates Freud's mendacity, and this without even a passing reference to the creative work of his predecessors (Cioffi, 2005). First he cites[11] Freud's statement that: 'By this procedure Breuer succeeded [...] in relieving the patient of all her symptoms. The patient had recovered and had remained well and, in fact, had become capable of serious work' (p. 314) Then by way of antithesis he quotes from Jones to the effect that 'A year after discontinuing the treatment Breuer confided to Freud that she was quite unhinged and that he wished she would die and so be released from her suffering' (ibid.) For Cioffi it therefore follows almost syllogistically, as surely as Socrates was a mortal, that Freud was a liar. In this method we have a veritable philosopher's stone of historical research: no need to explore context, to question evidence, to interrogate the witnesses' statements, and with no notion that things might be other than they appear from the dismembered chunks of bleeding text lying brightly lit on the analytical slab.

For Cioffi, as for others working in the same genre, the telling of the history is easy, even though the resulting truth of this particular history lies solely in the very relating of the legend it creates and in the way the anti-psychoanalytic movement recounts to itself its own fantasies of the birth of the monster it despises. This is not to level a charge of bad faith at those who perpetrate this kind of settling of historical accounts, for that would be to denounce a reassuring fable-telling activity as though it were the result of a falsifying intention. But in this volume, in Borch-Jacobsen's (2005) opening six-page synopsis of the case summarising the highlights of his earlier book, as well as in Cioffi's one-paragraph snapshot later in the same volume, we find the modern apogee of treatments of Anna O. Just as for the psychoanalytic movement the complexities of Breuer's case eventually became characteristically reduced to a few garbled lines at the start of the introductory primers, we now see the mimicry of this in the opposing camp. Now that history has turned full circle and psychoanalysis has got what it deserves it seems that Anna O. is destined to remain a figurehead, where a mere gesture in her direction is enough to tell us everything that we need to know about the origins of the psychoanalysis to which she bore witness. What need for lengthy discussion or probing analysis? As a touchstone of everything that is wrong with the psychoanalytic enterprise the Anna O. case is now apparently as transparent and open as its history is closed.

This is all quite far removed from those two figures standing at the head of this whole body of secondary, interpretative literature: Jones and Ellenberger. They came from quite different traditions and in most respects proposed radically conflicting theses about the Anna O. case. Yet their work has somehow acted in concert to produce what is currently taken to be the accepted state of historical knowledge of the case of Bertha Pappenheim in her manifestation as Anna O. Jones set the ball rolling by recounting publicly Freud's story of the phantom pregnancy and by being the first to allege openly that Breuer's treatment was not the success customarily maintained. The fact that Jones predicated Breuer's purported failure solely on unpublished correspondence between Freud and his fiancée is often lost sight of, for when Ellenberger discovered that Bertha had stayed at the Sanatorium Bellevue for some months it was quite easy to see this as further evidence of therapeutic failure because of the ground already prepared by his predecessor. None of the correspondence evidence that Jones draws on relates in any way at all to the stay in Kreuzlingen, but this too normally goes unremarked, as does the fact that even though the terminal hysterical crisis story that Jones relates is widely discredited, it still functions in a latent form for many writers as further evidence of failure. There is a perceived convergence between a number of factors: the stay in Kreuzlingen, the evidence of Bertha Pappenheim's continued suffering for several years after Breuer completed his treatment (including further institutionalisation), the retrospective 'constructions' about the breaking of the transference put about in various forms by Freud himself. All these features of the case have conspired in the hands of commentators to appear consilient and to point in one direction: Breuer's treatment was essentially a failure. The only things that do not fit with this judgement are Breuer's case history itself and Freud's own publicly held view of it in subsequent years. It therefore follows in the interests of consistency that what was reported by both Breuer and Freud was, in all essentials, wrong. The history of the Anna O. case in the last 50 years has largely consisted of attempts to assimilate this latter notion, and different writers have been more or less troubled or more or less gleeful about its implications. It is of course a prime conclusion of this book that this judgement about Breuer and Freud cannot stand, and that it is the alternative versions given by the commentators of the last half century that require substantial revision where they are not to be jettisoned entirely, for the evidence they cite simply does not sustain the critical conclusions they reach. It is now time to turn, finally, to an exploration of some of the implications of this thesis.

Conclusion

Der Mensch muß bei dem Glauben verharren, daß das Unbegreifliche begreiflich sei; er würde sont nicht forschen.[1]

J. W. von Goethe, *Maximen und Reflexionen* (1829)

The principal aim of this book has been to revisit the contemporary evidence currently available concerning the Anna O. case with the aim of assessing how far it sustains the view that is nowadays widely held that Breuer's treatment of his patient was essentially a failure. If this view is accepted it follows that the conclusion of Breuer's case study of 1895 was, at the very least, misleading to the extent that it implied greater success than was in fact the case, and in so far as Freud himself knew of this, then he too was complicit in Breuer's deception of his readers. The main burden of the argument in this book has been to reject this position, but before reviewing the implications of this it would perhaps be well to summarise the conclusions so far.

Close examination of Breuer's original 1882 report on Bertha Pappenheim reveals a number of significant features. If we accept this report as an honest account of how the case emerged and developed from Breuer's point of view (and no one seems to have seriously doubted this) then it appears that for quite some time Breuer was uncertain about the exact nature of his patient's ailments. Although he was called in to treat a cough that he quickly diagnosed as 'hysterical', he also soon became aware of the serious state of his patient's mental health, which, as might be expected at the time, he provisionally regarded as a separate condition from any hysteria which might also be present. As the symptoms evolved under his care, he gradually settled on a diagnosis of hysteria, which itself seemed to be grounded in an underlying unknown illness that had to be left to follow its natural course. One of the principal peculiarities of the illness were the states of absence into which his patient recurrently fell, which, while not features of hysteria in themselves, became the basis on which hysterical symptoms were able to take root. When Breuer eventually decided on a diagnosis of hysteria, this was in more than one respect a negative conclusion, signalling merely that there was no clear alternative somatic cause for his patient's problems. This meant that Breuer was thinking in terms of a general functional disorder of the nervous system that had both localised manifestations in disturbances of movement, sight, and so on, as well as more wide-ranging psychical effects, summarised in the concept of 'hysterical psychosis'. But when coupled with the severity of his patient's condition the diagnosis was also such that there was no clearly defined programme of treatment of the kind that might have followed a diagnosis of a non-hysterical ailment, beyond working on a day-to-day basis to manage the illness under whatever circumstances the patient presented.

It is often pointed out that the patient herself produced her own 'treatment', in so far as what came to be the cathartic method gradually emerged in the course of the illness. In the nature of the case this is not so surprising, for if the diagnosis of hysteria meant that there was no immediately available therapeutic action that could be adopted, and if the severity of the patient's condition meant that the usual rest cures, massage, electricity and so on, would be either impractical or of no clear immediate benefit, then Breuer would have had little alternative but to watch and wait. Eventually even this régime of non-intervention became impossible to sustain as the patient's mental condition (though not her physical state) deteriorated sharply after her father's death, necessitating her removal to Inzersdorf sanatorium for several months. In the course of her illness it became clear to those around her that Bertha gained a degree of relief when she was able to recount stories connected with her daytime phantasies and Breuer eventually turned this into a systematic technique, which he began to employ regularly. Already in the 1882 report there is evidence that Breuer came to consider the role of suppressed affect to be important in the production of symptoms, and conversely the expression of the affect, by means of articulating the event that gave rise to it, appeared to him to alleviate the symptom in question. However, Breuer made no attempt to account for this phenomenon theoretically.

When the treatment came to an end in June 1882 it appears to have been entirely at the wish of Bertha herself, and there is no evidence that

Breuer broke off the treatment. During the treatment itself the documentation reveals no evidence of any clearly expected outcome, and it simply records the gradual improvements in the patient's condition. The overwhelming impression given is that what Breuer thought of as the underlying illness was managed, rather than radically confronted, and when its major manifestations subsided this seems to be because the illness had simply pursued its course. Indeed there were some symptoms that Breuer never considered to be hysterical, and which just disappeared.

By the time the treatment finished Bertha was in a position to leave Vienna to visit relatives for a few weeks before she went to the Sanatorium Bellevue in Kreuzlingen to convalesce. When she arrived at the sanatorium there were two significant remaining problems. First there was a very painful facial affliction, diagnosed as trigeminal neuralgia, from which she had been suffering for over two years, indeed for some months before the presumed onset of her hysterical condition in the summer of 1880. Secondly, she was dependent on morphine, which was needed to control the facial pain. Although one of the principal objects of the stay in Kreuzlingen was to wean Bertha from the morphine, this was not achieved by the time she left at the end of October, and the doctor's report at the end of her stay reflects the extent to which the facial disorder was the principal residual symptom remaining from Bertha's previous two years of suffering. By the end of her stay, there was still a daily recurrence of the hysterical inability to speak German every evening, but this occasioned Bertha herself no great distress and was the subject of only a passing comment by the Bellevue doctor. This problem diminished even further in the succeeding months, although the same could not be said of the trigeminal neuralgia, which persisted in plaguing her and required the continued use of morphine. Breuer declined to resume his treatment of her, but neither the indications about Bertha's condition in Freud's own correspondence from 1883 onwards nor the information we have about further periods of institutionalisation lend support to the notion that severe hysterical symptoms persisted. That she continued to suffer is beyond doubt, but there is no evidence that points to this resulting from anything other than facial neuralgia. Although in addition there may have been a regular recurrence of the states of absence in which she had fallen prey to hysteria in the first place, these were neither hysterical symptoms as such, nor did they seem to cause Bertha much torment compared with her physical pain.

As far as Breuer and Freud's retrospective view of the case is concerned it seems that from quite early on they considered that the narcotic dependence had interfered with the recovery from the hysteria, but this did not affect their overall evaluation of the success of the new treatment. Beyond this, they held that the method that Breuer had discovered could hope for no more than the removal of any hysterical symptoms remaining once the main hysterical illness had resolved itself. There was never any claim that the cathartic method could cure acute hysteria, let alone remove the underlying hysterical state. Breuer and Freud recommended the cathartic method in general in 1895 solely as a means of removing residual hysterical symptoms, and in the particular case of Anna O. they never claimed that the method had cured her hysteria. It is true indeed that the end of the case study presents a picture of the patient that is less than complete as a depiction of her total medical condition: there is no reference to her stay in Kreuzlingen, no mention of the facial neuralgia, the dental operation or any drug dependence. But the function of Breuer's chapter on Anna O. in the *Studies on Hysteria* was to illustrate by means of a case history a new method of examining and treating hysterical phenomena, not to give a full account of the medical history of a patient and all her afflictions as such. Any case study that is framed with the purpose of demonstrating the viability of a particular thesis will have to be based on choices about the inclusion and exclusion of particular characteristics of the patient's overall state, and these will be determined by the delimitation of the phenomenon under study. If it appeared to Breuer that there were certain aspects of Bertha Pappenheim's condition that were not to do with her hysterical pathology then it would make no sense for him to include them, any more than we would expect a case study in ophthalmology to include full reports on the patient's bunions. The available evidence suggests that whatever gave rise to Bertha's dental operation, her facial neuralgia and the consequent narcotic dependence was not considered by Breuer to be related to hysteria, and there was therefore nothing untoward about his decision to omit them from the published case study.[2]

Evidence from Freud's correspondence with his fiancée from the 1880s reveals that Freud knew that the treatment of Bertha Pappenheim had caused Breuer significant problems in his relationship with his wife, and that these were instrumental in his declining to treat Bertha further. This is quite likely to have been at the point when it became apparent in the autumn of 1882 that Bertha's stay in Kreuzlingen had not achieved what had been hoped for and that further medical care would be necessary. There is no suggestion in the contemporary evidence that Breuer ever broke off the treatment, and not a hint that Freud in 1883 thought that this had been the case. When Freud in that year wrote to Martha of

Breuer withdrawing completely from his activity as a physician of Bertha Pappenheim there is nothing in the context to imply that this refers to the ending of the treatment in June of the previous year, rather than some indeterminate time afterwards. All the evidence from later years suggests that when Freud retold the story of the ending of the treatment, this was based on an entirely different set of considerations from what would have been known to him immediately in its aftermath.

After the breakdown of his relationship with Breuer, Freud developed his own distinctive view of the Anna O. case that was largely based on hindsight. This was in the main connected with his conclusion that sexual factors played an indispensable aetiological role in hysteria, and that therefore Bertha Pappenheim's pathology must at root have been a sexual one, despite first appearances. Freud's theory of the aetiological role of sexuality did not emerge until after he had completed the treatment of the patients who were to be represented in his own case histories in the *Studies on Hysteria*, and so the potential for illustrating his own novel views on the basis of the material he was presenting was comparatively limited. The main constraint was of course that Breuer did not agree with him. While Breuer was perfectly willing to acknowledge the role of sexuality in some cases of hysteria, he would not concede that it was always and necessarily a requisite factor. As a working, but uneasy compromise between their two positions it was agreed that none of the case histories would be directed towards revealing Freud's newly emergent position, and that in their general formulations the authors would each openly respect the other's views. But the tensions of this compromise are evident in a number of places in the *Studies*, and the working relationship between Freud and Breuer broke down even before publication. Freud could never come to terms with Breuer's reluctance to accept his new sexual theory, and he saw Breuer's resistance as quite irrational. It was therefore a short step to linking the theory of sexuality with the idea that the patient's emotional life must inevitably come into play in the course of the relationship with the doctor and thus seeing the Anna O. case in retrospect as being a prime example of an unresolved transference relationship. Similarly it also required no great leap for Freud also to come to believe that Breuer's failure to recognise this was not based on considerations of evidence and rationality, but on his own emotional resistance to the pervasiveness of sexuality in neurosis and its treatment, or what would later be known by psychoanalysts as an aspect of the doctor's counter-transference.

The correspondence in 1883 between Freud and Martha predominantly focused on Breuer's over-accommodation to the demands of his patient, at least as far as his domestic circumstances were concerned. Martha feared her own claims over her future husband might at some point be challenged in this way, but there is no evidence of direct knowledge by either of the couple that any situation of impropriety had arisen or even that Bertha had developed any disturbing emotional over-involvement with Breuer. When Freud advanced years later his own reconstruction of what had happened, this was never a narrative built on the basis of a plain and simple familiarity with the details of the case, so much as a piecing together within the framework of the new theory of sexuality and the power of transference the hints of difficulty that had been given to him by Breuer. All the evidence that we have from Freud's own pen about the tale of Breuer breaking off the treatment and Bertha Pappenheim's phantom pregnancy reveal that he always conceded that this was a reconstruction, but when the story began to circulate informally in his proximate circle it appears that the hypothetical element of this became lost. This, of course, does not exonerate Freud from responsibility for the propagation of a narrative concerning what all available indications suggest never actually happened, but any *a priori* supposition without direct evidence that this was simply a deliberate, malicious fiction on Freud's part sacrifices any possibility of advancing an understanding of what actually might have been in play here.

Freud's memory for dates and details was notoriously poor.[3] Having known for more than a decade after the event itself that Breuer had significant difficulties during the extended treatment of Bertha Pappenheim and having come in the meantime to the conclusion that not only must Breuer have become over-involved in the case but that Bertha too must have exhibited signs of a transference engagement that Breuer himself could never acknowledge because of his own internal resistance, it was but a small step to reconstruct a dramatic end to the whole therapeutic relationship. This may even have involved Freud displacing in his memory to the following year the event in 1881 when Breuer did indeed have to extricate himself from the treatment to a certain degree and have Bertha committed to Inzersdorf after the death of her father. Where the detail of the hysterical childbirth came from and whether it too may have emerged from fragments of data that Freud pieced together years afterwards remains something of a mystery even though it has a certain psychoanalytic logic to it if one sexualises Anna's relationship to her father at the point of the onset of her illness in the way that Eitingon and then Freud both did. While on the one hand it is a most peculiar set of details to have invented from nothing, on the other there is no evidence from the time that the story is true. But even if we set aside this particular episode there is no doubt that Freud considered the Anna O. case, rightly or wrongly, to be a partial failure. The failure lay in Breuer's inability to acknowledge even a decade later what had been under his nose, and this continuing inability to negotiate the transference relationship with his patient became central to Freud's retrospective accounts of the case.

This is the key fact that must be taken into consideration when reflecting on the accounts of the Anna O. case narrated in their various forms by numbers of Freud's followers. For if they reported on the basis of his authority that the case had not been a complete success, then it is crucial to note that they did not do so because he told them of Bertha's subsequent institutionalisation or that she continued to suffer for many years afterwards, but that they followed his story of Bertha's putative hysterical crisis at the end of the treatment and Breuer's inability to handle this. It was this supposed event that in Freud's mind was the index of Breuer's failure. Even in the case of Freud's letter to Tansley where he does mention institutionalisation (for an inflated three quarters of a year), this is predicated on Breuer's flight from his patient, not on a failure of the treatment as such.

It was Ernest Jones who was the first to broach publicly the possibility that the case had not been as successful as Breuer had made out and to do so on grounds that were independent of Freud's own testimony of Bertha's hysterical crisis. However, his evidence was drawn from the betrothal correspondence to which he had privileged access, but which on close inspection reveals nothing more than the possibility that Bertha continued to suffer extreme pain from her neuralgia and bouts of her 'absence' in the evenings as much as five years later. They do not show that Breuer's treatment of her hysterical symptoms had failed. Jones's whole account is something of a patchwork of evidence of dubious provenance, and while many commentators have rightly been guarded about accepting the hysterical childbirth story, the same cannot be said for his declaration of Breuer's failure. This was given an indirect but spurious credibility by Ellenberger's discovery of the Kreuzlingen case notes and by the whole scenario that he constructed, which he thought cast doubt on both Breuer's and much of Jones's versions of the case. But Ellenberger's own work on the Anna O. story was severely flawed. Convinced at the outset about the essential unreliability of Breuer and Jones, and misreading both of them, Ellenberger presented conclusions that were radically at variance with the genuinely new empirical evidence that he had discovered. This was effected by means of a persistent disregard of the unreliability of some of his sources, an insufficient attention to detail and a sustained readiness to maintain that his evidence told a contrary story to that which it patently portrayed to anyone willing to approach it with an open mind.

It is therefore particularly unfortunate that the version of events as told by Ellenberger has, to all intents and purposes, remained the story of Anna O. as told today. For all historical work on the Anna O. case since has taken Ellenberger's story for granted and merely elaborated further in one or other direction the same tale of Breuer's failure. If we are now to abandon this as essentially a modern fiction, where does that leave the Anna O. case today and what is implied by the argument of this book for future scholarship?

In the first place, the case cannot be considered as now definitively closed and laid to rest. This is not simply because others may wish to contest the findings and arguments of this book, but because as a matter of principle there is always the possibility of further evidence coming to light which may change the picture again. Most of the argument advanced here has not been based on new evidence, but on a reading of existing data which differs radically from most other current interpretations. But the fact that such a radically variant reading is possible is an index of just how ambiguous some of this data is and how widespread the gaps in it are. At one level there is no paucity of data, and its range is really quite wide. It includes, among other things, Breuer's original published case history, the original Kreuzlingen case notes, Pappenheim family correspondence, Freud's published addenda to the case, his remarks in correspondence and comments made by his followers. Yet given the historical spread of this data and the unreliability of so much of it in relation to what it tells us about exactly what happened in the Anna O. case, it is not so very surprising that no clear picture emerges when it is considered in its totality. But this is precisely the problem with so much of the commentary on the case: it greatly exaggerates the extent to which the data points unequivocally in one particular direction. Historians of this episode generally seem to have felt at liberty to develop their own variation of the case, and in the last 50 years this has been increasingly to tell the story of the ramifications of Breuer's failure. In specific instances and on particular details these positions are contradicted, or at least rendered highly problematic, by one or other piece of the extant evidence, as the review of the literature in the latter half of this look has attempted to show. But in some cases too much certainty is predicated on what is, to say the very least, an incomplete picture, and alternative possibilities become elided in the rush to conviction. To be sure, if each piece of evidence is stripped from its broader circumstances and every piece of ambiguity and every slight inconsistency in the sources is resolved in favour of the argument that Breuer's treatment of Anna O. was essentially a failure, then this conclusion seems to be almost inevitable. But once the individual fragments of data are considered in their context, and once it is recognised that these pieces of evidence were not created for the sole purpose of betraying a single latent 'truth' about the case some one hundred years afterwards, then it surely has to be recognised that the story told by this book is also consistent with all the evidence, and at least has the additional merit of pointing towards the resolution of some hitherto puzzling contradictions.

The conclusion arrived at here that Breuer's 1895 case history was not essentially misleading, and that Freud did not participate in a fraudulent attempt to cover up a failure in the interests of his emergent discipline of psychoanalysis is perhaps a novel one, given the last 50 years of Freud scholarship, but it is not for this reason that it must remain in a certain sense provisional. It is a thesis that is conditional on the currently available evidence, but which could quite possibly be undermined should further evidence come to light. Hitherto unknown correspondence or additional medical documentation could indeed reveal that Bertha Pappenheim still suffered from hysterical symptoms years after her treatment with Breuer had ended, or that Freud was complicit with Breuer in deceiving his public about the value of the case. There is nothing to preclude, as a matter of principle, the position on the Anna O. case that has generally been adhered to for the last 50 years from being true, but the contention here is that currently the state of the evidence is such that it cannot continue to be sustained with any confidence.

While it is still theoretically possible that further evidence may be discovered that supports the idea of Breuer's failure, it must be added that there is an amount of circumstantial evidence why this is unlikely to be the case. If Breuer's enterprise had been essentially unsuccessful, and if therefore both he and Freud had been guilty of dissembling when they published the *Studies on Hysteria* in 1895, the risks to both would have been quite considerable. First there was a whole network of doctors who both knew Bertha Pappenheim and treated her, including Hermann Breslauer and Emil Fries, the directors at Inzersdorf, Robert Binswanger and Dr Laupus at Kreuzlingen and Carl Bettelheim in Vienna. Any of these might have been likely to read the *Studies* and to recognise their former patient. Even if the ambitious Freud might have been tempted to exaggerate the success of the case, the cautious and well-established

Breuer, with one of the best medical reputations for general practice in Vienna, would surely have had too much to lose in gambling in this way to acquire a piece of fame, even if he had been so inclined. Secondly, there was Bertha Pappenheim's family. Although by the time the *Studies* were published Bertha and her mother been living in Frankfurt for some seven years, they still had relatives back in Vienna who were well-connected. It could not be assumed by either Breuer or Freud that one of these might not become aware of what claims were being made about the treatment of one of their kin and protest if these were fraudulent. The fact that there is no evidence of any such objection by either colleagues or family is less significant than an appreciation of the risk that Breuer in particular would have run had doubts been circulated, even privately, amongst his circle.[4]

Even in Frankfurt there is circumstantial evidence, albeit of a negative kind, that no one who knew of Breuer's treatment of Bertha Pappenheim had reservations about the claims he made about it. In 1886, some four years after Breuer's treatment of Bertha, Ludwig Edinger, the celebrated neurologist, had married Anna Goldschmidt, who was the daughter of a cousin of Bertha's mother, herself a Goldschmidt by birth. Thus Bertha Pappenheim and Ludwig Edinger became second cousins by marriage. His wife, Anna Edinger, became prominent in Frankfurt as a strong proponent of women's rights and as a pioneer social worker, like Bertha herself. Ludwig and Anna Edinger's son, Friedrich, was in 1914 to marry Dora Meyer, who, as Dora Edinger, eventually became responsible for the compilation of materials relating to Bertha Pappenheim's life and work that formed the basis of her 1963 publication. In that book, Dora Edinger reveals that Bertha's illness had been known about within the family. She writes:

> This illness was only known to her family, also the fact that she had been treated by the eminent Viennese doctor, Dr Josef Breuer, and that he frequently discussed her case with his younger friend, Sigmund Freud, until it was finally taken up, over ten years later, as 'Fräulein Anna O.' in the collection of case histories the two doctors published in 1895. (Edinger, 1963, p. 12)

In the English edition of her book further information is given:

> When she was in her early twenties she suffered a serious breakdown. Her family knew about it – it was a cousin who informed Jones. I heard about it from a relative who was also Bertha Pappenheim's

good friend, Louise Goldschmidt; my father-in-law Ludwig Edinger, Neurologist, (1855–1918), who was a second cousin by marriage, later confirmed it. (Edinger, 1968, pp. 14–5)

Louise Goldschmidt was married to a cousin of Anna Edinger, and was therefore another second cousin of Bertha Pappenheim. So although Bertha's illness and her treatment by Breuer was only known about within her family, and not among her later co-workers, this knowledge seems to have been widespread, even among her more distant relatives. What is particularly significant here is that Ludwig Edinger was familiar with the identity of Bertha Pappenheim and Anna O. It may well be that this was solely through being a member of her extended family, but there is also a possibility that Edinger had a professional interest in his relative's case by virtue of being her doctor. This was certainly the opinion of Dora Edinger, who wrote in a private letter in 1957, discovered by Gerald Kreft, as follows:

I do not know whether I wrote to you that I always knew that B.P. was Anna O.; I believe that later my father-in-law [Ludwig Edinger] was her doctor. Freud had a very high regard for him, but this was not based on a reciprocity. My father-in-law shied away from Freud's conclusions – consciously at least. (Edinger, cited in Kreft, 1996, p. 221)

As this is the only direct, though hardly conclusive evidence we have of Edinger being Bertha Pappenheim's doctor, Kreft evaluates the consequential possibilities carefully. It could simply be an error on Dora Edinger's part; perhaps it was only because he was a family member that Ludwig Edinger knew of the identity of Bertha Pappenheim and Anna O. Alternatively it could be that it was only many years after her arrival in Frankfurt that Edinger became her doctor. But given his status as Frankfurt's leading neurologist onwards Kreft considers it a strong possibility that Bertha took him as her doctor from the time she arrived there in the late 1880s (pp. 221–2).

Somewhat tenuous corroboration of the possibility that Edinger was Bertha Pappenheim's doctor is given by details deriving from the person who became her doctor in later years. In 1995 the psychoanalyst and scholar of hypnosis, Erika Fromm, wrote to Kreft:

No one in Frankfurt knew that BP was Anna O., and when Ernest Jones published, in 1953, that she was, I read it (because I am a psychoanalyst) and wrote to my father, who by that time was living in

Israel. He was astonished [...] He had read the 'Studien über Hysterie', but it never occurred to him that Bertha Pappenheim could be Anna O. (Cited in Kreft, 1999, p. 212)

What is significant about this is that Kreft had learnt that Erika Fromm's father, Dr Siegfried Oppenheimer, had been Bertha Pappenheim's doctor in Frankfurt, but only from about 1918 onwards. As 1918 was the year in which Ludwig Edinger died, it is quite possible that this was the event that prompted Bertha Pappenheim to seek a new doctor.[5]

Even if Edinger had not been Bertha Pappenheim's doctor, he certainly knew of her past history and of her treatment by Breuer. This is important because there is indirect evidence of Edinger having a high regard for the Breuer/Freud method of treatment. For apart from being a neurologist, Edinger had a close interest in matters to do with psychological medicine and hypnosis. In fact in 1909 he published in the *Deutsche Medizinische Wochenschrift* a brief review of the newly published second edition of the *Studies on Hysteria*:

> In a new, unchanged imprint we have here the work from which Freud's studies on several psychological processes proceed. It was reviewed exhaustively at the time; that a new reprint became necessary shows how lively is the interest of the whole of medicine [*der Ärzteschaft*] in this instructive book. (Edinger, cited in Kreft, 1996, p. 208)

Two years later he wrote:

> Suggestion in hypnosis played a large role about twenty years ago; doctors and patients, more than today, stood under the conviction that there is given here a powerful curative factor, and on that basis we had at that time better successes than today (...) [This] also led in large part to the doctors learning [in the meantime] to concern themselves very much more intensively (...) with the psyche of the patient and to our experiencing how much is to be achieved here by a judicious analysis of mental life and a suggestive management. (Edinger, cited in Kreft, 1996, p. 222; ellipses in Kreft's text)

Although Breuer did indeed use suggestion with Bertha Pappenheim, his overall method is very much more in line with what Edinger refers to as an analysis of mental life, but neither here nor in his earlier review, does he express any reservations about the kind of treatment that was exemplified in Breuer's approach to his patient. As Kreft remarks (p. 223), if there was anyone at all, apart from Freud and Breuer, who was in a position to judge Breuer's conclusion of his case study, then it was Ludwig Edinger, whether his knowledge derived from Bertha being his patient or whether it was just as a family member. Surely if Edinger had the least suspicion that Breuer's case study was fundamentally inaccurate or misleading, he would have indicated as much, even if only obliquely, either in his general discussions of psychotherapeutic method or in his specific review of the *Studies on Hysteria*.

To be sure there is a certain amount of supposition implied in this, and the suggestion made here depends on the absence of a critical strain in Edinger's writing, rather than positive confirmation of specific knowledge. Nevertheless in trying to construct an overall impression of the case there is an obligation to consider the possibilities raised by all the evidence.

A similar sign that all might well have been just as it seemed is given by a further private reference by Freud to the case, which, while being quite slight in its implications, is nevertheless perhaps indicative of how Freud regarded his mentor's work with Bertha Pappenheim just a few years after its completion. In 1886, shortly after his return from studying under Charcot in Paris, where he had been dazzled by his discovery of Charcot's work on hysteria, Freud completed and published a translation of a set of his lectures (Charcot, 1886). Naturally he sent a copy to Breuer, but when he did so, he inscribed it as follows: 'To his most highly esteemed friend, Dr. Josef Breuer, secret master of hysteria and other complicated problems, in silent dedication, the translator' (cited in Swales, 1989, p. 292). Given how close the intellectual and personal relationship between Freud and Breuer had been up to 1886 it is not surprising that Freud should write such a flattering tribute, but it is striking that this should include, of all things, a reference to Breuer's mastery of hysteria, particularly when it was Charcot himself who was deemed by many to be pre-eminent in this field. Charcot, it should be remembered, had no great interest in the detailed analysis of particular hysterical symptoms, and according to Freud's version of events many years afterwards, he showed no great curiosity about Breuer's work with Bertha Pappenheim when Freud informed him of it (Freud, 1925, pp. 19–20). Yet Freud in 1886 clearly did think that Breuer had made inroads into the study of hysteria that went beyond what Charcot had achieved, for the reference to 'the secret master of hysteria' must surely refer to what Freud by then knew of Breuer's treatment of Bertha Pappenheim. But what possible motive could he have had for bestowing such a specific compliment if he thought at the time that the case had been the failure that much of the secondary literature of the last 50 years would have us believe? Whatever notions Freud constructed in later years about how the treatment may have ended, in 1886, nine years before the publication of the *Studies*, his private opinion seems to have been that Breuer had achieved something of note.

These pieces of circumstantial evidence taken in isolation indicate very little about Breuer's treatment of Bertha Pappenheim, but all together they do not sit easily with the most common picture of it found in much of the current literature. But why is it that this picture has been so resilient? How has such a mistaken conception of the origins of psychoanalysis managed to take root and to sustain itself for so long? While the seeds of this were sown by Freud in his retrospective accounts of the case, both public and private, it was when they were taken up in an even more distorted form by Jones that the genie really escaped from the bottle. But the history of this accumulated fiction is not a case of simple factual error; issues to do with the history of psychoanalysis are inseparable from its politics of contestation and dispute, and Freud in particular was well aware of this. When he repeated Breuer's claim that the element of sexuality was astonishingly undeveloped in his famous first patient, he commented as follows:

> I have often wondered why the critics did not more often cite this assertion of Breuer's as an argument against my contention of a sexual aetiology in the neuroses, and even to-day I do not know whether I ought to regard the omission as evidence of tact or of carelessness on their part. (Freud, 1914, p. 11)

Having opened such a pathway on behalf of his supposed critics he of course quickly covers the trail by asserting that there was in fact a sexual aetiology in the case, but that Breuer was unable to recognise and deal with it because he did not perceive the nature or significance of the transference relationship. Privately he was able to add to his followers that this failure had its consequences for the patient in the hysterical crisis that ensued, and to remark further that Breuer had no further dealings with this patient because of this. While the contemporary evidence suggests that this did not at all happen in the way Freud said, it cannot be assumed that the version of the end of the treatment that Freud propagated years later was simply a massive act of fraudulent bad faith on his part. While we can be fairly sure that Bertha herself decided when to end the treatment and that at the point when this happened there was no great hidden crisis of any kind, this does not indicate that Freud's story was simply a malevolent invention. Indeed we know that Breuer did indeed decline to undertake any further treatment of his patient, that Bertha did undergo a massive crisis that Breuer was unable to deal with, resulting in her institutionalisation for a period of some months, and we also have reason to believe that the emotional rapport between doctor and patient was particularly intense. But it appears that these factors did not all combine at the time and under the circumstances that Freud was in later years to maintain. However, given that we also know that a dispute about the aetiological role of sexuality was one of the key factors in the ending of the relationship between Breuer and Freud it is not entirely surprising that Freud, with the aid of a memory for detail that was always less than totally reliable, pieced together all the historical details in the way that he did. Yet while this was not necessarily a deliberate distortion, it undoubtedly served the interests of the fundamental tenets of psychoanalysis, in particular the role of sexuality and the transference, while at the same time preserving Freud's essential role in their discovery.

The part played by Jones in spreading the myth of Breuer's failure is a slightly different one, yet it too is rooted in the politics of psychoanalysis. Jones did not approach the subject as either a pure witness or a disinterested historian, but as an insider who had known Freud well and as his semi-official biographer. The origins and motivations of his task are explicit in the very opening sentence of his preface: 'This is not intended to be a popular biography of Freud: several have been written already, containing serious distortions and untruths' (Jones, 1953, p. iii).

Further on he wrote:

> Ill-natured people were already at work disparaging his character, and this could be rectified only by a still further exposition of his inner and outer life.
>
> Freud's family understandingly respected his wish for privacy, and indeed shared it. They often sheltered him from a merely inquisitive public. What changed their attitude later was the news of the many false stories invented by people who had never known him, stories which were gradually accumulating into a mendacious legend. They then decided to give me their whole-hearted support in my endeavour to present as truthful account of his life as is in my power. (ibid.)

Of course the struggle was not just about the disparagement of Freud's character, and it very rarely has been; the battles around biographical issues have mostly been related to the fundamental theories of psychoanalysis and attempts to either reinforce or undermine them, and these have been endemic to psychoanalysis ever since its foundation. But while Jones was certainly committed to the cause of psychoanalysis, his biography cannot be regarded as a mere piece of propaganda in furtherance of the movement or of the preservation of Freud's reputation at all costs. In relation to the quarrel with Breuer, for example, Jones expressed his own view that at the personal level this was more of Freud's making than Breuer's (p. 178) and even that Freud's reaction to Breuer had something neurotic in it (p. 338). Yet on the specific question of the character of the Anna O. case, even though Jones's account was certainly the most critical then published, it had the immediate effect of extending into the public domain the version of events that Freud had been putting about in private, and thereby supporting the underlying message of the importance of sexuality and the transference and of Freud's part in the discovery of this. Even where Jones was also the first to call into question (albeit spuriously) the effectiveness of Breuer's treatment on the grounds of Bertha's subsequent history, this extended the same thesis just one step further through the implication that the failure to recognise and resolve the transference was a key factor in the patient's repeated relapses. But this was the point at which Jones unwittingly made the initial breach in the floodgates that was to culminate in the widespread acceptance that the Anna O. case represented a marked failure, for this significant revision that Jones made to the published history has remained largely intact, hugely reinforced (again spuriously) by the discoveries of Ellenberger.

The idea that Breuer's treatment of Bertha Pappenheim was in the end a failure ironically serves almost every party's interests. For pro-Freudians it demonstrates that whatever may have been the significance of Breuer's achievement, the resolution of Bertha's symptoms could be only apparent rather than real without a recognition of the power of sexuality and the grip of the transference, which only Freud was able to attain. For anti-Freudians the absence of a cure demonstrates that even in its first faltering step, psychoanalysis was steeped in failure, and, moreover, a failure that has been largely hidden in the 'official' histories, starting of course with the very publication of the case history by Breuer and Freud themselves in 1895.

Yet it would be a mistake to reduce the historiography of psychoanalysis to the simple history of competing interests, because even the most motivated of partisans are bounded by at least some notion of credible evidence if their version of events is not to appear totally without foundation. However, sufficient latitude is usually available in the selection, interpretation and presentation of the data to enable the necessary compromise between apparent objectivity and inner conviction to be effected fairly effortlessly in most cases. This means that given the politics of the psychoanalytic movement, both its supporters and detractors are able to avail themselves quite easily of the often piecemeal, hazy and fragmented nature of the available evidence and to become convinced that their way of telling the story is the only plausible one. A more dispassionate approach requires the avoidance of jumping to firm conclusions on particular points where the evidence is unclear, ambiguous or contradictory, and guarding against making assumptions about individual motivation on the part of historical actors where the evidence does not immediately quite square with what one might expect to be the case. Historical evidence is rarely as clear cut as one would wish it to be and due allowance must be made for those occasions where a first appearance of clarity is in fact deceptive. No historical thesis can be properly sustained that does not at least make a reasonable attempt to consider all the available evidence in its appropriate context and to consider the full range of possibilities of interpretation.

If this book has achieved its goals it will have raised questions about the currently prevailing standards of historical interpretation in the field of psychoanalysis and the part these have played in the writing into its history of the Anna O. case. It is time that historians of psychoanalysis approached this case anew, which, paradoxically, implies in many ways turning the clock back to a time before the mythic figure of Anna O. became a pawn in the fight over the heart of psychoanalysis. This itself, of course, is a contentious proposal, which many may not find acceptable, but if the argument and evidence presented here at least encourage a degree of scepticism about the received history of the founding case of psychoanalysis, then something of value will have been achieved.

Appendix: Chronology

Date	Event	Source	This book
23 June 1880	Family travels to Ischl.	Swales (1988) p. 59	
17 July 1880	Beginning of first (latent incubation stage) of illness; Bertha sits up at night nursing her father.	Hirschmüller (1989) p. 278	p. 16
Beginning of September 1880	Family returns to Vienna.	Hirschmüller (1989) p. 280	
End of November 1880	Breuer first visits Bertha because of nervous cough.	Hirschmüller (1989) p. 280	pp. 19–22, 151
Beginning of December 1880	Bertha's convergent squint appears.	Breuer and Freud (1895) p. 23	
11 December 1880	End of latent stage of illness. Bertha takes to bed; start of second (manifest) stage of illness.	Breuer and Freud (1895) p. 23	pp. 16, 21, 25
March 1881	Bertha overcomes aphasia, regains movement and begins to speak in English.	Breuer and Freud (1895) p. 25	
1 April 1881	Bertha leaves bed for first time since December.	Breuer and Freud (1895) p. 25	pp. 22, 182
5 April 1881	Father dies; end of second (manifest) stage of illness. Start of third (persistent somnambulism) stage.	Breuer and Freud (1895) pp. 22, 25	pp. 16, 22-4, 26, 58, 66, 112, 126, 152, 176
Approx. 15 April 1881	Krafft-Ebing consulted.	Hirschmüller (1989) p. 285	p. 20
7 June 1881	Bertha taken to Inzersdorf.	Breuer and Freud (1895) p. 28	pp. 23, 32, 42, 66, 101, 189

Date	Event	Source	This book
First week of July 1881	Breuer leaves for five-week holiday trip.	Hirschmüller (1989) pp. 287, 288	p. 183
Mid-August 1881	Breuer returns from holiday trip.	Hirschmüller (1989) p. 287	p. 183
End of August 1881	Bertha goes to Vienna with Breuer for eight days.	Hirschmüller (1989) p. 288	p. 24
Beginning of November 1881	Bertha leaves Inzersdorf to live with her mother in Vienna.	Hirschmüller (1989) p. 289	pp. 24-5, 144-5
4 November 1881	Breuer writes to Binswanger concerning prospective admission to Bellevue for convalescence should Bertha's acclimatisation to her family fail.	Hirschmüller (1989) p. 292	pp. 25, 145, 176
Beginning of December 1881	End of third (persistent somnambulism) stage of illness.	Hirschmüller (1989) p. 278	p. 16
December 1881	Bertha begins reliving one year in past.	Breuer and Freud (1895) pp. 32–3	pp. 66-7
February 1882	Dental operation on left upper jaw.	Hirschmüller (1989) p. 302	pp. 129-31, 143, 191
11 March 1882	Birth of Dora Breuer.	Ellenberger (1970) p. 483	pp. 65, 67
Mid-March 1882	Onset of severe facial neuralgia.	Hirschmüller (1989) p. 301	p. 131
7 June 1882	Treatment by Breuer ends as hysteria comes to a close on anniversary of committal to Inzersdorf.	Breuer and Freud (1895) p. 40	pp. 16, 29, 32, 42, 63, 93, 101, 102, 189
19 June 1882	Bertha goes to Karlsruhe to stay with relatives; Breuer writes to Binswanger concerning prospective admission to Bellevue.	Hirschmüller (1989) p. 294	pp. 28, 29, 32, 63, 134

Date	Event	Source	This book
12 July 1882	Bertha enters Bellevue five weeks after end of treatment by Breuer.	Hirschmüller (1989) p. 112	pp. 28, 63, 177
21 July 1882	Letter from Robert Binswanger to Recha Pappenheim. He reports that Bertha's loss of her mother tongue occurs only on odd occasions in the evening for a matter of minutes.	Hirschmüller (1989) p. 300	
23 July 1882	Letter from Fritz Homburger to Robert Binswanger. Bertha reporting facial pains during the day and regular speech disturbances in the evenings.	Hirschmüller (1989) p. 298	
Mid-August 1882	Letter from Robert Binswanger to Recha Pappenheim contemplating surgical treatment of Bertha's neuralgia.	Hirschmüller (1989) p. 301	pp. 26, 130
27 August 1882	Letter from Recha Pappenheim in Karlsruhe to Robert Binswanger advising against surgery; neuralgia closely connected to psychic processes.	Hirschmüller (1989) p. 301	p. 26
Approx. beginning of October	Report by Bertha on her inability to speak German.	Hirschmüller (1989) pp. 296–7	pp. 30-1, 32, 34, 177
5 October 1882	Letter from Robert Binswanger to Recha Pappenheim reporting that Bertha is just as dependent on morphine as she ever was.	Hirschmüller (1989) p. 303	p. 101
7 October 1882	Letter from Recha Pappenheim in Karlsruhe	Hirschmüller (1989) pp. 303–4	p. 101

Date	Event	Source	This book
	to Robert Binswanger, reporting that Breuer is unable to take over treatment.		
15 October 1882	Letter from Recha Pappenheim in Vienna to Robert Binswanger. Bertha has told her that her facial neuralgia is worse rather than better and her morphine consumption has therefore increased.	Hirschmüller (1989) p. 304	
29 October 1882	Bertha leaves Bellevue for Karlsruhe.	Hirschmüller (1989) p. 290	pp. 29, 31
8 November 1882	Letter of thanks from Bertha Pappenheim in Karlsruhe to Robert Binswanger, in which she reports still having to rely on syringe.	Hirschmüller (1989) p. 306	p. 31
25 December 1882	To Frankfurt for family visit.	Hirschmüller (1989) p. 307	p. 31
28 December 1882	To Mainz for family visit.	Hirschmüller (1989) p. 307	p. 31
4 January 1883	Letter from Fritz Homburger to Robert Binswanger reporting that English speaking had occurred for about an hour in the evening from time to time two weeks after her arrival and that the neuralgic pains had persisted.	Hirschmüller (1989) p. 307	pp. 31, 6
22 January 1883	Letter from Martha Bernays to Minna Bernays; Bertha reported to be completely cured.	Freud and Bernays (2005) p. 47	p. 33
13 July 1883	Letter from Freud to Martha Bernays relating discussion with Breuer about Bertha Pappenheim.	Freud (1961) p. 55	

Date	Event	Source	This book
30 July 1883	Bertha enters Inzersdorf Sanatorium.	Hirschmüller (1989) p. 115	p. 33
5 August 1883	Letter from Freud to Martha Bernays reporting that Breuer wishes Bertha were dead so she could be free of her suffering.	Forrester (1990) p. 26	pp. 34, 138, 148, 187
31 October 1883	Letter from Freud to Martha Bernays. Tells her that Bertha is in a sanatorium getting rid of her pains and morphine poisoning and gives account of Breuer's withdrawal as Bertha's doctor.	Borch-Jacobsen (1996) pp. 40–1	pp. 34-5, 99, 103, 187, 190
2 November 1883	Letter from Martha Bernays to Freud imagining herself in the position of Breuer's wife.	Appignanesi, L. and Forrester, J. (1992) p. 82; Library of Congress	pp. 103-4, 187
4 November 1883	Letter from Freud to Martha Bernays reassuring his fiancée about being different from Breuer.	Appignanesi, L. and Forrester, J. (1992) p. 82; Library of Congress	pp. 104-5
13 January 1884	Letter from Breuer to Robert Binswanger reporting Bertha in good health with no pains or other troubles.	Hirschmüller (1989) p. 310	p. 35
17 January 1884	Bertha leaves Inzersdorf Sanatorium.	Hirschmüller (1989) p. 115	p. 33
4 March 1885	Bertha enters Inzersdorf Sanatorium.	Hirschmüller (1989) p. 115	p. 33
2 July 1885	Bertha leaves Inzersdorf Sanatorium.	Hirschmüller (1989) p. 115	p. 33
28 November 1886	Letter from Martha Bernays to Minna and Emmeline Bernays; Bertha apparently extraordinarily well.	Library of Congress	p. 35

Date	Event	Source	This book
1 February 1887	Letter from Martha Bernays to Emmeline Bernays reporting visit from Bertha whose illness has taken its toll.	Library of Congress	p. 35
31 May 1887	Letter from Martha Bernays to Emmeline Bernays reporting Bertha quite miserable. After 5 in the evening she gets into one of her states.	Library of Congress	pp. 35-6
30 June 1887	Bertha enters Inzersdorf Sanatorium.	Hirschmüller (1989) p. 115	p. 33
18 July 1887	Bertha leaves Inzersdorf Sanatorium.	Hirschmüller (1989) p. 115	p. 33
14 November 1888	Registered address in Frankfurt.	Hirschmüller (1989) p. 372	pp. 116-7

Notes

Preface

1. The greatest difficulties are situated where we're not looking for them. (The English translations of the quotations from Goethe at the head of each chapter are based on those made by Elisabeth Stopp and published in the Penguin Edition of Goethe's *Maxims and Reflections* (1998), edited by Peter Hutchinson.)

Introduction: The changing history of a case history

1. The unreasonable thing about otherwise reasonable people is that they don't know how to sort out what someone is saying when he's not really put it as precisely as he should have done.
2. These will be discussed below.
3. Micale (1995, pp. 59–62) gives a brief but useful survey of some of this literature and Macmillan (1997, pp. 10–12; pp. 631–3) likewise looks at some of the problems associated with it.

1 The 1882 documents

1. The present moment is a sort of public: you have to deceive it so that it imagines you are doing something; then it leaves you alone to carry on in secret with what its descendants will surely view with astonishment.
2. The Latinism '*hystericis*' used by Breuer here could most literally be translated as 'hysterics', although this has connotations in English of a general attack of fits or convulsions, rather than a range of hysterical symptoms, as Breuer intends. The passage quoted is a modified translation of the German, since the rendering in the published English edition (p. 279) masks the point of the distinction between the absences and the hysterical symptoms that is much clearer in the original: 'In solcher Weise traten eine ungemeine Menge von hystericis immer zuerst im Affect oder in der Absence auf, die sich dann immer häufiger wiederholten...' (Hirschmüller, 1978, p. 351).
3. Fritz Schweighofer appears to be rare in the secondary literature in noticing this crucial distinction in Breuer's work: 'The hypnosis and hypnoid states assume a central place in Breuer's presentation. They are in fact not symptoms of Bertha's hysteria, but according to Breuer's ideas, the element, so to speak, in which the described symptoms and their aetiology emerge' (Schweighofer, 1987, p. 100).
4. It is interesting to note how closely some aspects of Bertha's presenting symptoms resembled the phenomena observed in mild epileptic attacks. In a lecture given in 1879, the great English neurologist, John Hughlings Jackson gave a detailed description, based on accounts of his patients, of the 'dreamy states' that can often precede an epileptic attack and which can occur by themselves as the results of mild epileptic discharges. Patients would describe feeling lost, or as though they were somewhere else, and sometimes as though past ideas

had become blended with the present. One patient, in reporting his feeling that he had two minds, prompted Jackson to comment that the expression 'double consciousness' is quite correct to describe such experiences. One common sensation experienced in such cases is the feeling of having been in the same situation or surroundings before, and Jackson describes this as a 'reminiscence' (Jackson, 1931, pp. 296–8). Although this is not quite the same usage as Breuer and Freud's (1895, p. 7) use of the term in the *Preliminary Communication* Jackson's discussion of the notion in the light of previous writings on the subject brings it closer. For example, he cites a French authority on the subject: 'Falret says that many become epileptic after some strong emotion or profound terror, and, at each fresh attack, see in their mind or under their eyes the painful circumstances or the frightful scenes which produced the disease in them the first time' (Jackson, 1879, p. 298). Jackson himself, in justifying his use of the term 'reminiscence' in relation to the dreamy states, remarks: 'Of necessity, the positive mental state – as also that of ordinary dreaming and the positive mental state in ordinary insanity – must be a revival of *formerly acquired* states of some sort, although in new and grotesque combinations' (p. 296, emphasis in original).

Jackson's reference to French authorities is significant in the present context because he notes that the dreamy states he describes have attracted little attention, although they have long been described by the French (p. 298) and it is therefore not perhaps so surprising that Breuer would use the French term to describe Bertha's odd states. In an article on epilepsy published in 1888 in Villaret's *Handwörterbuch der Gesamten Medizin*, the same French term is used in a description of the mild epileptic attack or *petit mal* (Villaret, 1888, p. 517). Given the close entanglement between hysteria and epilepsy in the late nineteenth-century history of medicine it is by no means odd that they should draw on the same vocabulary and symptom imagery.

5. The differences between these categories of affliction at the end of the nineteenth century are widely documented in the secondary literature on the history of psychiatry. For recent surveys see Shorter (1992, Ch. 8; 1997a, Ch. 4). As Ulrike May-Tolzmann points out, relationships between the categories of neurosis and psychosis are made even more complicated by the fact that during the second half of the nineteenth century, more attention began to be paid to the psychic symptoms of neuroses, while, conversely, causes of psychoses were increasingly sought in somatic conditions. In this way the two terms almost began to exchange their original senses. The hybrid terms of psychoneurosis and neuropsychosis emerged in this period of change as increasing emphasis was given to the psychical component of the major, general neuroses, such as hysteria, neurasthenia and epilepsy (May-Tolzmann, 1998, p. 342–3). See also Hirschmüller (1989, pp. 362–3) and May-Tolzmann (1996, pp. 78–82).

6. Mikkel Borch-Jacobson's reading of this passage betrays no awareness of the important contemporary distinction between hysteria and mental illness. He writes:

Note the strangeness of this 'however.' It seems at first to contradict Breuer's reasoning – Why would Bertha Pappenheim be mentally ill *in spite of* being hysterical? – but makes perfect sense in the context of what follows: '*Those around her still saw nothing of this.*' Clearly, Breuer held to his diagnosis *in spite of* the Pappenheim family's incredulity, and perhaps even *in opposition to* the family's opinion in the matter. (Borch-Jacobson, 1996, pp. 81–2, emphases in original)

Because Borch-Jacobsen is reliant on present-day notions of hysteria as a mental illness, his commentary misses the point Breuer is making and leads him instead into an otherwise unsupported construction about the family scenario. There is no evidence at all of the family being incredulous or otherwise doubting Breuer's diagnosis; they knew nothing of it simply because at that stage the symptoms were not visible to them, as Breuer himself has already made clear. The real implications of his 'however' are more than adequately covered by Hirschmüller's earlier commentary on it in the light of the contemporary distinction between hysteria and psychosis (1989, p. 109). He draws attention to Freud's own note on this in an early article on hysteria: 'A psychosis in the psychiatrist's sense of the word is not a part of hysteria, though it can develop on the foundation of the hysterical status and is then to be regarded as a complication' (Freud, 1888, p. 49).

7. Between 1882 and 1895 of course, Charcot had given increased prominence to the hereditary factor in the predisposition to hysteria and linked it to the already-existing idea of degeneration. The fact that Freud's case histories do not pay much attention to his patients' hereditary backgrounds perhaps indicates (by contrast with Breuer) how far he was already distancing himself from Charcot's views under the influence of his own theory of defence.

8. There is further evidence that perhaps Breuer maintained a clearer distinction between Bertha's hysteria and other aspects of her condition than is sometimes apparent. After Bertha's return from Inzersdorf later in the year, Breuer wrote in November 1881 to Robert Binswanger about the possibility of a stay in the Sanatorium Bellevue. In this letter he says that 'her illness was caused by the death of her father' (Hirschmüller, 1989, p. 293). Given that Bertha had been in his care for at least six months before her father died, this makes no sense unless we understand the reference to illness here as referring solely to the specific crisis that she entered in April 1881.

9. 'Affection' is a rather misleading translation of the German 'Affect', which could be rendered more naturally in English as simply 'affect'.

10. Although the significance of the suppressed affect, which was later to play such an important role in the theory of catharsis, is clearly noted by Breuer in his 1882 account, Johann Reicheneder (1990, pp. 319–28) is surely correct when he cautions against the idea that Breuer's theoretical understanding of this phenomenon was already developed at this point. The whole issue of how the Bertha Pappenheim of the 1882 report evolved into the Anna O. of the 1895 *Studies* warrants further consideration and analysis.

11. The infra-orbital and zygomatic are two branches of the maxillary (upper jaw) division of the trigeminal nerve. The significance of this will be examined later.

12. It must be remembered that Breuer's 1882 report relates the story of his patient only up to the end of 1881 and there is no detailing at all of the fourth and final phase of the illness. Therefore all of the singularities of this final phase that Breuer relates in the published version have no counterpart in the earlier report.

13. 'Psychoses' has to be understood in the contemporary sense discussed above of 'psychic disturbances', and without the modern connotation.

14. Laupus's observation on Bertha's loss of her mother tongue each evening is worthy of note: 'The evening occurrence of the loss of her mother tongue, however, which was also observed here, lay wholly outside the usual scope of hysteria' (Hirschmüller, 1989, p. 292). It may be that Laupus is commenting on the unusual range of Bertha's hysterical symptoms, but it could also be that he was expressing a doubt as to whether this odd phenomenon could really be accounted for by the diagnosis of hysteria at all.

15. Hirschmüller (1989, p. 296) dates the document as 'about the middle of 1882', but internal evidence suggests rather later than this. Bertha arrived at the sanatorium on 12 July and she records that she experienced periods of 'timemissing' in the first two months of her stay (p. 297). This means that her account could not have been written earlier than mid-September. However, she continues that she has not had these periods for 'some weeks' (ibid.) and this would seem to indicate a date of writing no earlier than October. If this is correct then it coincides rather nicely with Bertha's note in her opening paragraph that her total inability to speak German had lifted about four months previously and since then had only returned in the evening under the circumstances she goes on to describe. Four months previously would be more or less exactly the point at which her treatment with Breuer would have terminated. Hirschmüller not unreasonably heads this document as Bertha's report on her illness, but this is perhaps a little too sweeping and could be misleading. Bertha herself writes about her inability to communicate in German: 'The physicians point it out as something very strange and but rarely to be observed; therefore I will try to give, as well, as a person who never has made any medical studies, can do, a short account of my own observations and experiences considering this terrible estate' (Hirschmüller, 1989, pp. 296–7). It therefore seems that the statement (prompted perhaps by her doctors) was intended as a subjective account of the strangest aspect of her condition while she was actually in that state, rather than as a full commentary on her case.

2 Subsequent evidence

1. People who contradict and quarrel ought to bear in mind that not every language is intelligible to every person. For surely everyone only hears what he understands.

2. The fact that Bettelheim – a friend of Breuer's from his student days (Hirschmüller, 1989, p. 116) – made the referral suggests that if indeed Breuer had been the Pappenheim family doctor for some years (p. 101) he no longer retained this position. The internist Carl Bettelheim (28/9/1840–26/7/1895) was born in Pressburg (the town from which Bertha's father and grandfather also originated) and after he graduated as a doctor in 1866, he worked as an assistant to Johann Oppolzer, from 1868 until 1870 (Eisenberg, 1893, p. 26). Breuer occupied a similar position during the same years (Hirschmüller, 1989, p. 20–3) and both men also studied under Brücke. Freud also knew Bettelheim, having worked with him on a physiological project in the mid-eighties (Jones, 1953, p. 220) and he presumably had a

continuing acquaintance with him up to Bettelheim's death in 1895, since we learn from a newspaper report in the evening edition of the *Neue Freie Presse* on 29 July 1895 that both Freud and Breuer had attended his burial in the cemetery at Döbling the day before. If Bettelheim knew Bertha Pappenheim well then this would not only give Breuer a continuing source of information about her condition, but Freud as well. It is of course also remotely possible (given their common town of origin) that Bettelheim had been engaged as the family doctor by Bertha's father, and that it was he who referred Bertha to Breuer in 1880, although Breuer's apparently extensive knowledge of the family (Hirschmüller, 1989, pp. 276–7) does tend to speak against this.

3. Freud (or his informant) makes an error here for Inzersdorf.
4. 'Auch bei Bertha bin ich gewesen diese Woche, hab aber nur ihre Mutter getroffen, die sehr freundlich war, B. soll es außerordentlich gut gehen, sie lernt jetzt zum Zeitvertreib Schneidern.' (Library of Congress)
5. 'Bertha meldete sich gleich für den andern Nachmittag bei mir zur Jause an und war auch gestern da mit der Cousine Anna, beide waren sehr gemütlich und der dicke Willi hat sie abgeholt. Bertha ist ganz wie früher in ihrem Wesen; in der Erscheinung hat sie sehr gealtert, das Haar ist beinahe ganz grau und die Frische der Augen ganz eingebüßt.' (Library of Congress)
6. 'Gestern mittag besuchte Bertha mich auf einen Augenblick, sie ist doch wieder ganz elend, nach 5 Uhr abends bekommt sie ihre Zustände und ist dann ganz unbrauchbar, den ganzen Tag über ist sie fesch und wohl, soll aber wieder gar nichts essen, das ist doch ganz furchtbar traurig, nicht wahr?' (Library of Congress)

3   The publication of the case study

1. When two people are really happy about one another, one can generally assume that they are mistaken.
2. In terms of the Anna O. case of course, this means what Breuer initially described as her 'absences'.
3. It is perhaps necessary to be reminded that the full title of this work is: *On the Psychical Mechanism of Hysterical Phenomena: Preliminary Communication*. It is not about the psychical mechanism of the hysterical condition, but of a category of its manifest symptoms: 'we cannot conceal from ourselves that this has brought us nearer to an understanding only of the *mechanism* of hysterical symptoms and not of the internal causes of hysteria' (Breuer and Freud, 1895, p. 17). Freud's more ambitious claims in relation to hysteria were to come later.
4. The phrase, 'prototype of a cathartic cure' is often given by Ellenberger in quotation marks as though he were quoting an exaggerated claim made by Breuer, Freud or one of their followers. In fact the phrase seems to originate with Ellenberger himself (Ellenberger, 1966, p. 95; Ellenberger, 1970, pp. 444, 487). Interestingly enough, though little noted in the secondary literature, the words 'catharsis' or 'cathartic' appear nowhere in Breuer's original notes, in the Anna O. case itself or in his own theoretical chapter in the *Studies on Hysteria*. Outside the *Preliminary Communication*, Breuer appears never to have used the term in print.

5. Forrester and Cameron have noted a comparable disjunction in a later comment by Freud on the Anna O. case between on the one hand, the hysterical symptoms and on the other, a different disease progressing in accordance with its own temporality. They also note the consistency of this with other accounts by Freud, dating from later years, and how these always seem to emphasise symptoms and their removal, rather than the cure of a disease as such (Forrester and Cameron, 1999, p. 934).

6. Translation modified. Strachey perpetrates an unaccountable mistranslation here. The original German is: 'Auf diese Weise schloß auch die ganze Hysterie ab.' This he rendered as: 'In this way too the whole illness was brought to a close.'

7. The suddenness of all this is still more pronounced in the original German, where the whole section from 'On the last day' to 'previously exhibited' is delivered in a single sentence, giving the impression of an even more breathless rush to conclude the report.

8. The entry for 'Convalescence' (*Rekonvaleszenz*) in that same practical handbook for medical practitioners for which Freud wrote his article on hysteria consists of the following:

> Convalescence is the period of recovery, that is the time that a patient still needs after the course of an illness and thus even after the disappearance of the last symptom of illness, in order to restore again the strength lost through the illness. The convalescent is therefore in himself a healthy person, but he is still weak and not yet back to normal capability; consequently there can only be a real convalescence after severe illnesses. (Villaret, 1891, p. 596)

4 Freud's account: Reconstructions

1. What is expressed by word of mouth must be dedicated to the present, to the moment; what is written down should be dedicated to what is far away, to what is yet to come.

2. This phrase is in English in the original. It was coined by the Duke of Wellington who used it via the medium of the King's speech to Parliament in 1828 to refer to the Battle of Navarino that had taken place in October the previous year (Woodhouse, 1965, p. 163). In this battle a combined British, French and Russian squadron had sunk the Turkish-Egyptian fleet. The dispatch of the squadron to this region of the Mediterranean had been intended merely to intimidate the Ottoman and rebel Greek forces into suspending their reciprocal hostilities, and the infliction of such a devastating blow to Turkish power had been neither planned nor anticipated. The effective destruction of the Turkish navy had far-reaching consequences extending for decades to come, and Wellington was horrified at the disturbance of regional stability. It rendered Turkish resistance to Greek rebellion hopeless and thus paved the way for Greek independence from the Ottoman Empire, it breached the traditionally friendly relations between Britain and Turkey and it fundamentally upset the balance of power in Europe by leaving the Turks significantly more vulnerable to Russian ambitions in the region. As an invocation of an extended metaphor for what Freud claimed Breuer had unintentionally unleashed in his treatment of Anna O., his use of the phrase

seems particularly apt, but the extent to which this would have been known to him remains an open question.

3. Even though Strachey makes these textual connections, received his own version of the end of the treatment directly from Freud and refers directly to Jones's account of it, he nowhere mentions explicitly the hysterical child-birth episode. Whether this omission is insignificant, whether it was because Freud did not tell him this part, or whether he simply doubted its reliability is not clear.

4. Freud states in a letter to Jung on 21 November that it had been explained to him that chimney-sweeping is regarded as a good omen because it is symbolic of coitus (Freud and Jung, 1974, p. 267). This is surely to be attributed to Eitingon's paper, which not only comments on the sexual symbolism of Anna's description of her talking cure as 'chimney-sweeping' but also explicitly casts Breuer in the role of chimney-sweep (Eitingon, 1998, p. 24).

One faint trace of a possible influence in the other direction may perhaps be detected in a curious point Eitingon makes towards the end of his paper. After alluding to the theatrical restaging of the snake hallucination that Anna surrendered herself to at the end of the treatment, Eitingon raises a doubt about the consequence of this: 'Could the fruit of this abandonment simply be the cure? Given the uncertainty, or rather the lack of catamnestic data, no doubt may be raised about the declaration of the book that Anna would soon thereupon become definitively healthy (?)' (p. 26).

Yet while Eitingon denies that there are grounds for doubt, Hirschmüller observes in an editorial footnote at that point that the question mark in parentheses appears to indicate that he does indeed have doubts about the claim. It would seem that having written the statement Eitingon inserted the punctuation at a later time to indicate his own second thoughts about its soundness. Both the statement and the added punctuation were then carried over into the typed version of the paper. On the other hand the construction of the sentence in German (unlike in English) means that the mere addition of a question mark turns the sentence into a straightforward question. It may therefore be that only the parentheses were added as an afterthought.

Moreover, while it is true that Breuer gives very little in the way of catamnestic, or follow-up data about his patient he does say two things. First that she was free from the disturbances she had previously exhibited, and secondly that it was sometime before she regained her mental balance entirely. So leaving aside for the moment exactly what Breuer was intending should be encompassed by these two statements, he does make some assertions about the aftermath of the treatment which Eitingon appears on the face of it either to ignore or not to accept. For while Breuer certainly indicates that the treatment had been successful, his reference to a lack of mental balance would render doubtful any impression that Anna was restored to total health with immediate effect. But why does Eitingon ignore this statement and imply that Breuer had given Anna an immediate clean bill of health? In fact he seems to treat this part of the case as though there were something that Breuer was not revealing. Does it not appear that the doubt that Eitingon expresses in his paper was not in fact something that had arisen spontaneously from reading the case study, but that he was perhaps privy to some inside information revealed by Freud that he could only allude to without being explicit about exactly what was involved? Such questions will have to remain as no more than speculations for the present, as a small oddity of punctuation is not sufficient to point to any clear conclusions on this matter. Thanks are due to Michael Schröter for providing for examination a copy of the key part of the Eitingon's typescript and also to him and to Ernst Falzeder for help in elucidating this passage.

5. As with many of Eissler's interviews the style is conversational, the transcript manifestly not always accurate and the punctuation irregular. On top of this, Jung's hesitations and ellipses in this particular case make the precise detail difficult to convey. The general import is fairly straightforward, however, and the free translation with amended punctuation given here is an attempt to convey it more clearly than in the original. In particular, the odd reference to 'my hands' means we have to assume that Jung is mimicking what he remembers as Freud's own account, for as we see in the notes from his 1925 seminar, Jung was under the mistaken impression that Freud was actually present to witness Anna's crisis. Alternatively, 'meine Hände' ('my hands') could conceivably be a mistranscription for 'seine Hände' ('his hands') although analysis of the original tape recording would be necessary for greater clarification of exactly what Jung said. All in all, precisely what Jung is quoting as opposed to reporting is not completely clear, and the quotation marks added here in the translation are not intended as definitive.

For the record, the original (uncorrected) transcription reads as follows:

J [...] Und, zum Beispiel: Die, die, Breuer und Freud, Die Studien über Hysterie – – am Schluss heisst es also: Sie war geheilt, nicht wahr, – – die mit dem chimney-sweeping

E Ja

J Es heisst, sie sei geheilt worden. Ach, sie war doch nicht geheilt! Wie sie in meine Hände kam, da hat sie, hat sie ja gleich wie Breuer als geheilt sie entlässt, da hat sie einen grossen hysterischen Anfall gemacht, worin sie, und hat dazu geschrien: jetzt kommt das Kind des Dr. Breuer! Wir brauchen das Kind, nicht!? Ja, aber das gehört doch in die Krankengeschichte! (*lacht*)

E Ja

J Nein!?

E Ja

J No ja, sagt er, das macht einen schlechten Eindruck, und so weiter, nicht wahr!

The transcript is on open access in the Library of Congress. Thanks are due to Peter Swales for providing the details cited here and to Ernst Falzeder, Wilhelm Hemecker, Johannes Reichmayr and Julia Swales for assistance with the interpretive difficulties of this passage.

6. In the letter to Tansley he maintains that his guesses or suppositions (*Vermutungen*) about the course of events (*Hergang*) with Breuer's first patient were certainly correct (Forrester and Cameron, 1999, p. 930).

7. In a later summary of his own book and in the light of reading Eitingon's paper on Anna O., Borch-Jacobsen shifts his position and confidently ascribes

the origin of the whole story to Eitingon himself, now relieving Freud of the credit even for casual invention (Borch-Jacobsen, 2005, p. 30). But leaving aside his assumption that Freud had no part in this detail of Eitingon's talk (also the fact that he misspells Eitingon's name, postdates by over a year to December 1910 the seminar where he gave the paper and also misdates its eventual publication) Borch-Jacobsen overlooks that the paper itself reveals a certain logic in the whole account. Starting as Eitingon does from an incestuous phantasy of coition, a consequential sequence of pregnancy and childbirth is hardly random. This is not at all to suppose that the event as conveyed by Freud happened or even to give credence to his and Eitingon's retrospective interpretations, but merely to point out that in this context the story is far from arbitrary or a mere piece of inventive psychoanalytic gossip.

If Borch-Jacobsen is simply dismissive of Freud's story in the Zweig letter, Kurt R. Eissler's rejection of the whole scenario is particularly vehement. Not only does he deny the veracity of Freud's construction as 'a baseless product of his imagination' (Eissler, 2001, p. 26) but he characterises him here as 'ungrateful, indiscreet and slanderous' (p. 177). The intemperance of Eissler's denigration of Freud on this point might have been partly redeemed if it had accompanied a plausible account of how the construction may have come into being in the first place. But all Eissler is able to offer is the suggestion that Freud's manifest hostility to Breuer was both a covert self-reproach because he himself had taken flight from the implications of Breuer's discovery until he discovered the transference in the Dora case, and also a product of his unexpressed ambivalence to his own father. But even if these are real psychoanalytic insights, they cannot compensate for the absence of an explanation that is a little more securely grounded in historical data.

8. Reeves on this point misreads Jones as suggesting that Bertha was committed to the institution at 'Gross Enzersdorf' straight after the display in front of Breuer. In fact this reference by Jones does not relate to Bertha's stay in any institution immediately at the end of her treatment but to one of her later periods of institutionalisation back in Vienna, and he appears to know nothing of her period in Kreuzlingen. Jones does not say when the institutionalisation he refers to took place, and Reeves simply assumes that it was when the treatment ended. His supposition that Freud or Jones could be mistaking Kreuzlingen for Inzersdorf and therefore possibly also displacing the false pregnancy to a year later than it had actually happened is therefore incorrect, but this does not affect significantly the main thread of his argument. As we shall see below, Ellenberger (1966) makes a similar error, but with more severe consequences.

9. There is perhaps some circumstantial evidence by analogy that might retrospectively suggest such a possibility to Freud. As we have seen in Eitingon's discussion of the case, he posits a coition phantasy in July 1880 when Anna is sitting by her father's bedside, followed by a phantasy of pregnancy when she became bedridden for several months towards the end of the year. It was only on 1st April 1881 that Anna left finally her bed again having ended her 'pregnancy', almost exactly nine months after the bedside scene (Freud and Breuer, 1895, p. 25). Both Freud and Eitingon would have been familiar with this kind of a mechanism because it occurs in the Dora case history, where Freud informs his patient that an attack of appendicitis occurring nine months after a phantasy of defloration had enabled her to realise a phantasy

of childbirth (Freud, 1905a, pp. 103–4). Eitingon draws several parallels between Anna O. and Dora, and it may even be that this part of the Dora case was the inspiration for the corresponding element in his (and perhaps Freud's) reinterpretation of Anna's symptoms.

10. Breuer puts in his 1882 report that he returned after his holiday in the middle of August 1881 (Hirschmüller, 1989, p. 287) and that he had been absent for five weeks (p. 288). The Gmunden cure lists record that it was on 16 July, therefore roughly four weeks before, that Mathilde Breuer along with other people (children and servants) took up holiday residence there. This leaves open the possibility that Breuer and his wife had visited Venice for a week or so before this date, although whether any trip to Venice ever actually took place must remain in some doubt, since the only evidence for it comes from the account given by Jones (1953, p. 247), about which there is reason to hold other reservations, as will be seen below. Thanks are due to Peter Swales for kindly providing the data from the cure lists.

11. Also to be taken into account is Breuer's curious reference to Bertha receiving injections of morphine because of severe convulsions (Hirschmüller, 1989, p. 295). When she was in Kreuzlingen, withdrawal of the morphine led on more than one occasion to convulsive attacks (p. 290). If Freud knew about this, then it too may have been drawn into the retrospective diagnosis of hysterical childbirth.

5   Defence and sexuality

1. If people knew where what they are looking for is situated, they wouldn't be looking for it at all.
2. Discussion of the issues surrounding the split between Breuer and Freud in both its theoretical and personal aspects is well encompassed by Jones (1953), Andersson (1962), Levin (1978) and Hirschmüller (1989).
3. Translation modified. The emphasis on Breuer's responsibility is heightened stylistically by the repetition of his name at the beginning of the second sentence, but in Strachey's translation he mollifies this by substituting 'him' for Breuer's name. He also wrongly closes the quotation marks after 'hysteria', rather than *'sine quâ non'*.
4. Translation modified. Cranefield's translation of *'sich lösen'* (Forel, 1968, p. 397) as 'be resolved' loses something of the implication that we have already noted in Breuer's discussion of the case that the illness followed its own course, rather than actively disappearing as a direct result of therapy.

6   Transference and the Faustian imperative

1. What is not original is unimportant and what is original is always marked by the frailties of the individual.
2. See Makari (1992) for an extended discussion of the origins of this early concept of the transference in the notion of the 'false connection' and its derivation from the hypnotic tradition. Although Freud's later writings on the transference clearly have their roots in this stage of his work, in the interests of historical accuracy we must take care not to compress all his writings on this topic into a single position. As Hirschmüller notes, at this point Freud had not yet drawn a connection between the sexual aetiology of the

neuroses and a necessarily erotic transference relation – this was only spelled out in his later work (Hirschmüller, 1989, pp. 398–9). But this means of course that as his view on this became clearer, so also did his conviction about the full nature of Breuer's error and its implications.

3. It is interesting to consider why Freud first made his criticisms of Breuer public only in 1914, but had not done so earlier in his Clark lectures in the United States in 1909, where the Anna O. case had also been discussed at some length. After all, Freud's conclusions about the deficits of Breuer's treat-ment originated in his break from him in the 1890s. In 1909 Freud satisfied himself with merely marking the distance between the work that he had done with Breuer and his own theory of the erotic basis of the neuroses which succeeded it. There is no hint of the presumed transference problems that he was later to disclose. This absence cannot be explained entirely by the nature of his American audience, for whom such details in an introductory lecture series might be considered a little abstruse. This is because in writing up his lecture notes for publication afterwards Freud took the opportunity to make some significant revisions, and in the same letter of 21 November 1909 to his American host, Stanley Hall, in which he asked permission to do this he also asked if he might allow his Viennese publisher to produce a German version of the lectures that he had given 'in outline' (*als Programmschrift*) in Worcester (Rosenzweig, 1992, p. 362–3). Freud clearly published his lectures with a view to his German-speaking audience as well, and in a letter to Jung on the same date he notes of his revisions: 'I am putting in a few defensive, or rather, aggressive remarks' (Freud and Jung, 1974, p. 265).

For his part, Borch-Jacobsen claims that it was crucial for Freud to be able to demonstrate that the case had a sexual base because rival critics, led by the psychiatrist August Forel, not only reproached him with having abandoned the cathartic method but also invoked against him the case of Anna O., whom Breuer had described as being completely asexual (Borch-Jacobsen, 2005, p. 29). Freud himself refers to the first aspect of this:

> ...certain opponents of psycho-analysis have a habit of occasionally rec-ollecting that after all the art of psycho-analysis was not invented by me but by Breuer. This only happens of course, if their views allow them to find something in it deserving attention; if they set no such limits to their rejection of it, psycho-analysis is always without question my work alone. (Freud, 1914, p. 8)

However, Borch-Jacobsen gives no evidence for his assertion that the case of Anna O. was used in any serious way against Freud in this connection or that any such consideration influenced him. Indeed this is unlikely to have been a factor because in referring to Breuer's claim that the sexual element in Anna was astonishingly undeveloped, Freud himself remarks: 'I have always wondered why the critics did not more often cite this assertion of Breuer's as an argument against my contention of a sexual aetiology in the neuroses...' (p. 11).

The decision finally to air his view of Breuer's shortcomings on the sexual element in the Anna O. case in public in 1914 is most probably bound up predominantly with the split from Jung, the politics of which motivated Freud to produce his *On the History of the Psychoanalytic Movement*, written during the first two months of 1914. In a letter to Abraham on 26 October 1913, Freud writes: 'At the first lecture yesterday I realized the complete analogy between the first running away from the discovery of sexuality behind the neuroses by Breuer and the latest one by Jung. That makes it the more certain that this is the core of Ψα' (Freud and Abraham, 2002, p. 202). Sexuality and the transference form the main subjects of the explicit criticisms that Freud directs at the Swiss school in the concluding part of *On the History of the Psychoanalytic Movement* (Freud, 1914, pp. 60–6) and he no doubt intended to make visible his perception of the parallels between Breuer's and Jung's repudiations of what to Freud had become the essence of psychoanalysis. In the light of his comment to Abraham we may infer that in revealing something of his perception of the ending of the Anna O. treatment in public for the first time, this was not so much a criticism of his former collaborator as an attack on Jung and the Swiss school, with Jung cast in the role of a new edition of Breuer. Jung will of course have heard from Freud some years previously a more elaborated version of the end of the treatment than the one Freud gives here. He will have known too of the significance that Freud attributed to it and that it was not just a concoction created for the purposes of publication at this particular juncture.

4. Freud's primary intended audience for the publication was probably the Burghölzli school of psychiatrists, from which quarter an interest in his work had already been publicly signalled in a review by Eugen Bleuler in April 1904 (Freud, 1985, p. 461). For a reconstruction of the most likely circumstances surrounding the publication of the Dora case, see Tanner (2002, pp. 102–6).

5. In his 1909 paper Max Eitingon drew a number of explicit parallels between Dora and Anna O. to the extent of referring to Dora metaphorically as Anna's younger sister (Eitingon, 1998 p. 26). One specific comparison he draws is on the point of breaking off the treatment, where, without any justification from the case history as written by Breuer, he casts this as an act of revenge on Anna's part (p. 24) just as Freud did for Dora.

6. This pathologising of the normal will not, of course, be to everyone's taste, but it does carry its corollary in the converse proposition that in Freud and psychoanalysis there is a reciprocal tendency to normalise the pathological. It is a paradox of Freud's work that while he often retains the conventional categories of the normal and the pathological, in practice these terms are radically threatened and often dissolved entirely. This is most evident in respect of the absence of a simple divide between 'normal' and 'abnormal' sexuality that is pervasive in the *Three Essays on the Theory of Sexuality* (Freud, 1905b) but is also followed through into the theory of neurosis where Freud, for example, writes that:

> [...] psycho-analysis has demonstrated that there is no fundamental difference, but only one of degree between the mental life of normal people, of neurotics and of psychotics. A normal person has to pass through the same repressions and has to struggle with the same substitutive structures; the only difference is that he deals with these events with less trouble and better success. (Freud, 1913, p. 210)

What is deemed to be psychologically 'pathological' is to all intents and purposes an essentially practical and pragmatic question as far as psychoanalysis is concerned. But then this is just a particular application of the principle that in all fields of inquiry (including so-called conventional medicine) the division between the normal and pathological is a normative one – pathology is never 'objectively' inscribed in phenomena as such. This is implicitly recognised in Freud's character analysis in the letter to Tansley: while the renunciation of sexuality was in some sense clearly abnormal, it was, paradoxically, the price of remaining healthy in other respects. Freud was not the first to refuse to base his therapeutics in a refusal to separate the normal and the pathological as different orders of reality. The *locus classicus* of this position is probably the work of the great nineteenth-century physiologist, Claude Bernard. In his 1865 study of experimental medicine Bernard wrote:

> Medicine necessarily begins with clinics, since they determine and define the object of medicine, i.e., the medical problem; but while they are the physician's first study, clinics are not the foundation of scientific medicine; physiology is the foundation of scientific medicine because it must yield the explanation of morbid phenomena by showing their relations to the normal state. We shall never have a science of medicine as long as we separate the explanation of pathological from the explanation of normal, vital phenomena. (Bernard, 1957, p. 146)

Whether Freud was actually right or not about the nature and origin of Bertha Pappenheim's later character is, of course, another matter.

7. Comparison with Freud's own account in his *Autobiographical Study* (Freud, 1925, p. 20) suggests that this was the main source of Zweig's version of the case.

8. In the German original there is not even a paragraph break at this point, unlike in the English translation (Freud, 1968, p. 427).

7   The birth of the legend: Ernest Jones

1. You never go further than when you no longer know where you are going.

2. Jones had already asked Freud in 1928 about when he had learnt of the Pappenheim case from Breuer. Freud replied with an erroneous dating: 'You are right in assuming that Breuer's reports of his case date from about 1884. Our relationship began gradually about 1882; in 1885 I went to Paris' (Freud and Jones, 1993, p. 652). Freud was generally quite unreliable about dates, but this particular error is perhaps indicative of how casual he could be about specific details. Little wonder that accounts of the Anna O. case vary so widely among those of his followers who may have learnt something of it directly from him. Why Jones, in his first draft, stated that Freud may possibly have known of the case even while Breuer was still treating Anna O. is not presently to be ascertained.

3. The letters of 19 March 1952 and 30 March 1952 from Anna Freud to Jones are in the Jones archive at the Institute of Psychoanalysis in London.

4. A different translation by Jeffrey M. Masson is given in Forrester (1990, p. 19) but this is less satisfactory than the rendering by Peter J. Swales used by Borch-Jacobsen. Freud's original German is given in Borch-Jacobsen (1997, p. 51). Currently published German versions of the Freud and Martha letters of

5 August, 31 October, 2 November and 4 November 1883 are somewhat unreliable and should be used with care. Forrester gives a slightly erroneous version of the original German of one sentence from the letter of 2 November (Forrester, 1990, p. 320), which Borch-Jacobsen integrates into an unavoidably inauthentic reproduction of the rest of its immediate context, making clear which is which in a footnote (Borch-Jacobsen, 1997, p. 52). His rendering of Freud's reply of 4 November is, for similar reasons of unavailability of the original, a paraphrase. Israëls acknowledges Forrester for providing the German original for an extract from the letter of 5 August (Israëls, 1999, p. 145) but does not then reveal that his own German version of the letter of 31 October is not similarly authentic but a fresh retranslation back into German of Masson's English version of Freud's text. On the other hand, his renderings of the extracts from the letters of 2 and 4 November are mostly accurate (pp. 159–160). All these letters are now on unrestricted access in the Sigmund Freud Collection of the Manuscript Division of the Library of Congress, Washington.

5. Es ist merkwürdig, der armen Bertha ist nie ein anderer Mann näher getreten als ihr jeweiliger Arzt, ach die hätte als Gesunde schon das Zeug dazu, dem vernünftigsten Manne den Kopf zu verdrehen, ist das ein Unglück mit dem Mädchen, nicht wahr – Lach mich nur recht aus Liebster, mich hat die Geschichte heut Nacht kaum schlafen lassen, ich hab mich so lebhaft in die verschwiegene Frau Mathilde hineinversetzt bis ich halb wachend empfand halb träumte, an ihrer Stelle zu sein und in der Lage von der Du gestern geschrieben, was mich in solche Aufregung gebracht daß ich eine brennende Sehnsucht nach Dir empfand [...].

6. Du hast ganz Recht zu erwarten, dass ich Dich recht auslachen werde. Ich thue es hiemit auf's Kräftigste. Bist Du so eitel zu glauben, daß Dir die Leute Deinen Geliebten, oder später Deinen Mann streitig machen werden? O nein, der bleibt ganz Dein u. Dein einziger Trost muß sein, daß er es selbst nicht anders will. Um Schicksale zu haben wie Frau Mathilde, muß man die Frau eines Breuer's sein, nicht wahr? Wenn Du mich aber recht lieb hast, freue mich ganz ungeheuer, ich brauche keine andere Neigung als die Deine. The final sentence of this quotation has previously been omitted from published extracts of this letter.

7. One other known source of the story of the hysterical childbirth that seems at first sight to be a likely candidate as the basis for Jones's account must in all probability be disqualified. The possibility that Jones had seen Freud's letter to Stefan Zweig seems to be precluded by correspondence in the Jones Archives at the Institute of Psychoanalysis in London. It was not until after the publication of the first volume of Jones's biography that he received a letter in April 1954 from Manfred and Hannah Altmann, the brother and sister-in-law of Zweig's second wife who committed suicide with him in 1942, discussing Ernst Freud's request for access to the letters from Freud to Zweig. In fact Jones wrote in a letter (now in the Library of Congress) to Anna Freud on 10 April that he had just received the letters from Zweig's sister-in-law, and in a further letter to Strachey on 3 December 1954 (in the Jones Archives) he indicated that by this time he had read them. A further remote possibility is that Kurt R. Eissler alerted Jones to this story, having been told it in his August 1953 interview with Jung, although this would entail a very late amendment to Jones's text, which was published at the end of 1953. But the fact that the

final version in Jones's papers exists in the form of a handwritten passage on a slip of paper in amongst the leaves of his earliest handwritten draft of the chapter perhaps suggests an earlier source.

8. We may note in passing that if this is a corrupt account of the Anna O. story it shares in common with Jung's version of the end of the treatment the notion that Freud had been present at the crisis, though whether this is more than coincidence must remain a matter of speculation. Thanks are due to Peter Swales for providing a copy of the passage from Jekels's essay and also credit for the suggestion (Swales, 1986, p. 39) that this is a corruption of the Anna O. story.

8   The development of the legend: Henri Ellenberger

1. Whoever misses the first buttonhole can't get properly buttoned up.
2. Ellenberger gathered information on Bertha Pappenheim's family background during his trip to Vienna in the summer of 1963 (Ellenberger, 1993, pp. 370–1). This discrepancy between the biographical data published on Bertha Pappenheim's death and what had been published within the psychoanalytic literature had already been noted by Karpe (1961, p. 10). Jones states in his biography that: 'Her mother, who was somewhat of a dragon, had come from Frankfurt and took her daughter back there for good at the end of the eighties' (Jones, 1953, p. 248). This comes from the additional paragraph of biographical data about Bertha Pappenheim that Jones inserted relatively late in the day. Some of the information in it comes from the memorial article that was published on Bertha Pappenheim's death in 1936, but the statement about returning to Frankfurt on the late eighties clearly does not, nor is it given by Breuer in the case history. Jones's source is most likely to be a member of the family contacted through Ena Lewisohn, Jones's informant about the memorial article. In her article on Bertha Pappenheim's later life (Jensen, 1961, p. 120), Ellen Jensen too, like Karpe, has already noted the discrepancy between the 1881 date given in the 1936 obituary and the Breuer case history, but unlike Ellenberger she does not attempt to resolve the contradiction in one direction or the other.
3. Even in this case Ellenberger should surely have noted that in all probability this was a mistake that Jones had inherited from Freud, since he records in his 1932 letter to Stefan Zweig that Breuer's daughter was born shortly after the end of the treatment (Freud, 1961, p. 409).

   Borch-Jacobsen (1996, p. 32) states on the basis of a reference in a family letter to Jones that the error about the date of Dora Breuer's birth was immediately pointed out to him by Breuer's relatives, but that Jones failed to correct this in his next edition, despite his promise to do so. The letter in question does not state explicitly what the error was and Borch-Jacobsen leaps to his conclusion without firm evidence. In fact he is almost certainly mistaken in his accusation here, since the error in question that Jones made (and which he *did* correct in subsequent editions) was to say that Dora Breuer committed suicide in New York, when in fact she killed herself in Vienna on 15 January 1942 to escape the Nazis. Ellenberger points out this error (1966, p. 95).
4. Even these first two sections are not spared minor errors, including (p. 480) a wrong birthdate for Bertha Pappenheim (it should be 1859, not 1860); the

claim (p. 482) that when she was in the sanatorium Breuer visited her every three or four days (Breuer gives no information about how often he saw her); the assertion (ibid.) that the patient had 'announced in advance that she would be cured by the end of June 1882, in time for her summer vacation' (in fact she decided she would be cured by 7 June, the anniversary of the day she was moved into the country). These slips do not affect the main substance of Ellenberger's argument.

5. Edinger rewrote the biographical introduction to the book for the English edition, so it differs in some significant respects from the earlier German version.

6. Borch-Jacobsen's summary of the photographic finding adds muddle to Ellenberger's own confusion. He reports that the photograph was taken at a time when Anna O. was 'supposed to be hospitalised' (Borch-Jacobsen, 2005, p. 26). But supposed by whom? Certainly not Breuer, nor even at this point Ellenberger. Jones's only reference to institutionalisation is to the period she spent in Inzersdorf a year later, for he of course knew nothing of the stay in Kreuzlingen. As we shall note below, Ellenberger does indeed later wrongly suppose that Bertha spent time in a sanatorium near Vienna in 1882, and it is perhaps this that has infected Borch-Jacobsen's account.

7. Ellenberger even now misreports details of Breuer's institutionalisation of his patient, though in a different way from his previous publications. While in the earlier versions he has Bertha in the institution for a whole year from June 1881, in this summary he now correctly says that she returned to Vienna in the autumn, but then invents the following: 'However, her condition became worse in December 1881, so that she had to be taken back to the country-house' (Ellenberger, 1972, p. 269). There is no evidence whatsoever for this claim. This 1972 essay was reprinted along with others by Ellenberger in 1993. The editor of the volume notes that both he and Ellenberger made minor textual amendments in the preparation of the new edition (Ellenberger, 1993, p. x) and so for present purposes the original version of Ellenberger's article will be used.

8. It must surely be regarded as a supreme irony that Ellenberger's blunder in thinking that Bertha was supposed to be in a sanatorium near Vienna in 1882 should apparently have led him to one of the most significant discoveries of modern psychoanalytic scholarship. For if we are to believe his 1972 account of his discovery of the Kreuzlingen documents, it was this wrong initial assumption that Bertha had been institutionalised in 1882 that led him to look for traces of Bertha in a sanatorium further afield, under the influence of the photograph from Konstanz. The full passage reads: 'What was Bertha doing in riding habit in Konstanz, Germany, at the time when she was supposed to be severely sick in a sanitarium near Vienna? Mrs. Edinger suggested that she could actually have been treated in one of the sanitariums which existed in that part of Europe. Actually there was one famous sanitarium, in the little Swiss town of Kreuzlingen, quite close to Konstanz: the Sanatorium Bellevue' (Ellenberger, 1972, pp. 273–4). Given the significance of Ellenberger's consequent discovery of the original case notes it would perhaps be hard to begrudge him this apparent piece of luck.

9. When Ellenberger came to publish a French edition of his magnum opus in 1974 he took the opportunity to revise the 1970 text on Anna O. in the light of his Kreuzlingen discovery. He did this in the main by incorporating large

sections from his 1972 paper, and these are carried forward to the more recent French edition (1994). However, on the issue of the photograph there are two suppressions. There is no longer a questioning of the consistency between Bertha's appearance in riding habit in Konstanz and Breuer's supposed testimony that she was severely ill in a sanatorium near Vienna, nor any sign of the alleged contrast between the photograph and Breuer's portrait of a homebound young lady with no outlets for her energies (Ellenberger, 1994, p. 512). Ellenberger clearly knew that there was something wrong with the analysis he had published in 1970 and in a slightly different form in 1972, but he did not carry through the wider implications of this even in the revised French text. There were no comparable excisions relating to conclusions about the photograph when the 1972 paper came to be re-published by Micale in 1993.

10. In the revised version of this paper published in 1993, Ellenberger has reined in his expectations a little and substituted 'uninformative' for 'disappointing' (Ellenberger, 1993, p. 269). On the contrary, to a reader with no prior preconceptions the report is very informative precisely because of what it does *not* contain.

9   The maturation of the legend: The derivative literature

1. Some people keep on knocking at the wall with a hammer and imagine that they are hitting the nail on the head every time.

2. On the other hand, the supremely talented Josef Breuer of the dental world still languishes in anonymity, since we do not know who carried out this pioneering operation.

3. Max Rosenbaum's (1984) opening essay in a series of present-day reinterpretations of the Anna O. case is a good example of such a piece. It welds together a variety of fragments of historical information and secondary interpretation of it into an historically-continuous, narrative presentation of how things really were that reads as if there were no doubts about the details or contradictions between their sources.

4. This may be partly a result of depending solely on Strachey's rendering of the events and his erroneous substitution of 'illness' for 'hysteria' when he says 'the whole illness was brought to a close' (Breuer and Freud, 1895, p. 40). Although Macmillan does not cite this passage in his earlier paper, he does so in his later recapitulation of the case (Macmillan, 1997, p. 9).

5. Pollock (1973, p. 330) makes the same erroneous assumption. It is entirely understandable given Ellenberger's misleading presentation of the case notes on this point.

6. Without referring to Israëls's work, Borch-Jacobsen has subsequently replicated the exact structure of Israëls's argument on this point. On the basis of the letter of 31 October he first charges Freud with later inverting the roles of Breuer and Anna O. in respect of who was smitten with whom, and then in the same breath accuses Freud of a falsehood in also alleging that Breuer had said nothing to him about the circumstances of the ending of the treatment, when the letter demonstrates that Breuer had in fact told him quite frankly what had gone on (Borch-Jacobson, 2005, p. 29). So the same letter that provides no evidence for what Freud later claimed to be true is also supposed to demonstrate that the truth he claimed never to have been told was really known to him all along.

7. It is at least partly on the basis of an erroneous transcription of Martha's letter that John Forrester signals his own view in his discussion of the same correspondence that both Bertha Pappenheim's transference and Breuer's counter-transference are adumbrated in these letters (Forrester, 1990, pp. 20–3). He also works on the same doubtful assumption, later made by Israëls too, that where Breuer's breaking off of the treatment is under discussion Freud and Martha must be referring to the events of June 1882, rather than somewhat later.

8. Borch-Jacobsen compresses a number of questionable assumptions and dubious readings into a tight space when he comments on this aspect of Bertha's treatment. When he links the surgery of February to the increase of the patient's pain the following month, he jumps to an inference that even Bertha's mother – surely better informed – did not make. Having made this leap he then reasonably enough regards the operation as 'apparently bungled', and attributes this insight to Schweighofer. But not only is there no evidence to suggest that the dental operation was bungled, Schweighofer in fact takes the opposite view to that suggested. As we have seen, he thinks that the operation was performed in order to treat Bertha's long-standing jaw affliction and that in this respect the operation was entirely successful as it led eventually to Bertha's recovery from other symptoms as well (Schweighofer, 1987, p. 149).

9. See Shorter (1990) for a discussion of the differences between the various kinds of private residential facilities available in central Europe in the late nineteenth century.

10. While in his 1996 book Borch-Jacobsen builds no substantial argument from this particular fabrication, this is not so in his later work. In an article published three years later Borch-Jacobsen repeats the claim made in his book, but this time without citing any evidence at all for it: 'Indeed, we know that Breuer told the story of Anna O. to his young colleague Freud, making no attempt to conceal the disastrous outcome of the treatment' (Borch-Jacobsen, 1999, p. 57). Having established this as his premise he then builds a whole fictitious narrative on top of it, sweeping in along the way all kinds of further assumptions that make the story a good one:

> One would expect that plain good sense would have dissuaded Freud from following the same dead end. But that would be ignoring Freud's lifelong propensity to sacrifice facts upon the altar of his pet theories. Freud was at the time keeping abreast of Charcot's, Janet's and Delboeuf's research on 'desuggestion' under hypnosis of traumatic memories, and he was quick to reread (or, if you prefer, to rewrite) the story of Anna O. in light of the theories of the Salpêtrière. In 1888, at a moment when he had no reason to think that Bertha Pappenheim was going to recover and when he himself had not yet tried the cathartic method on any of his patients, he triumphantly wrote in an encyclopedia article on 'Hysteria': 'It is even more effective if we adopt a method first practiced by Josef Breuer in Vienna...' (ibid.)

It should be borne in mind here throughout this passage that the evidence for Breuer communicating the disastrous outcome of the treatment is not only non-existent, but is nevertheless supposed by Borch-Jacobsen in his book to date from November 1882. The result is a complete derangement of chronology as we are told that Freud was 'at the time' keeping abreast of Charcot, Janet and Delboeuf and writing an article in 1888, still with no reason to think that Bertha Pappenheim was going to recover, though we are not told the evidence for this either. It is rather ironic in the circumstances that Borch-Jacobsen prefaces this passage with a rebuke to Freud and 'countless psychoanalysts' for rewriting and doctoring the narrative of the Anna O. case, for in Borch-Jacobsen's own narrative readers have a valuable opportunity indeed to witness 'history in the making.'

11. Incidentally from a quite wrongly referenced source. But no matter; this is an error indicative of a particular approach to sources rather than a substantial one affecting the taut logic of the demonstration.

Conclusion

1. Man must persist in the belief that the incomprehensible is, in fact, comprehensible; else he would cease to do research.
2. One slight qualification needs to be entered here. As a close comparison between Breuer's published account and the original report for Binswanger shows, the former was very much based on the latter. As a medical report for a colleague, the 1882 document would indeed have been written as a rounded account of the patient's general condition, rather than as a more closely focused exposition of a narrow range of symptoms and their treatment. There is some evidence that for this reason the published case is something of a compromise, being rather too inclusive compared with how it might have been if it had been composed from scratch. Breuer himself concedes: 'Although I have suppressed a large number of quite interesting details, this case history of Anna O. has grown bulkier than would seem to be required for a hysterical illness that was not in itself of an unusual character. It was, however, impossible to describe the case without entering into details, and its features seem to me of sufficient importance to excuse this extensive report' (Breuer and Freud, 1895, p. 41). Breuer's judgement that the illness was not in itself of an unusual character reads a little oddly to present-day sensibilities, though this does again suggest that some of its more extravagant features may not have been conceived by Breuer as hysterical in the narrow sense. It should also be noted that apart from a passing reference to a transitory facial pain in the spring before the onset of her illness, there is no mention of the facial neuralgia in Breuer's 1882 report; there is also no record of the dental operation, nor of the morphine dependence. To be sure, these would most naturally have featured in the record of the final period of treatment during the first half of 1882, and this section is missing from the report, either because it was not transcribed, or, perhaps more likely, because it was never written. Nevertheless the point remains that the general aim of the published case study would be to include only what was relevant, and as we have good reason to think that the neuralgia and its consequences were not thought by Breuer to be hysterical, we cannot be totally surprised that they are not recorded.
3. In a letter preserved in the Jones archive at the Institute of Psychoanalysis in London, James Strachey wrote to Ernest Jones in 1951: 'Freud was quite

extraordinarily inaccurate about details. He seems to have had a delusion that he possessed a "phonographic memory". Actually a large proportion – I should say the majority – of his literary quotations turn out to be slightly wrong if you verify them. And he constantly contradicts himself over details of fact. When we did the case histories we sent him long lists of these – most of which he then put right in the Ges. Schriften & later editions.'

4. In fact Wilhelm and Emma Pappenheim, Bertha's cousin and his wife, both signed an effusive letter of greetings sent to Breuer on his seventieth birthday by many of his patients, colleagues and friends (Hirschmüller, 1989, p. 262).

5. Thanks are due to Gerald Kreft for his assistance with the historical data on this point and for sharing details of his private correspondence with Erika Fromm. It is interesting to note that Oppenheimer was completely oblivious to the identity of Anna O. and Bertha Pappenheim, and this suggests that no details of Bertha's medical history prior to her move to Frankfurt in the late 1880s had been preserved anywhere in whatever medical record Oppenheimer will presumably have inherited.

References

Alam, C. & Merskey, H. (1994) What's in a Name? The Cycle of Change in the Meaning of Neuralgia. *History of Psychiatry*. Vol. 5, Part 4, No. 20, pp. 429–74.

Andersson, O. (1962) *Studies in the Prehistory of Psychoanalysis*. Norstedts: Svenska Bokförlaget, Scandinavian University Book.

Appignanesi, L. & Forrester, J. (1992) *Freud's Women*. London: Weidenfeld & Nicolson Limited.

Bernard, C. (1957) *An Introduction to the Study of Experimental Medicine*. New York: Dover Publications, Inc.

Bernheim, H. (1890) *Suggestive Therapeutics: A Treatise on the Nature and Uses of Hypnotism*. Edinburgh and London: Young J. Pentland.

Bjerre, P. (1920) [1916] *The History and Practice of Psychoanalysis*. Boston: Richard G. Badger, The Gorham Press.

Borch-Jacobsen, M. (1996) *Remembering Anna O.: A Century of Mystification*. New York and London: Routledge.

Borch-Jacobsen, M. (1997) Anna O. zum Gedächtnis: eine hundertjährige Irreführung. München: Wilhelm Fink Verlag.

Borch-Jacobsen, M. (1999) Is Psychoanalysis a Scientific Fairy Tale? *Narrative*. Vol. 7, No. 1, pp. 56–70.

Borch-Jacobsen, M. (2005) La vérité sur le cas de Mlle Anna O. In Meyer, C. et al. (eds) *Le Livre noir de la psychanalyse*. Paris: les arènes, pp. 25–30.

Breuer, J. & Freud, S. (1895) Studies on Hysteria. *Standard Edition Vol. II*. London: The Hogarth Press.

Brill, A. A. (1948) *Lectures on Psychoanalytic Psychiatry*. London: John Lehmann.

Charcot, J.-M. (1886) *Neue Vorlesungen über die Krankheiten des Nervensystems inbesondere über Hysterie. Autorisirte deutsche Ausgabe von Dr. Sigm. Freud*. Leipzig und Wien: Toeplitz und Deuticke.

Charcot, J.-M. (1991) *Clinical Lectures on Diseases of the Nervous System*. London: Routledge.

Cioffi, F. (2005) Épistémologie et mauvaise foi: le cas du freudisme. In Meyer, C. et al. (eds) *Le Livre noir de la psychanalyse*. Paris: les arènes, pp. 306–27.

Cranefield, P. F. (1958) Joseph Breuer's Evaluation of his Contribution to Psychoanalysis. *International Journal of Psycho-analysis*. Vol. 39, pp. 319–22.

de Paula Ramos, S. (2003) Revisiting Anna O.: A Case of Chemical Dependence. *History of Psychology*. Vol. 6, No. 3, pp. 239–50.

Dufresne, T. (2003) *Killing Freud: Twentieth-Century Culture and the Death of Psychoanalysis*. London; New York: Continuum.

Edinger, D. (Hg.). (1963) *Bertha Pappenheim. Leben und Schriften*. Frankfurt am Main: Ner-Tamid-Verlag.

Edinger, D. (1968) *Freud's Anna O.* Highland Park, Illinois: Congregation Solel.

Ehrenfels, C. von (2006) In Hemecker, W. (Hg.), *Briefwechsel zur Psychologie*. Graz: Leykam Buchverlag.

Eitingon, M. (1998) Anna O. (Breuer) in psychoanalytischer Betrachtung: Wien X. 1909. *Jahrbuch der Psychoanalyse*. Vol. 40, pp. 14–30.

Eisenberg, L. (1893) *Das Geistige Wien. Künstler- und Schriftsteller-Lexikon. Zweiter Band. Medicinisch-naturwissenschaftlicher Theil*. Wien: C. Daberkow's Verlag.

Eissler, K. R. (2001) *Freud and the Seduction Theory: A Brief Love Affair*. Madison, Connecticut: International Universities Press, Inc.

Ellenberger, H. F. (1966) Review of Edinger, D. (Hg.), Bertha Pappenheim, Leben und Schriften. *Journal of the History of the Behavioural Sciences*. Vol. 2, pp. 94–6.

Ellenberger, H.F. (1970) *The Discovery of the Unconscious: The History and Evolution of Dynamic Psychiatry*. New York, NY: Basic Books, Inc.

Ellenberger, H. F. (1972) The Story of 'Anna O': A Critical Review with New Data. *Journal of the History of the Behavioural Sciences*. Vol. 8, pp. 267–79.

Ellenberger, H. F. (1993) In Micale, M. S (ed.), *Beyond the Unconscious: Essays of Henri F. Ellenberger in the History of Psychiatry*. Princeton, New Jersey: Princeton University Press.

Ellenberger, H. F. (1994) *Histoire de la découverte de l'inconscient*. Paris: Fayard.

Forel, A. (1968) *Briefe. Correspondance*. Bern und Stuttgart: Verlag Hans Huber.

Forrester, J. (1990) *The Seductions of Psychoanalysis*. Cambridge: Cambridge University Press.

Forrester, J. & Cameron, L. (1999) 'A Cure with a Defect': A Previously Unpublished Letter by Freud Concerning Anna O. *International Journal of Psychoanalysis*. Vol. 80, No. 5, pp. 929–942.

Freud, S. (1888) Hysteria and Hysteroepilepsy. *Standard Edition Vol. I*. London: The Hogarth Press.

Freud, S. (1892) Sketches for the 'Preliminary Communication' of 1893. *Standard Edition Vol. I*. London: The Hogarth Press.

Freud, S. (1893) On the Psychical Mechanism of Hysterical Phenomena: A Lecture. *Standard Edition Vol. III*. London: The Hogarth Press.

Freud, S. (1894) The Neuro-Psychoses of Defence. *Standard Edition Vol. III*. London: The Hogarth Press.

Freud, S. (1904) Freud's Psycho-analytic Procedure. *Standard Edition Vol. III*. London: The Hogarth Press.

Freud, S. (1905a) Fragment of an Analysis of a Case of Hysteria. *Standard Edition Vol. VII*. London: The Hogarth Press.

Freud, S. (1905b) Three Essays on the Theory of Sexuality. *Standard Edition Vol. VII*. London: The Hogarth Press.

Freud, S. (1910) Five Lectures on Psycho-analysis. *Standard Edition Vol. XI*. London: The Hogarth Press.

Freud, S. (1913) On Psycho-analysis. *Standard Edition Vol. XII*. London: The Hogarth Press.

Freud, S. (1914) On the History of the Psycho-analytic Movement. *Standard Edition Vol. XIV*. London: The Hogarth Press.

Freud, S. (1915) Observations on Transference-Love (Further Recommendations on the Technique of Psycho-analysis, III). *Standard Edition Vol. XII*. London: The Hogarth Press.

Freud, S. (1925) An Autobiographical Study. *Standard Edition Vol. XX*. London: The Hogarth Press.

Freud, S. (1926) The Question of Lay Analysis. *Standard Edition Vol. XX*. London: The Hogarth Press.

Freud, S. (1961) In Freud, E (ed.), *Letters of Sigmund Freud 1873–1939.*. London: The Hogarth Press.

Freud, S. (1968) In Freud, E. & Freud, L. (Hsg.), *Briefe 1873–1939*. Frankfurt am Main: S. Fischer Verlag.

Freud, S. (1985) In Masson, J. M. (ed.), *The Complete Letters of Sigmund Freud to Wilhelm Fliess 1887–1904*. Cambridge, MA: Belknap Press of Harvard University Press.

Freud, S. & Abraham, K. (2002) In Falzeder, E. (ed.), *The Complete Correspondence of Sigmund Freud and Karl Abraham 1907–1925*. London: Karnac.

Freud, S. & Bernays, M. (2005) In Hirschmüller, A. (Hg.), *Sigmund Freud/Minna Bernays Briefwechsel 1882–1938*. Tübingen: edition diskord.

Freud, S. & Binswanger, L. (2003) In Fichtner, G (ed.), *The Freud-Binswanger Correspondence 1908–1938*. London: Open Gate Press.

Freud, S. & Ferenczi, S. (1993) In Brabant, E., Falzeder, E. & Giampierini-Deutsch, P. (eds), *The Correspondence of Sigmund Freud and Sándor Ferenczi. Volume 1, 1909–1914*. Cambridge, MA: Belknap Press of Harvard University Press.

Freud, S. & Jones, E. (1993) In Paskauskas, R. A (ed.), *The Complete Correspondence of Sigmund Freud and Ernest Jones*. Cambridge, MA: Belknap Press of Harvard University Press.

Freud, S. & Jung, C. G. (1974) In McGuire, W. (ed.), *The Freud/Jung Letters*. Cambridge, MA: Harvard University Press.

Goshen, C. E. (1952) The Original Case Material of Psychoanalysis. *American Journal of Psychiatry*. Vol. 108, pp. 829–34.

Hirschmüller, A. (1978) *Physiologie und Psychoanalyse in Leben und Werk Josef Breuers*. Jahrbuch der Psychoanalyse/Beiheft 4. Verlag Hans Huber.

Hirschmüller, A. (1989) *The Life and Work of Josef Breuer: Physiology and Psychoanalysis*. New York: New York University Press.

Hirschmüller, A. (1998) Max Eitingon über Anna O. *Jahrbuch der Psychoanalyse*. Vol. 40, pp. 9–13.

Hodgkiss, A.D. (1991) Chronic Pain in Nineteenth-Century British Medical Writings. *History of Psychiatry*. Vol. 2, Part 1, No. 5, pp. 27–40.

Israëls, H. (1999) *Der Fall Freud: Die Geburt der Psychoanalyse aus der Lüge*. Hamburg: Europäische Verlagsanstalt/Rotbuch Verlag.

Jackson, J. H. (1931) Lectures on the Diagnosis of Epilepsy. (1879) In Taylor, J. (ed.), *Selected Writings of John Hughlings Jackson. Vol.1*. London: Hodder & Stoughton, pp. 276–307.

Jensen, E. (1961) Anna O. Ihr Späteres Schicksal. *Acta Psychiatrica et Neurologica*. Vol. 36, pp. 119–31.

Jones, E. (1953) *Sigmund Freud: Life and Work. Volume I: The Young Freud 1856–1900*. London: The Hogarth Press.

Jones, E. (1955) *Sigmund Freud: Life and Work. Volume II: Years of Maturity 1901–1919*. London: The Hogarth Press.

Jung, C. G. (1989) In McGuire, W (ed.), *Analytical Psychology: Notes of the Seminar Given in 1925*. Princeton, New Jersey: Princeton University Press.

Kaplan, R. (2004) O. Anna: Being Bertha Pappenheim – Historiography and biography. *Australasian Psychiatry*. Vol. 12, No. 1, pp. 62–68.

Karpe, R. (1961) The Rescue Complex in Anna O.'s Final Identity. *Psychoanalytic Quarterly*. Vol. 30, pp. 1–27.

Kreft, G. (1996) In Plänkers, H. et al. (Hg.), Zur Archäologie der Psychoanalyse in Frankfurt: Fundstücke und Perspektiven um Ludwig Edinger. *Psychoanalyse in*

Frankfurt am Main. Zerstörte Anfänge. Wiederannäherungen. Entwicklungen. Tübingen: Edition Diskord, pp. 195–234.

Kreft, G. (1999) Anna O. und/oder Bertha Pappenheim... Umschreibung eines Desiderats anläßlich der Edition des nachgelassenen Manuskripts (1959) von Max M. Stern (1895–1982) In Lilienthal, U. & Stiehm L. (Hg.). *Den Menschen zugewandt leben. Festschrift für Werner Licharz.* Osnabrück: secolo Verlag, pp. 205–37.

Levin, K. (1978) *Freud's Early Psychology of the Neuroses.* Hassocks, Sussex: Harvester Press.

Macmillan, M. B. (1977) The Cathartic Method and the Expectancies of Breuer and Anna O. *International Journal of Clinical and Experimental Hypnosis.* Vol. 25, No. 2, pp. 106–18.

Macmillan, M. B. (1997) *Freud Evaluated: The Completed Arc.* Cambridge, MA: MIT Press.

Makari, G. (1992) A History of Freud's First Concept of Transference. *International Review of Psycho-analysis.* Vol. 19, Part 4, pp. 415–32.

May-Tolzmann, U. (1996) *Freuds frühe Klinische Theorie (1894–1896). Wiederentdeckung und Rekonstruktion.* Tübingen: Edition Diskord.

May-Tolzmann, U. (1998) 'Obsessional Neurosis': A Nosographic Innovation by Freud. *History of Psychiatry.* Vol. 9, Part 3, No. 35, pp. 335–353.

Merskey, H. (1992) Anna O. Had a Severe Depressive Illness. *British Journal of Psychiatry.* Vol. 161, pp. 185–94.

Meyer, C. (ed.) (2005) *Le Livre noir de la psychanalyse.* Paris: les arènes.

Micale, M. S. (1995) *Approaching Hysteria: Disease and its Interpretations.* Princeton, New Jersey: Princeton University Press.

Nunberg, H. & Federn, E. (eds) (1967) *Minutes of the Vienna Psychoanalytic Society. Volume II: 1908–1910.* New York: International Universities Press, Inc.

Orr-Andrawes, A. (1987) The Case of Anna O.: A Neuropsychiatric Perspective. *Journal of the American Psychoanalytic Association.* Vol. 35, No. 2, pp. 387–419.

Pollock, G. H. (1968) The Possible Significance of Childhood Object Loss in the Josef Breuer-Bertha Pappenheim (Anna O.)–Sigmund Freud Relationship. I. Josef Breuer. *Journal of the American Psychoanalytic Association.* Vol. 16, pp. 711–39.

Pollock, G. H. (1972) Bertha Pappenheim's Pathological Mourning: Possible Effects of Childhood Sibling Loss. *Journal of the American Psychoanalytic Association.* Vol. 20, pp. 476–93.

Pollock, G. H. (1973) Bertha Pappenheim: Addenda to Her Case History. *Journal of the American Psychoanalytic Association.* Vol. 21, pp. 328–32.

Pollock, G. H. (1984) Anna O.: Insight, Hindsight and Foresight. In Rosenbaum, M. & Muroff, M. (eds), *Anna O. Fourteen Contemporary Reinterpretations.* New York: The Free Press.

Rank, O. (1958) *Beyond Psychology.* New York: Dover Publications, Inc.

Rank, O. (1973) *The Trauma of Birth.* New York, Evanston, San Francisco, London: Harper Torchbooks.

Rank, O. (1996) In Kramer, R (ed.), *A Psychology of Difference; The American Lectures.* Princeton, New Jersey: Princeton University Press.

Reeves, C. (1982) Breuer, Freud and the Case of Anna O: A Re-examination. *Journal of Child Psychotherapy.* Vol. 8, pp. 203–14.

Reicheneder, J. G. (1990) *Zum Konstitutionsproze der Psychoanalyse.* Jahrbuch der Psychoanalyse, Beiheft 12. Stuttgart-Bad Cannstatt: Frommann-Holzboog.

Rosenbaum, M. (1984) Anna O. (Bertha Pappenheim): Her History. In Rosenbaum, M. & Muroff, M. (eds), *Anna O. Fourteen Contemporary Reinterpretations*. New York: The Free Press, pp. 1–25.

Rosenbaum, M. & Muroff, M. (eds) (1984) *Anna O. Fourteen Contemporary Reinterpretations*. New York: The Free Press.

Rosenzweig, S. (1992) *Freud, Jung and Hall the King-Maker: The Historic Expedition to America (1909) with G. Stanley Hall as Host and William James as Guest*. St. Louis, MO: Rana House Press.

Schweighofer, F. (1987) *Das Privattheater der Anna O*. München; Basel: Ernst Reinhardt Verlag.

Shorter, E. (1990) 'Private Clinics in Central Europe' 1850–1933. *Social History of Medicine*. Vol. 3, pp. 159–95.

Shorter, E. (1992) *From Paralysis to Fatigue: A History of Psychosomatic Illness in the Modern Era*. New York: The Free Press.

Shorter, E. (1997a) *A History of Psychiatry; from the Era of the Asylum to the Age of Prozac*. New York: John Wiley & Sons Inc.

Shorter, E. (1997b) What was the Matter with 'Anna O.': A Definitive Diagnosis. In Dufresne, T. (ed.) *Freud Under Analysis: History, Theory, Practice. Essays in Honor of Paul Roazen*. Northvale, New Jersey: Jason Aronson Inc, pp. 23–34.

Swales, P. J. (1986) *Freud, Breuer and the Blessed Virgin*. Privately circulated typescript of a lecture given in 1986.

Swales, P. J. (1988) Anna O. in Ischl. *Werkblatt. Zeitschrift für Psychoanalyse und Gesellschaftskritik*. Jg. 5, Nr. 1/2, pp. 57–64.

Swales, P. J. (1989) Freud, Cocaine, and Sexual Chemistry; The Role of Cocaine in Freud's Conception of the Libido. In Spurling, L. (ed.) *Sigmund Freud: Critical Assessments. Vol. 1*. London; New York: Routledge 273–301.

Tanner, T. A. (2002) Sigmund Freud and the *Zeitschrift für Hypnotismus*. *Arc de Cercle*. Vol. 1, No. 1, pp. 75–142.

Thornton, E. M. (1986) *The Freudian Fallacy: Freud and Cocaine*. (Revised edition.). London: Paladin Books.

Villaret, A. (ed.) (1888) *Handwörterbuch der Gesamten Medizin. I. Band*. Stuttgart: Verlag von Ferdinand Enke.

Villaret, A. (ed.) (1891) *Handwörterbuch der Gesamten Medizin. II. Band*. Stuttgart: Verlag von Ferdinand Enke.

Wetterstrand, O. G. (1890) *Hypnotism and its Application to Practical Medicine*. London: G. P. Putnam's Sons.

Woodhouse, C. M. (1965) *The Battle of Navarino*. London: Hodder and Stoughton.

Zweig, S. (1933) Mental Healers: Franz Anton Mesmer, Mary Baker Eddy, Sigmund Freud. London: Cassell and Company Limited.

Index